A History of Christian Thought

PAUL TILLICH

A History of
Christian Thought

Edited by Carl E. Braaten

HARPER & ROW, PUBLISHERS
New York and Evanston

LIBRARY OF CONGRESS CATALOG CARD NUMBER: 68-17592

Contents

Preface

THIS edition of Tillich's lectures on the history of Christian thought is a revision of the text of the second edition, 1956. The first edition was composed of lectures which Tillich delivered during the spring semester, 1953, at Union Theological Seminary in New York. They were stenographically recorded and transcribed by Peter H. John and distributed by him in a small edition. In his "Preface to the Second Edition" Peter John stated that he had "tried to correct errors in typography, orthography, and some errors in transcription." Then he acknowledged that "a thorough revision of the text for matters of style and content is of course still necessary, and will perhaps be undertaken in a future edition." Ideally, a completely revised edition should have been produced with the assistance of Tillich himself. Without his help this revision could not be as thorough as might have been hoped. Although I have been liberal in making changes in matters of style, I have dealt with the content in a conservative manner.

Tillich's *A History of Christian Thought* may be viewed as a complement to his *Perspectives on Nineteenth and Twentieth Century Protestant Theology*, and both together may be regarded as two volumes of Tillich's interpretation of the classical Christian tradition. The latter begins about where the former leaves off. There is some overlapping at the point of the demise of Protestant Orthodoxy and the rise of the Enlightenment. A student of the intellectual history of Christianity and of contemporary theology will find it necessary to read both works to appreciate the full sweep of Tillich's grasp of the tradition. They reveal the historical depth of Tillich's insights more directly than his systematic volumes and essays.

These lectures on the history of thought appear in print at a time when the understanding of history has become the central task and most urgent problem of current theological reflection. They offer evidence of how Tillich himself handled history. For Tillich the past was pregnant with the present, and the study of it like a pathway into the future. The only one who can be alive to the present and open to the future is the one who is in dialogue with the past, who can interpret its monuments and understand its movements. This volume will be a demonstration of the power of history for one who never immersed himself in the past as an escape from the present. History comes alive to the student who permits Tillich to introduce him to its vitalities.

Most of Tillich's students are already familiar with these lectures. It is hoped, however, that the present edition will serve the needs of a new generation of theological students who did not experience the good fortune to have Tillich as their teacher or contemporary. It has been an honor for me to edit this work as well as the *Perspectives*. I wish to express profound gratitude to Mrs. Hannah Tillich and to Robert C. Kimball, the executor of the estate of Paul Tillich, for their permission to have these lectures published. To Robert H. Fischer, my colleague, I am grateful for suggestions he made for improving the text.

Oxford, England   CARL E. BRAATEN
September, 1967

Introduction:
The Concept of Dogma

ALL human experience implies the element of thought, simply because the intellectual or spiritual life of man is embodied in his language. Language is thought expressed in words spoken and heard. There is no human existence without thought. The emotionalism that is so rampant in religion is not more but less than thinking, and reduces religion to the level of sub-human experience of reality.

Schleiermacher emphasized the function of "feeling" in religion and Hegel emphasized "thought", giving rise to the tension between them. Hegel said that even dogs have feeling, but man has thought. This was based on an unintentional misunderstanding of what Schleiermacher meant by "feeling", one that we often find repeated even today. Yet it expresses the truth that man cannot be without thought. He must think even if he is a most pious Christian without any theological education. Even in religion we give names to special objects; we distinguish acts of the divine; we relate symbols to each other and explain their meanings. There is language in every religion, and where there is language there are universals or concepts that one must use even at the most primitive level of thought. It is interesting that this conflict between Hegel and Schleiermacher was anticipated already in the third century by Clement of Alexandria who said that if animals had a religion, it would be mute, without words.

Reality precedes thought; it is equally true, however, that thought shapes reality. They are interdependent; one cannot be abstracted from the other. We should remember this when we come to the discussions on the trinity and christology. Here on the basis of much thought the church fathers made decisions which have influenced the life of all Christians ever since, even the most primitive.

There is also the development of methodological thought which proceeds according to the rules of logic and uses methods in order to deal with experiences. When this methodological thought is expressed in speaking or writing and communicated to other people, it produces theological doctrines. This is a development beyond the more primitive use of thought. Ideally such a development leads to a theological system. Now a system is not something in which to dwell. Everyone who dwells within a system feels after some time that it becomes a prison. If you produce a systematic theology, as I have done, you try to go beyond it in order not to be imprisoned in it. Nevertheless, the system is necessary because it is the form of consistency. I have found that students who express the greatest misgivings about the systematic character of my theology are the very ones who are most impatient when discovering two of my statements that contradict each other. They are unhappy to find one point in which the hidden system has a gap. But when I develop the system further to close this gap, they feel that is a mean attempt on my part to imprison them. This is a very interesting double reaction. Yet it is understandable, because if the system is taken as a final answer, it becomes even worse than a prison. If we understand the system, however, as an attempt to bring theological concepts to a consistent form of expression in which there are no contradictions, then we cannot avoid it. Even if you think in fragments, as some philosophers and theologians (and some great ones) have done, then each fragment implicitly contains a system. When you read the fragments of Nietzsche—in my opinion the greatest fragmentist in philosophy—you can find implied in each of them a whole system of life. So a system cannot be avoided unless you choose to make nonsensical or self-contradictory statements. Of course, this is sometimes done.

The system has the danger not only of becoming a prison, but also of moving within itself. It may separate itself from reality and become something which is, so to speak, above the reality it is supposed to describe. Therefore, my interest is not so much in the systems as such, but in their power to express the reality of the church and its life.

The doctrines of the church have been called dogmas. In

former times this type of course used to be called "the history of dogma". Now we call it "the history of Christian thought", but this is only a change in name. Actually, nobody would dare to present a complete history of what every theologian in the Christian Church has thought. That would be an ocean of contradictory ideas. The purpose of this course is quite different, namely, to show those thoughts which have become accepted expressions of the life of the church. This is what the word "dogma" originally meant.

The concept of dogma is one of those things which stand between the church and the secular world. Most secular people are afraid of the dogmas of the church, and not only secular people but also members of the churches themselves. "Dogma" is like a red cloth waved before the bull in a bull fight; it provokes anger or aggressiveness, and in some cases flight. I think the latter is most often the case with secular people in relation to the church. To understand this we have to examine the history of the concept of dogma, which is very interesting.

The first step in this history is the use of "dogma" derived from the Greek word *dokein*, which means "to think, imagine, or hold an opinion". In the schools of Greek philosophy preceding Christianity *dogmata* were the doctrines which differentiated the various schools from each other, the Academics (Plato), the Peripatetics (Aristotle), the Stoics, the Skeptics, and the Pythagoreans. Each of these schools had its own fundamental doctrines. If someone wanted to become a member of one of these schools, he had to accept at least the basic presuppositions which distinguished that school from the others. So even the philosophical schools were not without their *dogmata*.

In similar fashion the Christian doctrines were understood as *dogmata* which distinguished the Christian school from the philosophical schools. This was accepted as natural; it was not like a red cloth which produces anger. The Christian dogma in the early period was the expression of what Christians accepted when they entered Christian congregations, at great risk and with a tremendous transformation of their lives. So a dogma was never just a theoretical statement by an individual; it was the expression of a reality, the reality of the church.

Secondly, all dogmas were formulated negatively, that is, as reactions against misinterpretations from inside the church.

This is true even of the Apostles' Creed. Take the first article of the Creed, "I believe in God the Father Almighty, Maker of heaven and earth." This is not simply a statement that says something in itself. It is at the same time the rejection of dualism, formulated after a life-and-death struggle of a hundred years. The same is true of the other dogmas. The later they are, the more clearly they show this negative character. We may call them protective doctrines, for they were intended to protect the substance of the biblical message. To an extent the substance was fluid; of course, there was a fixed core, the confession that Jesus was the Christ. But beyond this everything was in motion. When new doctrines arose which seemed to undercut the fundamental confession, the protective doctrines were added to it. In this way the dogmas arose. Luther recognized this fact that the dogmas were not the result of a theoretical interest, but arose from the need to protect the Christian substance.

Since each new protective statement was itself subject to misinterpretation, there was always the need for sharper theoretical formulations. In order to do this it was necessary to use philosophical terms. This is how the many philosophical concepts entered into the Christian dogmas. It was not that people were interested in them as philosophical concepts. Luther was very frank about this; he openly declared that he disliked terms like "trinity", "*homoousios*", etc., but he admitted that they must be used, however unfortunate, because we have no better ones. Theoretical formulations must be made when other people formulate doctrines theoretically in such a way that the substance seems to be endangered.

The next step in the history of this concept was for dogmas to become accepted as canon law by the church. Law according to the canon is the rule of thought or behavior. Canon law is the ecclesiastical law to which everybody who belongs to the church must subject himself. Thus the dogma receives a legal sanction. In the Roman Church the dogma is part of canon law; its authority comes from the legal realm. This is in line with the general development of the Roman Church; the word "Roman" has the connotation of legalistic development.

However, the tremendous reaction against dogma in the last four centuries would perhaps not have been created without one further step: the ecclesiastical law became accepted as civil law by medieval society. This meant that the person who breaks the canonic law of doctrines is not only a heretic, one who disagrees with the fundamental doctrines of the church, but he is also a criminal against the state. It is this last point which has produced the radical reaction in modern times against dogma. Since the heretic undermines not only the church but also the state, he must be not only excommunicated but also delivered into the hands of the civil authorities to be punished as a criminal. It was this state of the dogma against which the Enlightenment was fighting. The Reformation itself was still pretty much in line with the prior development of dogma. But certainly since the Enlightenment all liberal thinking has been characterized by the attempt to avoid dogma. This trend was also supported by the development of science. Science and philosophy had to be given complete freedom in order to make possible their creative growth.

In his famous *History of Dogma* Adolph von Harnack raised the question whether dogma has not come to an end in view of its dissolution in the early period of the Enlightenment. He concedes that there is still dogma in orthodox Protestantism, but he believes that the last step in the history of dogma was reached when the Protestant dogma was dissolved by the Enlightenment. Since then there is really no dogma in Protestantism. Now this implies a very narrow concept of dogma, and Harnack is aware that he is using the concept in a narrow sense, namely, in the sense of the christological-trinitarian doctrine of the ancient church. Reinhold Seeberg emphasized that, on the contrary, the dogmatic development did not end with the coming of the Enlightenment, but is still going on.

Here we face a very important systematic question. Are there any dogmas in present-day Protestantism? Those of you who enter the ministry must take some kind of examination by the church, which is not so much an examination of knowledge as of faith. The churches want to know whether you agree with their fundamental dogmatic tenets. They often conduct these examinations in a very narrow way, without much understanding of the developments in theology since Protestant Orthodoxy. Many students have an inner revolt against these examinations of faith, but you should not forget that you are entering a particular group which is different from other groups. First of all, it is a Christian and not a pagan group; or it is a Protestant and not a

Catholic group; and within Protestantism it could be either an
Episcopalian or a Baptist group. Now this means that the church
has a justified interest in having those who represent it show
some acceptance of its foundations. Every baseball team demands
that its members accept its rules and standards. Why should the
church leave it completely to the arbitrary feelings of the individual? This is impossible.

It is one of the tasks of systematic theology to help the churches
to solve this problem in a way which is not too narrow-minded
and not dependent on the sixteenth- and seventeenth-century
theologians. There is some fundamental point which is accepted
if somebody accepts the church. I believe that it is not a matter
of the church requiring its ministers to accept a series of dogmas.
How could they honestly say that they have no doubts about any
of these dogmas? If they had no doubts, they would hardly be
very good Christians, because the intellectual life is as ambiguous as the moral life. And who would call himself morally perfect?
How then could someone call himself intellectually perfect? The
element of doubt is an element in faith itself. What the church
should do is to accept someone who says that the faith for which
the church stands is a matter of his ultimate concern, which he
wants to serve with all his strength. But if he is asked to say what
he believes about this or that doctrine, he is driven into a kind of
dishonesty. If he says he agrees completely with a given doctrine,
for example, the doctrine of the Virgin Birth, either he is dis-
honest or he must cease to think. If he cannot cease to think, he
must also doubt. That is the problem. I think the only solution on
Protestant soil is to say that this whole set of doctrines represents
one's own ultimate concern, that one desires to serve in this
group which has this basis as its ultimate concern. But one can
never promise not to doubt any one of these particular doctrines.

The dogma should not be abolished but interpreted in such a
way that it is no longer a suppressive power which produces dishonesty or flight. Instead it is a wonderful and profound expression of the actual life of the church. In this sense I will try to
show that in discussing these dogmas, even when they are expressed in the most abstract formulations by means of difficult
Greek concepts, we are dealing with those things which the
church believed to be the most adequate expression for its life
and devotion in its life-and-death struggle against the pagan and

Jewish worlds outside, and against all the disintegrating tendencies which appeared inside. My conclusion is that we should estimate the dogma very highly; there is something great about it. But it should not be taken as a set of particular doctrines to which one must subscribe. This is against the spirit of the dogma, against the spirit of Christianity.

CHAPTER I

The Preparation for Christianity

A. THE *Kairos*

ACCORDING to the apostle Paul there does not always exist the possibility that that can happen which, for example, happened in the appearance of Jesus as the Christ. This happened in one special moment of history when everything was ready for it to happen. We will now discuss the "readiness". Paul speaks of the *kairos* in describing the feeling that the time was ripe, mature, or prepared. This Greek word is an example of the richness of the Greek language in comparison with the poverty of modern languages. We have only one word for "time". The Greeks had two words, *chronos* and *kairos*. *Chronos* is clock time, time which is measured, as we have it in words like "chronology" and "chronometer". *Kairos* is not the quantitative time of the clock, but the qualitative time of the occasion, the right time. (Cf. its use in some of the Gospel stories.) There are things that happen when the right time, the *kairos*, has not yet come. *Kairos* is the time which indicates that something has happened which makes an action possible or impossible. We all experience moments in our lives when we feel that now is the right time to do something, now we are mature enough, now we can make the decision. This is the *kairos*. It was in this sense that Paul and the early church spoke of the *kairos*, the right time for the coming of the Christ. The early church, and Paul to a certain extent, tried to show why the time in which Christ appeared was the right time, how his appearance was made possible by a providential constellation of factors.

What we must do now is to show the preparation for Christian theology in the world situation into which Jesus came. We will do this from a theological point of view—there are others—and thus provide an understanding of the possibilities of a Christian theology. It is not as if the revelation from Christ fell down like a stone from heaven, as some theologians seem to believe. "Here it is; you must take it or leave it." This is contrary to Paul. Actually there is a universal revelatory power going through all history and preparing for that which Christianity considers to be the ultimate revelation.

B. THE UNIVERSALISM OF THE ROMAN EMPIRE

The actual situation into which the New Testament event came was the universalism of the Roman Empire. This meant something negative and positive at the same time. Negatively it meant the breakdown of national religions and cultures. Positively it meant that the idea of mankind as a whole could be conceived at that time. The Roman Empire produced a definite consciousness of world history, in contrast to accidental national histories. World history is now not only a purpose which will be actualized in history, in the sense of the prophets; instead it has become an empirical reality. This is the positive meaning of Rome. Rome represents the universal monarchy in which the whole known world is united. This idea has been taken over by the Roman Church, but applied to the pope. It is still actual in the Roman Church; it means that Rome still claims the monarchic power over all the world, following the Roman Empire in this. It is perhaps an important remark generally that we should never forget that the Roman Church is *Roman*, that the development of this church is influenced not only by Christianity but also by the Roman Empire, by its greatness and by its idea of law. The Roman Church took over the heritage of the Roman Empire. We should never forget this fact. If we are tempted to evaluate the Roman Church more highly than we should, we ought to ask ourselves: how many Roman elements are in it, and to what extent are they valid for us in our culture? We should do the same thing with the Greek philosophical concepts which created the Christian dogma. To what degree are they valid today? Of course, it is not necessary to reject something simply because it happens to be Roman or Greek, but neither is it necessary to accept something which the church has derived from Rome or Greece, even if sanctioned by a dogmatic decision.

C. Hellenistic Philosophy

Within this realm of one world, of a world history and monarchy created by Rome, we have Greek thought. This is the Hellenistic period of Greek philosophy. We distinguish the classical period of Greek thought, which ends with the death of Aristotle, from the Hellenistic period which includes the Stoics, Epicureans, Neo-Pythagoreans, Skeptics, and Neo-Platonists. This Hellenistic period is the immediate source of much of Christian thought. It was not so much classical Greek thinking but Hellenistic thought which influenced early Christianity.

Again I want to distinguish the negative and the positive elements in Greek thought in the period of the *kairos*, the period of the ancient world coming to an end. The negative side is what we would call Skepticism. Skepticism, not only in the school of the Skeptics but also in the other schools of Greek philosophy, is the end of the tremendous and admirable attempt to build a world of meaning on the basis of an interpretation of reality in objective and rational terms. Greek philosophy had undercut the ancient mythological and ritual traditions. At the time of Socrates and the Sophists it became obvious that these traditions were not valid any more. Sophism is the revolution of the subjective mind against the old traditions. But life must go on; the meaning of life in all realms had yet to be probed, in politics, law, art, social relations, knowledge, religion, etc. This the Greek philosophers tried to do. They were not people sitting behind their desks writing philosophical books. If they had done nothing but philosophize about philosophy, we would have forgotten their names long ago. But they were people who took upon themselves the task of creating a spiritual world by observing reality objectively as it was given to them, interpreting it in terms of analytic and synthetic reason.

1. *Skepticism*

This great attempt of the Greek philosophers to create a world of meaning broke down at the end of the ancient world and produced what I call the skeptical end of the ancient development. Originally *skepsis* meant "observing" things. But it has received the negative sense of looking at every dogma, even the *dogmata* of the Greek schools of philosophy, and thereby undercutting them. The Skeptics were those who doubted the statements of all schools of philosophy. What is perhaps even more important is that these schools of philosophy, for example, the Platonic Academy, took a lot of these skeptical elements into themselves. Skepticism did not go beyond probabilism, while the other schools became pragmatic. Thus a skeptical mood entered all the schools and permeated the whole life of the later ancient world. This skepticism was a very serious matter of life. Again it was not a matter of sitting behind one's desk and finding out that everything can be doubted. That is comparatively easy. Rather, it was an inner breakdown of all convictions. The consequence was— and this was very characteristic of the Greek mind—that if they were no longer able to render theoretical judgments, they believed that they could not act practically either. Therefore, they introduced the doctrine of *epochē*, which meant "restraining, keeping down, neither making a judgment nor acting, deciding neither theoretically nor practically." This doctrine of *epochē* meant the resignation of judgment in every respect. For this reason these people went into the desert with a suit or gown. The later Christian monks followed them in this respect, because they also were in despair over the possibility of living in this world. Some of the skeptics of the ancient church were very serious people, and drew the consequences which our snobbistic skeptics today are usually unwilling to do, who have a very good time while doubting everything. The Greek skeptics retired from life in order to be consistent.

This element of skepticism was an important preparation for Christianity. The Greek schools, the Epicureans, Stoics, Academics, Peripatetics, Neo-Pythagoreans, were not only schools in the sense in which we today speak of philosophical schools, for example, the school of Dewey or Whitehead. A Greek philosophical school was also a cultic community; it was half-ritual and half-philosophical in character. These people wanted to live according to the doctrines of their masters. During this period when the skeptical mood permeated the ancient world, they wanted certainty above all; they demanded it in order to live.

Their answer was that their great teachers, Plato or Aristotle, Zeno the Stoic or Epicurus, and at a later time, Plotinus, were not merely thinkers or professors, but they were inspired men. Long before Christianity the idea of inspiration was developed in these Greek schools; the founders of these schools were inspired. When members of these schools later entered into discussion with Christians, they said, for example, that Heraclitus, not Moses, was inspired. This doctrine of inspiration gave Christianity also a chance to enter into the world. Pure reason alone is not able to build up a reality in which one can live.

What was said about the character of the founders of these philosophical schools was very similar to what the Christians also said about the founder of their church. It is interesting that a man like Epicurus—who later was so much attacked by the Christians that only some of his fragments remain—was called *soter* by his pupils. This is the Greek word which the New Testament uses and which we translate as "savior". Epicurus the philosopher was called a savior. What does this mean? He is usually regarded as a man who always had a good time in his beautiful gardens and who taught an anti-Christian hedonistic philosophy. The ancient world thought quite differently about Epicurus. He was called *soter* because he did the greatest thing anyone could do for his followers: he liberated them from anxiety. Epicurus, with his materialistic system of atoms, liberated them from the fear of demons which permeated the whole life of the ancient world. This shows what a serious thing philosophy was at that time.

Another consequence of this skeptical mood was what the Stoics called *apatheia* (apathy), which means being without feelings toward the vital drives of life such as desires, joys, pains, and instead being beyond all these in the state of wisdom. They knew that only a few people could reach this state. Those who went into the desert as Skeptics showed that they were able to do so to a certain extent. Behind all this, of course, stands the earlier criticism of the mythological gods and the traditional rites. The criticism of mythology happened in Greece about the same time that Second Isaiah did it in Judea. It was a very similar kind of criticism and had the effect of undercutting the belief in the gods of polytheism.

2. The Platonic Tradition

We have dealt with the negative side in Greek thought at the time of the *kairos*. But there were also some positive elements. First we will take up the Platonic tradition. The idea of transcendence, that there is something that surpasses empirical reality, was prepared for Christian theology in the Platonic tradition. Plato spoke of essential reality, of "ideas" (*ousia*) as the true essences of things. At the same time we find in Plato, and even stronger in later Platonism and Neo-Platonism, a trend toward the devaluation of existence. The material world has no ultimate value in comparison with the essential world. Also in Plato the inner aim of human existence is described—somewhere in the *Philebus*, but also practically everywhere in Plato—as becoming similar to God as much as possible. God is the spiritual sphere. The inner *telos* of human existence is participation in the spiritual, divine sphere as much as possible. This element in the Platonic tradition was used especially by the Cappadocian Fathers of the church to describe the ultimate aim of human existence.

A third doctrine besides the idea of transcendence and the *telos* of human existence described the soul as falling down from an eternal participation in the essential or spiritual world, being on earth in a body, then trying to get rid of its bondage to the body, and finally reaching an elevation above the material world. This happens in steps and degrees. This element was also taken into the church, not only by all Christian mystics, but also by the official church fathers to a great extent.

The fourth point in which the Platonic tradition was important was its idea of providence. This seems to us to be a Christian idea, but it was already formulated by Plato in his later writings. It was a tremendous attempt to overcome the anxiety of fate and death in the ancient world. In the late ancient world the anxiety of accident and necessity, or fate, as we would call it today, represented by the Greek goddesses *Tychē* and *Haimarmene*, was a very powerful thing. In Romans 8, where we have the greatest hymn of triumph in the New Testament, we hear that it is the function of Christ to overcome the demonic forces of fate. The fact that Plato anticipated this situation by his doctrine of providence is one of his greatest contributions. This providence, coming from the highest god, gives us the courage to escape the vicissitudes of fate.

A fifth element was added to the Platonic tradition which came from Aristotle. The divine is a form without matter, perfect in itself. This is the profoundest idea in Aristotle. This highest form, called "God", is moving the world, not causally by pushing it from the outside, but by driving everything finite toward him by means of love. In spite of his apparently scientific attitude toward reality, Aristotle developed one of the greatest systems of love. He said that God, the highest form, or pure actuality (*actus purus*), as he called it, moves everything by being loved by everything. Everything has the desire to unite itself with the highest form, to get rid of the lower forms in which it lives, where it is in the bondage of matter. Later the Aristotelian God, as the highest form, entered into Christian theology and exerted a tremendous influence upon it.

3. *The Stoics*

The Stoics were more important than Plato and Aristotle together for the life of the late ancient world. The life of the educated man in the ancient world at this time was shaped mostly by the Stoic tradition. In my book, *The Courage to Be*, I have dealt with the Stoic idea of the courage to take fate and death upon oneself. There I show that Christianity and the Stoics are the great competitors in the whole Western world. But here I want to show something else. Christianity took from its great competitor many fundamental ideas. The first is the doctrine of the Logos, a doctrine that may bring you to despair when you study the history of trinitarian and christological thought. The dogmatic development of Christianity cannot be understood without it.

Logos means "word". But it also refers to the meaning of a word, the reasonable structure which is indicated by a word. Therefore, Logos can also mean the universal law of reality. This is what Heraclitus meant by it, who was the first to use this word philosophically. The Logos for him was the law which determines the movements of all reality.

For the Stoics the Logos was the divine power which is present in everything that is. There are three aspects to it, all of which become extremely important in the later development. The first is the law of nature. The Logos is the principle according to which all natural things move. It is the divine seed, the creative divine power, which makes anything what it is. And it is the creative power of movement of all things. Secondly, Logos means the moral law. With Immanuel Kant we could call this the "practical reason", the law which is innate in every human being when he accepts himself as a personality, with the dignity and greatness of a person. When we see the term "natural law" in classical books, we should not think of physical laws, but of moral laws. For example, when we speak of the "rights of man" as embodied in the American Constitution, we are speaking of natural law.

Thirdly, Logos also means man's ability to recognize reality; we could call it "theoretical reason". It is man's ability to reason. Because man has the Logos in himself, he can discover it in nature and history. From this it follows for Stoicism that the man who is determined by the natural law, the Logos, is the *logikos*, the wise man. But the Stoics were not optimists. They did not believe that everybody was a wise man. Perhaps there were only a few who ever reached this ideal. All the others were either fools or stood somewhere between the wise and the foolish. So Stoicism held a basic pessimism about the majority of human beings.

Originally the Stoics were Greeks; later they were Romans. Some of the most famous Stoics were Roman emperors, for example, Marcus Aurelius. They applied the concept of the Logos to the political situation for which they were responsible. The meaning of the natural law was that every man participates in reason by virtue of the fact that he is a human being. From this basis they derived laws far superior to many that we find in the Christian Middle Ages. They gave universal citizenship to every human being because everyone potentially participates in reason. Of course, they did not believe that people were actually reasonable, but they presupposed that through education they could become so. Granting Roman citizenship to all citizens of the conquered nations was a tremendous equalizing step. Women, slaves, and children, who were regarded as inferior beings under the old Roman law, became equalized by the laws of the Roman emperors. This was done not by Christianity but by the Stoics, who derived this idea from their belief in the universal Logos in which everyone participates. (Of course, Christianity holds the same idea on a different basis: all human beings are the children of God the Father.) Thus the Stoics conceived of the idea of a state embracing the whole world, based on the common rationality of everybody. This was something which Christianity could take up and develop. The difference was that the Stoics did not have the concept of sin. They had the concept of foolishness, but not sin. Therefore, salvation in Stoicism is a salvation through reaching wisdom. In Christianity salvation is brought about by divine grace. These two approaches are in conflict with each other to the present day.

4. *Eclecticism*

Eclecticism is another reality which was taken over by the Christian Church. This comes from a Greek word meaning to choose some possibilities out of many. Americans should not have contempt for this because in this respect as in so many others they are like the ancient Romans. The Eclectics were not creative philosophers like the Greeks. The Roman thinkers were often at the same time politicians and statesmen. As Eclectics they did not create new systems. Instead, they chose (Cicero, for example) the most important concepts from the classical Greek systems which they thought would be pragmatically useful for Roman citizens. From a pragmatic point of view they chose what would make possible the best way of living for a Roman citizen, as a citizen of the world state. The main ideas which they chose, which we find again in the eighteenth-century Enlightenment, were the following: the idea of providence, which provides a feeling of safety to the life of the people; the idea of God as innate in everybody, which induces fear of God and discipline; the idea of moral freedom and responsibility, which makes it possible to educate and to hold people accountable for moral failure; and finally the idea of immortality, which threatens with another world those who escape punishment in this one. All these ideas were in some way a preparation for the Christian mission.

D. THE INTER-TESTAMENTAL PERIOD

We come now to the Hellenistic period of the Jewish religion. In Judaism during the inter-testamental period there developed ideas and attitudes which deeply influenced the apostolic age, that is, Jesus, the apostles, and the writers of the New Testament.

The development in the idea of God during this period between the Testaments was toward a radical transcendence. God becomes more and more transcendent, and for this reason he becomes more and more universal. But a God who is both absolutely transcendent and absolutely universal has lost many of the concrete traits which the God of a nation has. For this reason names were introduced to preserve some of the concreteness of the divinity, names like "heaven". For example, in the New Testament we often find the term "kingdom of heaven" in place of "kingdom of God". At the same time, the abstraction is carried on under two influences: (1) the prohibition against using the name of God; (2) the struggle against anthropomorphisms, that is, seeing God in the image (*morphē*) of man (*anthropos*). Consequently the passions of the God of the Old Testament disappear and the abstract oneness is emphasized. This made it possible for the Greek philosophers, who had introduced the same radical abstraction with respect to God, and the Jewish universalists to unite on the idea of God. It was Philo of Alexandria, in particular, who carried through this union.

When God becomes abstract, however, it is not sufficient to hypostasize some of his qualities, such as heaven, height, glory, etc. Mediating beings must appear between God and man. During the inter-testamental period these mediating beings became more and more important for practical piety. First, there were the angels, deteriorated gods and goddesses from surrounding paganism. During the period when the prophets fought against polytheism, they could not play any role. When the danger of polytheism was completely overcome, as it was in later Judaism, the angels could reappear without much danger of a relapse into it. Even so, however, the New Testament is aware of this danger and warns against the cult of the angels.

The second type of figure was the Messiah. The Messiah became a transcendent being, the king of paradise. In the Book of Daniel, which is dependent on Persian religion, the Messiah is also called the "Son of Man" who will judge the world. In Daniel this term is probably used for Israel, but later it became the figure of the "man from above" as described by Paul in I Corinthians 15. Thirdly, the names of God are increased and become almost living figures. The most important of these figures is the Wisdom of God, which appears already in the Old Testament. Wisdom created the world, appeared in it, and then returned to heaven since it did not find a place among men. This is very close to the idea in the Prologue of the Fourth Gospel.

Another of these powers between God and man is the *shekinah*, the dwelling of God on earth. Another is the *memra'*, the Word of God, which later became so important in the Fourth Gospel. Still another is the "Spirit of God", which in the Old Testament means God in action. Now, however, it became a partly independent figure between the most high God and man. The Logos became most important for it united the Jewish *memra'* with the Greek philosophical *logos*. Logos in Philo is the *protogenēs huios theou*, the first-born Son of God. These mediating beings between the most high God and man to some extent replace the immediacy of the relationship to God. As in Christianity, particularly in Roman Catholic Christianity, the ever more transcendent idea of God was made acceptable to the popular mind by the introduction of the saints into practical piety. The official doctrine remained monotheistic; the saints were to receive only veneration, never adoration.

Between man and God there arose also another world of beings having great power, namely, the realm of demons. There were evil as well as good angels. These evil angels are not only the agencies of temptation and punishment under God's direction, but they are also a realm of power in opposition to God. This comes out clearly in Jesus' conversation with the Pharisees concerning the divine or demonic power in connection with his exorcism of demons. This belief in demons permeated the daily life of that time and was also the subject of the highest speculations. Although there was an element of dualism here, it never reached the state of an ontological dualism. Here again Judaism was able to introduce a number of ideas from Persia, including the demonology of Persian religion in which the demons have the same status as the gods, but it never lapsed into an ontological dualism. All the demonic powers derive their power from the one God; they have no standing on their own in an ultimate sense. This comes out in the mythology of the fallen angels. The evil angels as created beings are good, but as fallen they are evil angels, and therefore they are responsible and punishable. They are not simply creations of an anti-divine being. Here we have the first anti-pagan dogma.

Another influence from this period on the New Testament is the elevation of the future into a coming aeon. In the late apocalyptic period of Jewish history, world history was divided into two aeons, into this aeon in which we are living (*aiōn houtos*) and the coming aeon which is expected (*aiōn mellon*). This aeon is evaluated very pessimistically, while the coming aeon is awaited with ecstasy. The coming aeon is not only a political idea; it goes beyond the political hopes of the Maccabean period in which the Maccabees defended the Jewish people against tyranny. Nor was it a statement of the prophetic message; the prophetic message was much more historical and this-worldly. These apocalyptic ideas were cosmological; the whole cosmos participates in these two aeons. This aeon is controlled by demonic forces; the world, even nature itself, is ageing and fading away. One of the reasons for this is that man has subjected himself to the demonic forces and is disobedient against the law. Adam's fall has produced the universal destiny of death. This idea was developed from the brief story of the fall in Genesis into a system as we find it in Paul. This fall is confirmed by every individual through his actual sin. This aeon is under a tragic fate, but in spite of that the individual is responsible for it.

During this inter-testamental period the piety of the law gains in importance, in part replacing the piety of the cult. Of course, the temple still exists, but the synagogue is developed alongside it as a religious school. The synagogue becomes the form in which the decisive religious life develops. The law was not evaluated in the negative way in which we usually do it; for the Jews it was a gift and a joy. The law was eternal, always in God and pre-existent in the same way that later Christian theology said that Jesus was pre-existent. The contents of the law provided for the organization of the whole of life, down to the smallest functions. Every moment of life was under God. This was the profound idea of the legalism of the Pharisees which Jesus attacked so vigorously. For this legalism produces an intolerable burden. There are always two possibilities in religion if an intolerable burden is placed on thought and action; the first is the way of compromise, which is the way of the majority. This means that the burden is reduced to the point that it can be endured. The second is the way of despair, which was the way of people like Paul, Augustine, and Luther. In IV Esdras we read: "We who have received the law shall be lost because of our sins, but the law never will be lost." Here a mood is expressed which is reflected in many Pauline sayings, a mood that permeated late Judaism during the period between the Testaments. Many of these ideas left their imprint on the New Testament.

E. THE MYSTERY RELIGIONS

The mystery religions were also influential on early Christian theology. These mystery religions should not be equated with mysticism as such. Mysticism is something that we find in Philo, for example. He developed a doctrine of ecstasy, or *ek-stasis*, which means "standing outside oneself". This is the highest form of piety which lies beyond faith. This mysticism unites prophetic ecstasy with "enthusiasm", a word which comes from *en-theos-mania*, meaning to possess the divine. From this there comes finally the fully developed mystical system of the Neo-Platonists, for example, of Dionysius the Areopagite. In this mystical system the ecstasy of the individual person leads to a union with the One, with the Absolute, with God.

But besides this development of mysticism we have the even more important development of the concrete mystery gods. These mystery gods are in a sense monotheistic, that is, the person who is initiated into a given mystery has a concrete god who is, at the same time, the only god. However, it was possible to be initiated into more than one mystery. This means that the figures of the mystery gods were exchangeable. There is lacking here the exclusiveness of Yahweh in the Old Testament.

These mystery gods greatly influenced the Christian cult and theology. If someone is initiated into a mystery, as later the Christians initiated their members into the congregations by steps, he participates in the mystery god and in the experiences of that deity. In Romans 6 Paul describes such experiences with respect to Jesus in terms of participation in his death and resurrection. An ecstatic experience is produced in the mystery activities. Those who participate are brought into a state of deep sorrow over the death of the god, and then after a time they have an ecstatic experience of the god resurrected. The suffering god is described in these mysteries. Ever since the Delphic Apollo we have the idea of the participation of God in the suffering of man. Apollo at Delphi had to pay for the guilt of slaying the powers of the underworld which have their own rights. Then there are the methods of introduction through psychological means. Intoxication is brought about by a change of light and darkness, by ascetic fasting, by incense, sounds, music, etc.

These mysteries also had an esoteric character. Initiation could only follow upon a harsh process of selection and preparation. In this way the mystery of the performances was protected against profanation. Later in the Christian congregations a similar thing took place in order to protect against betrayal to the pagan persecutors.

F. THE METHOD OF THE NEW TESTAMENT

All of the elements we have discussed were a preparation for the rise of Christianity. The decisive preparation, however, was the event which is documented in the New Testament. Here we cannot present a New Testament theology, but we can show, by means of a few examples, how the New Testament received from the surrounding religions categories of interpretation and transformed them in the light of the reality of Jesus as the Christ. This means that there were always two steps, reception and transformation. The categories which had developed in the various religions, in the Old Testament, and in the inter-testamental period, were used to interpret the event of Jesus' appearance, but the meanings of these categories were transformed in being applied to him.

With respect to christology, for example, Messiah is the ancient prophetic symbol. This symbol was applied to Jesus by the early disciples, perhaps at the very beginning of their encounter with him. This was a great paradox. On the one hand, it was adequate because Jesus brings the new being; on the other hand, it was inadequate because many of the connotations of the term "Messiah" go beyond the actual appearance of Jesus. According to the records, Jesus himself realized the difficulty of this double judgment. Therefore, he prohibited his disciples to use this term. Now it may be that this is a later construction of the records;

but however that may be, it does mirror the double judgment that this category is both adequate and inadequate.

The same thing is true of the "Son of Man" concept. On the one hand, it is adequate, and perhaps used by Jesus himself, for it points to the divine power present in him to bring the new aeon. On the other hand, it is inadequate because the Son of Man was supposed to appear in power and glory.

The term "Son of David" was also used. It is adequate since he was supposed to be the fulfiller of all the prophecies. Yet it is inadequate because David was a king, so "Son of David" can indicate a political leader and king. Jesus resisted this misunderstanding when he said that David himself called the Messiah his Lord.

The "Son of God" is an adequate term because of the special relationship and intimate communion between Jesus and God. At the same time it is inadequate because "Son of God" is a very familiar pagan concept. The pagan gods propagated sons on earth. Because of this the words "only begotten" were added and he was called "eternal". The Jews had difficulty with this term because of its pagan connotations. They could speak of Israel as "Son of God" but they could not apply it to an individual.

The title "kyrios" means Lord; it is adequate because of its use in the Old Testament where it is an expression of divine power. At the same time it is inadequate because the mystery gods were also *kyrioi*, lords, and, furthermore, Jesus was pictured concretely as a finite being. It was adequate because the mystery gods were objects of mystical union, and so was Jesus. For Paul especially, a person could be in Christ (*en Christō*), that is, in the power, holiness, and fear of his being.

Finally, the concept "Logos" was adequate insofar as it expressed the universal self-manifestation of God in all forms of reality. In Greek philosophy and Jewish symbolism it is the cosmic principle of creation. Yet it is inadequate because the Logos is a universal principle, whereas Jesus is a concrete reality. His is a concrete personal life described by this term. This is expressed in the great paradox of Christianity: the Logos became flesh. Here we have a perfect example of how the meaning of a term, with all the connotations it had from the past, can be transformed in expressing the Christian message. The idea that the universal Logos became flesh could never have been derived from the

Greek thought. Therefore, the church fathers emphasized again and again that while the Greek philosophers possessed the idea of the universal Logos, what was peculiarly Christian was that the Logos became flesh in a personal life.

The greatness of the New Testament is that it was able to use words, concepts, and symbols which had developed in the history of religions and at the same time preserve the picture of Jesus who was interpreted by them. The spiritual power of the New Testament was great enough to take all these concepts into Christianity, with all their pagan and Jewish connotations, without losing the basic reality, namely, the event of Jesus as the Christ, which these concepts were supposed to interpret.

CHAPTER II

Theological Developments in the Ancient Church

A. THE APOSTOLIC FATHERS

WE come now to the apostolic fathers, the earliest post-biblical writers we know of, some of them even earlier than the later books of the New Testament. These apostolic fathers, Ignatius of Antioch, Clement of Rome, "The Shepherd" of Hermas, and others, were more dependent on a Christian conformism that had gradually developed than on the outspoken position of Paul in his Letters. Paul's influence during this period was felt more indirectly through John and Ignatius. The reason for this, at least in part, was that the controversy with the Jews was a matter of the past; Paul's conflict with the Jewish Christians did not have to be continued. Instead of that, the positive elements in the faith which could provide an understandable content for the pagans had to be brought out. In general one could say that in the period of the apostolic fathers the great visions of the first ecstatic breakthrough had disappeared, leaving in their place a given set of ideas which produced a kind of ecclesiastical conformity, and making the missionary work possible. Some people have complained about this development, deploring that so early after the second generation of Christians the power of the Spirit was on the wane. This is an unavoidable thing, however, in all creative periods. One needs only to think of the Reformation. After the breakthrough and after the second generation which received the breakthrough, a fixation or concentration on some special points begins. There are the educational needs to preserve what was given earlier.

Nevertheless, this period of the apostolic fathers is extremely

important, even though it may have considerably lost its spiritual
power in comparison with the preceding period of the apostles,
since it preserved what was needed for the life of the congregations. The first question to be asked was: Where could one find
the expression of the common spirit of the congregation? Originally the real mediators of the message were those who were
bearers of the Spirit, the "pneumatics", those who had the *pneuma*.
But as we know from Paul's first letter to the Corinthians,
especially chapter 12, he already encountered difficulties with the
bearers of the Spirit because they produced disorder. So he laid
stress on order together with the Spirit. In the Pastoral Epistles,
which were attributed to Paul, the emphasis on ecclesiastical
order became increasingly important. By the time of the apostolic
fathers the ecstatic spirit had almost disappeared. It was considered dangerous. And why, they asked, do we need it? Everything the Spirit had to say has already been classically expressed
in Scripture and tradition. Therefore, instead of the prophets who
traveled from place to place as the apostles did, we now have
definite norms and authorities arising in the Christian congregations. What were these norms and authorities?

The first and basic authority was the Old Testament. Next to
that was the earliest collection of writings which are now in the
New Testament. The limits of the New Testament had not yet
been definitely set. It took more than two hundred years for the
church to make a final decision on all the books in the New
Testament canon.

Besides these writings there was already a complex of dogmatic and ethical doctrines which had become traditional. In I
Clement these are called "the canon of our tradition". This tradition had various names, like truth, gospel, doctrine, and commandments. This, however, was a large amount of material; it
had to be narrowed down for those who were to be baptized. So
a creed was created which they could confess when they became
members of the church. This creed had a similarity to our present
Apostles' Creed, because its center was also christological.
Christology was at the center because this is what distinguished
the Christian communities from Judaism as well as paganism.

Baptism was the sacrament of entrance into the church. The
baptized person, who at that time, of course, was a pagan adult,
had to confess that he would accept the implications of his

baptism. Then he was baptized in the name of Christ. Later on the names of God the Father and the Spirit were added. As yet there were no accompanying explanations; this was faith and liturgy, not yet theology.

All these things were going on in the church. This church was the *ekklesia*, the assembly of God or Christ. The original meaning of *ekklesia* was "called out". They were called out of the houses and nations to form the church universal; they were called out of the barbarians, out of the Greeks and the Jews, to become the true people of God. Of course, the Jews anticipated this and were a kind of *ekklesia* themselves. But they were not the true people of God, for the true people of God are universally called out of all the nations. If this is the case, it becomes necessary for those called together unto the conformity of the ecclesiastical creed to distinguish themselves from those outside and from heretics inside. How can this be done? How is it possible to determine whether a doctrine conforms to the doctrines of the church instead of being introduced from barbarian, Greek, or Jewish teachings? The answer was that this can be done only by the bishop who is the "overseer" of the congregation. The bishop represents the Spirit who is supposed to be within the whole congregation. In the struggle against pagans, Jews, barbarians, and heretics, the bishop became more and more important. In his letter to the Smyrneans Ignatius wrote: "Where the bishop is, there the congregation should be." Prophets who appear may be right or wrong, but the bishop is right. The bishops were representatives of the true doctrine. Originally the bishops were not distinguished from the presbyters or elders. Gradually, however, the bishop became a monarch among the elders, giving rise to the monarchical episcopate. This is a natural development. If the authority which guarantees truth is embodied in human beings, it is almost unavoidable that there will be a tendency to narrow down upon one individual who holds the final decision. In Clement of Rome we already find traces of the idea of apostolic succession, that is, that the bishop represents the apostles. This shows clearly how early the problem of authority became decisive in the church and started a trend toward its fuller development in the Roman Church.

We shall now take up some of the special doctrines of this period. In view of the pagan world in which these Christians lived it was essential to emphasize above all a monotheistic idea of God. Thus the Shepherd of Hermas says: "First of all, believe that God is one, who has made all things, bringing them out of nothing into being." The doctrine of creation out of nothing is expressed here. Although we cannot find this doctrine explicitly in the Old Testament, it might be said to be implicit there, and certainly was expressed prior to Christianity by the Jewish theologians during the inter-testamental period. This doctrine was decisive for the separation of the early church from paganism.

Along the same line was the emphasis on the almighty God, the *despotēs*, as he was called, the powerful ruling Lord. Clement exclaims, "O great demiurge", speaking of him as the great builder of the universe and the Lord of everything. These concepts which seem so natural to us were important because they were a defense against paganism. Creation out of nothing means that God did not find an already pre-existent matter when he started to create. There was no matter which resists form, as it was in Neo-Platonic paganism, and which must therefore be transcended. Instead, the material world is an object of God's creation; it is good and must not be disparaged for the sake of salvation. The word "demiurge" was used in Plato and Gnosticism for something below the highest God. The highest God is beyond doing such a lowly thing as creating the world, and so he leaves that to the demiurge. This means that the divine reality is not present in the act of creation. Against this notion Clement says that the great demiurge is God himself; there is no dichotomy between the highest God and the maker of the world. Creation is an absolute act out of nothing. This implies God's almighty power. To say that God is almighty does not mean that God is one who sits on a throne and can do anything he wants to do like an arbitrary tyrant. Rather, almightiness means that God is the sole ground of everything created, and that there is no such thing as matter which resists him. This is the meaning of the first article of the Apostles' Creed: "I believe in God the Father Almighty, Maker of heaven and earth." We should read this with great awe, because by this confession Christianity separated itself from the dualistic interpretation of reality in paganism. There are not two eternal principles, an evil principle of matter as eternal as a good principle of form. The first article of the Creed is the great wall which Christianity erected against paganism. Without this wall christology inevitably deteriorates into gnosticism in which Christ is one of the cosmic powers alongside others, although perhaps the highest among them. Only in the light of the first article is the second article of the Creed meaningful. Do not reduce God to the second Person of the Trinity.

As the ruler of everything God has a plan of salvation. Ignatius in particular develops this idea of a plan of salvation. In his letter to the Ephesians he speaks of the "economy towards the new man". This is a wonderful summary of the Christian message. Economy here means "building a house". It is used for the structure of the relationships between God and the world. There is an economy of trinitarian thinking: Father, Son, and Spirit. Only all three together are God. There is an economy of salvation, that is the building up of the different periods which finally lead to the new man. This idea of the new man, the new creature or new being, as the aim of the history of salvation is an important contribution of these theologians. This economy of salvation is already present in the period of the Old Testament. So Ignatius says: "Judaism has believed towards Christianity." The Christ, the new man, is the perfect fulfillment in which the disruption of the old man is overcome and death is dissolved. This leads to Christology.

Generally one can say that Jesus as the Christ was considered to be a pre-existent spiritual being who had transformed the historical Jesus into an agent of his saving activity. The Spirit is a hypostasis in God, an independent power in complete union with God. The Son came into the realm of flesh. "Flesh" here always means historical reality. He accepted flesh; or the flesh co-operated with the Spirit in him. The Holy Spirit dwelt in the flesh which he chose. He became the Son of God by his service.

Alongside this there was another idea. One could also say that the first Spirit, the proton pneuma, became flesh. For instance, Ignatius said: "Christ is God and perfect man at the same time. He comes from the Spirit and the seed of David." This means that he is not only some spiritual power which has accepted flesh, but that he as the spiritual power has become flesh.

Another term that was used was iatros, physician. Salvation was still understood here as healing. This physician heals both fleshly and spiritually. Very mixed ideas were used to emphasize that something paradoxical has happened, that a divine spiritual power has appeared under the conditions of humanity and existence. Thus, he is depicted as one having genesis and at the same time without genesis; he has come into the flesh; he has entered into death. But he is God who came into flesh and in death has eternal life. He is both from Mary and from God; he is able to suffer and not able to suffer, because of his elevation to God.

Ignatius could say: "For there is one God who made himself manifest through Jesus Christ his Son, who is his logos, proceeding from his silence." And II Clement: "Being the first Spirit, the head of the angels, he became flesh. Being he who appears in human form, Christ is the word proceeding out of the silence." He proceeds from silence, *apo sigēs*. The Christ breaks the eternal silence of the divine ground. As such he is both God and complete man. The same historical reality is the one as well as the other, both as one person. One could speak of a double message (a *diplon kerygma*), the message that this same being is both God *and* man.

Here we see the chief religious interest of this whole period, the interest, as Clement says, to speak theologically of Christ as of God. "Brothers, so we must think about Jesus Christ as about God, for if we think small things about him, we can hope to receive small things only." The absoluteness of salvation demands an absolute divine Savior. We are confronted here by the problem of two possible ways of thinking: Did Christ come into the flesh, accepting it? Or did he come as the Logos, being transformed into it? Both types of christology already appear, taking on flesh, or being transformed into it.

The idea of the divine Logos breaking the silence of God is very profound. It means that the divine abyss in itself is without word, form, object, and voice. It is the infinite silence of the eternal. But out of this divine silence, the Logos breaks forth and opens up what is hidden in this silence. He reveals the divine ground.

The christology we find here is not a theoretical problem; rather, the christological problem is one side of the soteriological problem. The interest is to have a safe salvation; the desire is to get the courage which overcomes the anxiety of being lost. The question of salvation is the basis of the christological question. What is this salvation? The work of Christ is twofold, first, *gnōsis* (knowledge) and secondly *zōē* (life). This is the way salvation was conceived of in the early Greek church. Christ brings knowledge and life. Sometimes the two things are combined in the phrase *athanatos gnōsis*, immortal knowledge, knowledge of that which is immortal and which makes immortal.

Christ called us from darkness into light; he made us serve the Father of truth. He called us who had no being and willed that we have being, out of his new being. This means that knowledge brings being. Knowledge and being belong together; so do lie and non-being. Truth is being; new truth is new being. Whoever has this knowledge of being has saving knowledge. This has to be emphasized against a gross misunderstanding. Harnack and his followers viewed ancient Christianity as being infected by Greek intellectualism. There are two things wrong in this viewpoint. First, Greek intellectualism is an inappropriate term because the Greeks were extremely interested in truth. With but some exceptions, the truth they wanted to have was existential truth, truth concerning their existence, truth that saves them out of this distorted existence and elevates them to the immovable One. The early Christian congregations understood truth in the same way. Truth is not theoretical knowledge about objects, but cognitive participation in a new reality that has appeared in the Christ. Without this participation no truth is possible, and knowledge is abstract and meaningless. This is what they meant when they combined knowledge and being. Participating in the new being is participation in truth, in the true knowledge.

This identity of truth and being mediates life. Christ gives immortal knowledge, the knowledge which gives immortality. He is the Savior and leader of immortality. In his own being he is our imperishable life. He gives both the knowledge of immortality and the drug of immortality, which is the sacrament. Ignatius called the Lord's Supper the remedy against our having to die, the *antidoton tō mē apothanein*. There is a very profound meaning in this idea that the sacramental materials of the Lord's Supper are, so to speak, drugs or remedies which produce immortality. First of all, it shows that the apostolic fathers did not believe in the immortality of the soul. There is no natural immortality, otherwise it would be meaningless for them to speak about immortal life which Christ offers. They believed that man is naturally mortal, just as the Old Testament held that in paradise man was able to eat from the food of the gods, called the "tree of life", and to keep alive by participating in this divine power. Similarly the apostolic fathers taught that with the coming of Christ the situation of paradise has been re-established. Again we may participate in the food of eternity, which is the body and the blood of Christ. In doing this we build into ourselves a counter-balance to our natural having to die. Death is the wages of sin only insofar as sin is separation from God. Because of this sin God's power to overcome our natural having to die does not work any more. But with Christ's coming it works again. It works in a sacramentally realistic way in the materials of the sacrament of the Lord's Supper. In the light of this we can conclude that our traditional way of speaking of the immortality of the soul is not classically Christian doctrine, but a distortion of it, not in a genuine, but in a pseudo-Platonic sense.

B. THE APOLOGETIC MOVEMENT

The Apologetic movement can rightly be called the birthplace of a developed Christian theology. Christianity needed apologetics for different reasons. An *apologia* means a reply or answer to a judge in the court, if someone should accuse you. Socrates' *apologia*, for instance, was his answer to those who accused him. Likewise, Christianity expressed itself in terms of answers to particular accusations. Those who did this systematically are called the Apologists.

Answers were needed because of a double accusation against Christianity: (1) Christianity was a threat to the Roman Empire. This was a political accusation; Christianity undermines the structure of the empire; (2) Christianity was, philosophically speaking, nonsense, a superstition mixed with philosophical fragments. These two attacks supported each other. The philosophical attack was taken over by the political authorities and used in their accusations. Thus the philosophical attacks became dangerous in terms of their political consequences. Celsus, the physician and philosopher, was the most important representative of these attacks. It is important to know his thinking if we want to see how Christianity was regarded at that time by an educated Greek philosopher and scientist. Celsus saw Christianity as a mixture of fanatic superstition and piecemeal philosophy. According to him the historical reports in the Bible are contradictory and lack any certain evidence. Here for the first time we have historical criticism of the Old and New Testaments, something which will be repeated later again and again. In Celsus it is criticism motivated by hate. Later, in the eighteenth century, we witness a criticism moved by a love toward the reality which lies behind these reports.

In turning to Celsus' attack on Christianity, we find that one of the main points is the resurrection of Jesus. Celsus observed that this event, which is supposed to be so important, was witnessed only by adherents of the faith, and at first only by a few ecstatic women. The deification of Jesus is not any different from the processes of deification which we know of elsewhere in history. For example, Euhemerus, the Cynic, has given enough examples of the way in which a human being, a king or hero, was deified. What is particularly disgusting, Celsus said, is that when the stories are most incredible, as many of the Old Testament stories, they are explained away allegorically. Of course, this was actually done. An element of anti-Judaism is visible in Celsus' criticism of the Old Testament miracle stories. This is understandable because Celsus was directing his criticisms against the Jews as much as against the Christians.

Celsus charged that the descent of God contradicts the unchangeable character of God which the Christian writers had also strongly emphasized. But if the divine Being has descended to earth, why did this happen in a despised corner of the world, and why did it happen only once? Particularly disgusting to the educated pagan—and we have here another element of anti-Judaistic feeling—is the fight between the Jews and Christians whether the Messiah has or has not appeared. The argument from prophecy to fulfillment that was used so much by Christians is also a stupid one. Celsus was historically educated enough to see that the prophet did not anticipate a fulfillment in the terms in which the fulfillment happened. This is an especially sore point in all of church history. For the sound idea of a universal preparatory revelation was distorted into a mechanism of "foreseeing" events which later happened.

Celsus' deepest criticism of Christianity was neither scientific with respect to history nor philosophical with respect to the idea of incarnation; instead, it was one which arose out of a basically religious feeling. He said that the demonic powers which, according to Paul, had been conquered by Christ are actually ruling the world. The world has not changed since the beginning of Christianity. And Celsus adds that there is no sense in trying to overcome these powers; they are the real rulers of the world. Therefore, one should be obedient to the Roman rulers on earth; at least they have reduced the power of the demons to some extent—which is also a Pauline idea. They have established a certain order in which the demonic forces are limited. However questionable the Roman emperors may be as persons, they must be obeyed and venerated, for Rome has become great through obedience to the orders of this world, to the necessities of law and nature. Christians are guilty of undermining the greatness and the glory of Rome, and thus undercut the only power that can prevent the world from falling into chaos and the demons from having a complete victory.

That was a serious attack, one which has been heard frequently in the history of Christianity. Christians who had the same philosophical education that Celsus had tried to answer for the church. The Apologists did not answer the attacks so much on the level of historical criticism as on the philosophical level. They did it in a way which shows three things that characterize every apologetic. First of all, if you want to speak meaningfully with someone, there must be a common basis of some mutually accepted ideas. The truth that is common to both Christians and pagans must first be elaborated. If they have nothing in common, no conversation is possible and no meaningful address to the pagans is possible. A rule for all Christian missionary work is that the other one must understand what you say; but understanding involves at least partial participation. If the missionary speaks an absolutely different language, no understanding is possible. Thus, the Apologists had to show that there is something in common.

Secondly, the Apologists had to point out defects in the ideas of paganism. There are things which contradict the pagan ideas. It can be shown that for centuries pagan philosophers have brought forth criticisms of these ideas. This is the second step of apologetics, namely, showing the negativity in the other. Thirdly, it must be shown that one's own position is not to be accepted as something from the outside, but rather that Christianity is the fulfillment of a longing and desire in paganism. This is the apologetic form of theology which I use in my own systematic theology, that is, the correlation between question and answer.

There is, however, one danger in apologetics; the common ground may be overemphasized at the expense of the differences. Then you merely accept the other as he is, without giving him anything different. A way must be found between the two extremes of either throwing indigestible material at the other from an external position, or telling him what he already knows. The latter is the way liberal theology has often acted, while the former is the way of fundamentalism and orthodoxy.

1. *The Christian Philosophy*

Justin Martyr was perhaps the most important of the Apologists. In speaking of Christianity he said: "This is the only philosophy which I have found certain and adequate." What does this mean? Some anti-apologetic theologians interpret this as evidence that Christianity was dissolved into a philosophy. They say further that this is what every apologetic theology does to Christianity. But when Justin said that Christianity was a philosophy, we must understand what he meant by philosophy. Philosophy at that time referred to the spiritual, non-magical and non-superstitious character of a movement. So Justin was saying that Christianity is the only certain and adequate philosophy because it is not magical or superstitious. For the later Greeks philosophy was not only a theoretical but more a practical matter. It was a matter of existential interpretation of life, a matter of life and death for the existence of the people at that time. To be a philosopher ordinarily meant to belong to a philosophical school, a sort of ritual community in which the founder of the school was supposed to have had a revelatory insight into the truth. Acceptance into such a school was not a matter of having a Ph.D., but of being personally initiated into the atmosphere of this school.

Justin taught that this Christian philosophy is universal; it is the all-embracing truth about the meaning of existence. From this it follows that wherever truth appears, it belongs to the Christians. Truth concerning existence, wherever it appears, is Christian truth. "What anybody has said about the truth belongs to us, the Christians." This is not sheer arrogance. He does not mean that

Christians now possess all the truth, or that they alone discovered it. He means, in terms of the Logos doctrine, that there cannot be truth anywhere which is not in principle included in Christian truth. This is what the Fourth Gospel says: the Logos appeared, full of truth and grace.

And vice versa, Justin said: "Those who live according to the logos are Christians." He included people like Socrates, Heraclitus, and Elijah. He added, however, that the total logos which appeared in Christ has become body, mind, and soul. Therefore, the philosophers apart from Christianity are partly in error and even partly subjected to demonic inspirations which come from the pagan gods. The gods of the heathen are not non-existent; they are real demonic forces and have destructive power.

What does all this mean? It removes the impression that these Christians felt themselves to be just another religion. Actually we find here the negation of the concept of religion with respect to Christianity, as though it were one religion among others, and as though Christianity is right and all other religions wrong. The Apologists would not say that their *religion* is right, the others wrong, but that the Logos has appeared on which their religion is based. He is the full Logos of God himself, appearing in the center of his being, appearing in his totality. This is more than religion. This is truth appearing in time and space. So the word "Christianity" is understood not as a religion but as the negation of *all* religions. In virtue of its universality Christianity is able to embrace them all. Justin said what I think is absolutely necessary to say. If anywhere in the world there were an existential truth which could not be received by Christianity as an element of its own thinking, Jesus would not be the Christ. He would be merely one teacher alongside other teachers, all of whom are limited and partly in error. But that is not what the early Christians said. They said—and we should say—that if we call Jesus the Christ, or the Logos as the Apologists called him, this means that by definition there cannot be any truth which cannot in principle be taken into Christianity. Otherwise the application of the term "Logos" to Jesus as the Christ would not have been possible. This does not mean that this *Logos* knew all the truth; that would be nonsense and would destroy his humanity. But it does mean that the fundamental truth which has appeared in him is essentially universal, and therefore can take in every other truth. For this reason the early theologians did not hesitate to take in as much Greek philosophical truth as they could, and also as much Oriental mysticism as they could.

The appearance of the Logos in Christ makes it possible for even the most uneducated human being to receive the full existential truth. In contrast, the philosophers may lose it in discussing it. In other words, the Apologists are saying that Christianity is far superior to all philosophy. Since philosophy presupposes education, only a few human beings have access to its truth. Others are excluded from truth in its philosophical form. However, they are not excluded from the truth that is manifest through the Logos in a living person. The message of Jesus as the Christ is universal in embracing all mankind, all classes, groups, and social stratifications of mankind.

Another argument that was used in defense of Christianity was the moral power and action of those who belong to the church. Therefore, the Christian congregations could not be dangerous to the Roman Empire. They help to prevent the world from falling into chaos. Even more than the Roman Empire itself, they are supporters of world order. So Justin could say: "The world lives from the prayers of the Christians and from the obedience of the Christians to the law of the state. The Christians preserve the world, and on the other hand, for their sake God preserves the world."

2. *God and the Logos*

The philosophical idea of God is inborn in every human being. All the characteristics which Parmenides attributed to Being are here attributed to God—eternal, without beginning, needing nothing, beyond passions, indestructible, unchangeable, and invisible. There is, however, one point of difference between classical Greek philosophy and Justin's doctrine of God. This difference comes from the Old Testament and changes everything. It is the statement that God is the Almighty Creator! The moment this statement is made, the personal element enters the abstract and mystical description of God's identity. God as Creator is acting, and as the Almighty he is the acting power behind everything which moves.

It is interesting to observe that in such a statement about God,

Christian monotheism oscillates between the transpersonal element of Being and the personal element of God as Creator and, of course, also as Savior. This oscillation is necessary as soon as the idea of God is made an object of thought. One cannot escape some elements of the eternal, the unconditional, the unchangeable, etc. On the other hand, practical piety and our experience of creatureliness presuppose a person-to-person relationship. Christianity must oscillate between these two elements, because both elements are in God himself.

Between God and man there are angels and powers, some good and some evil. But their mediating power is insufficient. The Logos is the real mediator. It is difficult to explain what the word "logos" means, especially to those who are nominalists from birth. It is difficult because this concept is not the description of an individual being, but of a universal principle. If one is not used to thinking in terms of universals as powers of being, such a concept as Logos remains impossible to understand. The concept of the Logos can be explained best against the background of Platonism or medieval realism.

Logos is the principle of the self-manifestation of God. The Logos is God manifest to himself in himself. Therefore, whenever God appears, either to himself or to others outside himself, it is the Logos which appears. This Logos is in Jesus as the Christ in a unique way. And this, according to the Apologists, is the greatness of Christianity and the basis of its claim about salvation. For if the divine Logos in its fullness had not appeared in Jesus as the Christ, no salvation would be possible. This is an argument from existence, not from speculation. This means that the classical theologians start from the experience of salvation, and then proceed to speak of Jesus as the Christ in terms of the Logos.

The Logos is the first "work" or generation of God as Father. The Father, being eternal mind, has the Logos in himself; he is "eternally logical", as Athenagoras, one of the Apologists, said. Here "logical" does not mean that he can argue well; he leaves that to us. As "logikos" he is adequate to the principles of meaning and truth. God is not irrational will; he is called eternal *nous* (mind), and this means he has within himself the power of self-manifestation. This analogy is taken from our experience. There is no mental process that is going on in some way or other except

in silent words. Likewise, the inner spiritual life of God includes
the silent word in him.

There is a spiritual procession that goes out from the
Father to the world in which he manifests himself to himself and
to the world. But this procession does not produce separation.
The Word is not the same thing of which it is the Word. On the
other hand, the Word cannot be separated from that of which it
is the Word. The Word of God is not identical with God; it is the
self-manifestation of God. But if you separate it from God, it
becomes empty, without content. This is an attempt to describe
the meaning of the term "Logos," in analogy with the mental
processes of man. The process of generation of the Logos in
God—eternally, of course—does not make God small. He is not
less than he was by the fact that he generates his Word. So Justin
can say: "The Logos is different from God according to number,
but not according to concept." He is God; he is not *the* God, but
he is one with God in essence. Justin used also the Stoic doctrines
of the immanent and the transcendent Logos. The Logos in God
is *logos endiathetos*, that is the indwelling Logos. This eternal,
indwelling Logos, the Word in which God expresses himself to
himself, becomes with the creation the *logos prophorikos*, the
proceeding, outgoing Logos. The Logos is then a word that is
spoken toward the outside, toward the creature, through the
prophets and the wise men. Logos means both word and reason.
If one thinks in Old Testament terms, one would prefer to translate *logos* by "word"; if one thinks in Greek terms, as the Apologists did on the whole, then one would translate *logos* by "reason".
"Reason" here does not mean "reasoning", but refers to the
meaningful structure of reality.

As the immediate self-expression of the divine, the Word (the
Logos, form, or reason) is less than the divine abyss, because the
divine abyss is always the beginning, and out of the depths of
divinity his self-manifestation toward the world comes. The
Logos is the beginning of the generations of God; he has, so to
speak, a diminished transcendence or divinity. But if this is so,
how can he reveal God fully? This became a problem for later
times. As soon as the Apologists used the term "logos" the problem arose and could not be silenced any more. If the Logos is
the self-expression of God in movement, is he less than God or
fully God? One continued to call Christ God, but how could the

statement be made understandable to pagans that a historical individual who lived and died is to be called "God"? The difficulty was not the incarnation as such. "Incarnation" is one of the most ordinary events in Greek mythology and in all mythology. Gods come to earth; they take on animal, human, or plant form; they do certain things and then return to their divinity. Such a concept, however, could not be accepted by Christianity. The difficulty was that *this* Son of God, who was a historical man and not a mythical figure, is supposed to be the absolute and unique incarnation of God.

The incarnation is a once-for-all event; and it is not a particular element or characteristic of God which becomes incarnate. Rather, it is the very center of divinity which becomes incarnate, and to express this the idea of the Logos was used. The problem was to combine monotheism, which was emphasized so strongly against pagan polytheism, with the idea of Christ's divinity. Both aspects of Christ, his humanity and his universality, had to be kept together. This was the need of that time which the Apologists fulfilled. And therefore they were successful.

In the Apologists the incarnation is not the union of the divine Spirit with the man Jesus; rather, the Logos really *becomes* man. This transformation christology becomes increasingly important through the Logos doctrine. Through the will of God the pre-existent Logos has become man. He has been made *flesh*. Here we have the first clear decision for the transformation christology over against the adoptionist christology. If the Logos (or Spirit) adopted the man Jesus, then we have quite a different kind of christology from the idea that the Logos is transformed into flesh.

The saving gifts of the Logos are *gnōsis* (knowledge) of God, of the law, and of the resurrection. As the Logos Christ is, first of all, a teacher; not a teacher who teaches us many things he knows better than we, but a teacher in the Socratic sense of giving us existential power of being. The Logos gives us truth about God and moral laws which we are to fulfill through freedom. Thus a kind of intellectualization and some educational elements come into the doctrine of the Christ. This was a possible consequence of the Logos doctrine, and for this reason there have always been reactions against it.

C. Gnosticism

The Apologists defended Christianity against the philosophers and emperors. However, the threats to Christianity did not come only from the outside. A much greater danger came from the inside; this was the danger of gnosticism. The term "gnosticism" is derived from the Greek word *gnōsis*, meaning "knowledge". It does not mean scientific knowledge. *Gnōsis* is used in three ways: (1) as knowledge in general terms; (2) as mystical communion; (3) as sexual intercourse. All three meanings can be found in the New Testament. *Gnōsis* is a knowledge by participation. It is as intimate as the relation between husband and wife. It is not the knowledge resulting from analytic and synthetic research. It is a knowledge of union and of salvation, existential knowledge in contrast to scientific knowledge. The Gnostics were the Greek intellectuals; but they understood the cognitive function of man in terms of participation in the divine.

The Gnostics were not a sect; if anything, they were many sects. Actually, however, gnosticism was a widespread religious movement in the late ancient world. This movement is usually called syncretism. It was a mixture of all the religious traditions of that time. It spread all over the world, and was strong enough to penetrate Greek philosophy and the Jewish religion. Philo of Alexandria was a typical forerunner of gnosticism. It was also strong enough to penetrate Roman law and Christian theology.

The basic elements of this religious mixture are the following: (1) The destruction of the national religions by the conquests of Alexander and Rome. The great world empires undercut the national religions. This is the negative presupposition. (2) The philosophical interpretation of mythology. When you read the systems of the Gnostics, you have the feeling that they have rationalized mythology. And this feeling is accurate. (3) The renewal of the ancient mystery traditions. (4) The revival of the psychic and magical elements which appeared in the religious propaganda of the East. While the political movement went from West to East, the religious movement went from East to West. Hence, gnosticism was an attempt to combine all the religious traditions which had lost their genuine roots, and to unite them in a system of a half-philosophical, half-religious character.

There were many similarities and differences between the gnostic groups and original Christianity. Against the public tradition of the Christian churches, they claimed to possess secret traditions known only to the initiated. They rejected the Old Testament because it contradicted many of the their fundamental tenets, especially their dualistic and ascetic tendencies. The New Testament was not rejected but purged. Marcion was the man who tried to purge the New Testament, leaving the ten main Letters of Paul and the Gospel of Luke, which most clearly bears Pauline influence. Presumably, they did not contain elements which contradicted the basic ideas of gnosticism, as did the other Epistles and Gospels in the New Testament.

Marcion was not primarily a speculative philosopher, but a religious reformer. He founded congregations of followers which lasted for a long time. The title of his book is *Antitheses.* He was a Gnostic in his distinction between the God of the Old Testament and the God of the New Testament, the God of the law and the God of the gospel. He rejected the former and accepted the latter. This problem should not be seen in terms of the fantastic idea of two gods. Rather, it should be seen in terms of the problem with which Harnack wrestled at the end of his life. That is the problem whether the Old and New Testaments are not so different that they cannot be combined. Marcionism is a form of radical Paulinism which exists throughout church history. In the modern period we have it in the Barthian school, when the God of revelation is placed against the God of natural law. In natural law and in history man is thought to be by himself. Of course, this school does not speak of a second God; such a fantastic mythology would be impossible today. Rather, it speaks of a radical tension between the natural world of reason and of morality and the religious realm of revelation which stands against all other realms. This was Marcion's problem, and he solved it by a radical separation in terms of a gnostic dualism.

For the Gnostics the created world is evil; it was created by an evil god whom they equated with the God of the Old Testament. Therefore, salvation is liberation from the world, and had to be accomplished through ascetic means. There is no place for eschatology in this dualistic world view, for the end of the world is seen in the light of a dualism. A dualistic fulfillment is not a fulfillment; it implies a split in God himself.

The Savior is one of the heavenly powers, called "aeons" or "eternities". The word "eternity" does not have the connotation of timelessness here, but of cosmic power. The higher aeon, the savior aeon, the savior power of being, descends to earth and takes on human flesh. It is self-evident, however, that a divine power cannot suffer. So he takes on either a strange body, or a body which only seems to be a body, but he does not *become* flesh. (The early Christians rejected the Gnostics on this point.) The Savior descends to the different realms in which the various astrological powers rule. This has special reference to the planets, which were considered as astrological powers long after the Renaissance, even in Protestantism. He reveals the hidden weapons of these demonic powers by trespassing their realm and overcoming them on his descent. He brings down the seals of their power, their names and their characters. If you have the name of a demonic power, you are superior to it; if you call it by name, it falls down. One of the Gnostic texts says: "Having the seals, I shall descend, going through all aeons. I shall recognize all mysteries. I shall show the shape of the gods. And the hidden things of the holy path, called gnōsis, I shall deliver." Here we see the claim of the good God, of the power of mystery which comes down to earth.

The demonic powers are the representatives of fate. The human soul which has fallen into their hands is liberated by the Savior and by the knowledge he brings. One could say: What the Savior does in gnosticism is somehow to use white magic against the black magic of the planetary powers, the same powers of whom Paul in Romans 8 speaks when he says they have been subjected by Christ. Therefore, the magic power of the sacraments is acknowledged. The highest power comes to earth in them.

Besides these speculative and sacramental features, gnosticism had ethical values of community and asceticism. The ascent of the soul is demanded, following the Savior who has ascended. The Savior liberates from demonic powers for the sake of union with the fullness, the *plērōma*, the spiritual word. On the upward way the human soul meets these rulers; the soul tells the rulers what it knows about them. He knows their names, and therefore their mysterious power, the structure of evil they represent. When

he tells them their names, they fall down and tremble and cannot
stop the soul on its way any more. These poetic images show that
gnosticism was a religion of salvation from the demonic powers.
This was the problem of the whole period, both in and outside
of Christianity. Somehow man is better than his creator. Man
must be saved from the powers of the demiurge, the one who
created the world. But not all men are able to be saved. There
are three classes of human beings: the *pneumatikoi*, i.e., the
spiritual ones; the *psychikoi*, i.e., those who follow the soul; and
the *sarkikoi*, i.e., those who follow the flesh. The *sarkikoi* are
lost; the *pneumatikoi* are saved; but the middle group, the *psychikoi*, can go either way. In order to be elevated on high, man
must participate in the mysteries. These are mostly mysteries of
purification, and usually connected with baptism. The Spirit in
baptism enters the sacramental water and dwells in it. The Spirit
is brought down by a special formula of initiation.

These ideas formed a great temptation to Christianity. Christ
remained in the center of history as the bringer of salvation; but
he was put into the framework of the dualistic world view of
Hellenism. The religious mood of this period is beautifully expressed in the Acts of Andrew, one of the apocryphal writings.
"Blessed is our generation. We are not thrown down, for we have
been recognized by the light. We do not belong to time, which
would dissolve us. We are not a product of motion, which would
destroy us again. We belong to the greatness toward which we
are striving. We belong to him who has mercy towards us, to the
light which has expelled the darkness, to the One from whom we
have turned away, to the Manifold, to the Super-heavenly,
by whom we have understood the earthly. If we praise him,
it is because we are recognized by him." This is really religious piety, not mere speculation, as the critics of gnosticism have
said.

There are many people today who would like to renew gnostic
religion as their own daily expression of religious experience,
not because of the fantastic speculation, but because of the real
piety expressed in it. Gnosticism was a great danger for Christianity. If Christian theology had succumbed to this temptation,
the particular character of Christianity would have been lost. Its
unique basis in the person of Jesus would have become meaningless. The Old Testament would have disappeared, and with it the

historical picture of the Christ. All of this was avoided because of the work of the men whom we call the anti-gnostic fathers. These fathers fought against gnosticism and expelled it from the church.

D. The Anti-Gnostic Fathers

The first great Christian theologians developed their systems in opposition to—and partly in acceptance of—the ideas of gnosticism. Their defense against attacks from the outside was made in terms of the Logos doctrine. However, some of the spirit of the world which was conquered by Christianity entered into Christianity itself. The fight then had to be waged against a Christianized paganism. Such a fight, however, is never simply a negation, but always involves reception as well. The result of this partial rejection and partial reception of the religious mood of that time is what we call "early Catholicism". The theologians with whom we now have to deal are important because they represent this early Catholicism. They express ideas which grew out of a rejection and an acceptance of the pagan religious movement of their time. To do this they accepted the Logos doctrine which had been developed by the Apologists. But now they brought it constructively—not only apologetically—into a framework of Bible and tradition. In doing this they deprived this doctrine, at least partly, of its dangerous implications, one of them, of course, being a relapse into polytheism, tritheism, or ditheism. The greatness of theologians like Irenaeus and Tertullian is that they saw this danger, and used the Logos doctrine to develop constructive theological ideas in relation to the religious movements of their own period.

Irenaeus was the greatest of the anti-gnostic fathers, religiously speaking. He understood the spirit of Paul and had a feeling for what Paul's theology meant for the Christian Church. However, the Pauline doctrine that was important for Irenaeus was not so much the one with which Paul fought against Judaism —the doctrine of justification by grace through faith—but it was more the center of Paul's own teaching, his doctrine of the Holy Spirit. In some ways Irenaeus' theology stands closer to Protestant Christianity than most of early Catholicism; yet he was the father of early Catholicism—and ultimately not a Protestant—

inasmuch as the Pauline doctrine of justification through faith, which I like to call the "corrective side" in Paul's theology, was not at the center of Irenaeus' thought.

Tertullian was another anti-gnostic father, the master of Latin rhetoric. He was the creator of ecclesiastical terminology in the Latin language. He had a juristic mind, although not a jurist himself. He was possessed of a very aggressive temperament and a strong character. He understood the primacy of faith and the paradox of Christianity. But he was not artificially primitive, for he accepted the Stoic philosophy and with it the idea that the human soul is by nature Christian—*anima naturaliter christiana*. He also accepted the Logos doctrine of the Apologists, because he did not only accept the paradox of Christianity but, having a sharp rational mind, he believed that Greek philosophy could not surpass Christianity in rational sharpness and clarity.

The third anti-gnostic theologian was Hippolytus, more scholarly than the other two. He carried on polemics against the gnostic movement in his exegetical works and writings on church history. These three theologians saw clearly the situation of the early church. It is important for Protestants to see how early the main fundamentals of the later Roman system were already present in the third century.

1. *The System of Authorities*

The problem which the Gnostics posed for the church was in the realm of authority, the question whether the Holy Scriptures were decisive as over against the secret teachings of the Gnostics. The gnostic teachers said that Jesus had passed on secret insights to them during the forty days after his resurrection when he was together with his disciples. These insights formed the content of gnostic philosophy and theology. Against this notion the anti-gnostic fathers had to establish a doctrine of Scripture.

The Holy Scripture is given by the Logos through the divine Spirit. Therefore, it became necessary to fix the canon. The very foundations of the church were threatened by the intrusion of secret traditions which asserted quite different things from what the biblical writings said. Thus, the decision to fix the canon arose out of the life-and-death struggle with gnosticism. This meant that the church must always return to the classical period, namely, the apostolic period of Christianity. What was written at that time is valid for all later times; anything really new that comes later can never be canonical. This is one of the reasons that so many of the books in the Bible go under apostolic names even though they were written during the post-apostolic period.

That which is canonical, it was felt, must be canonical in an absolute sense, including the letters of the text. Here Christianity simply followed the legalistic interpretation of the law in Judaism in which every Hebrew letter in the Old Testament text has an open and a hidden meaning, and is absolutely inspired. This, of course, was not enough, because the Bible must be interpreted. This is true whenever the Bible is made an absolute norm. The Gnostics interpreted the Scriptures differently from the official church. Therefore, the principle of tradition was bound to come up. The tradition was identified with the *regula fidei*, the rule of faith. When this happened, not the Bible but the rule of faith became decisive, just as the confessional documents written after the Reformation became the decisive canon for theological instruction, and not the Bible.

The rule of faith was also called the canon of truth; something is true because it comes from the apostles. It is apostolic tradition (*traditio apostolica*) which is mediated through presbyters or bishops. This, however, is still too indefinite; there are too many elements in the tradition, ethical and dogmatic. So a concentrated summary of the Bible and the rule of faith was needed in connection with the confession at baptism, the main sacrament at that time. This, of course, presupposes that the bishops who are responsible for the rule of faith and the baptismal creed have the gift of truth. They have it because they are the successors of the apostles. Here already we have a clear expression of the episcopal doctrine of apostolic succession. The apostolic succession is most visible in the Roman Church, which was founded by Peter and Paul, according to these anti-gnostic fathers. Irenaeus says about this church: "To this church all nations must come, because of its greater principality, the church in which the apostolic tradition has been always preserved."

Thus we have a very impressive system of authorities: the Bible, the apostolic tradition, the rule of faith, the baptismal creed, and the bishops, created in the struggle against the Gnostics. What is astonishing is how early all this happened.

2. *The Montanist Reaction*

A reaction set in against the developing order, a reaction of the Spirit against the order, represented by a man named Montanus. This reaction was very serious, as evident in the fact that Tertullian himself later became a Montanist. This Montanistic reaction against ecclesiastical fixation of Christianity runs throughout church history in one form or other.

The Montanists had two basic ideas: the Spirit and the "end". The Spirit was suppressed by the organized church. There was a fear of spiritual movements because the Gnostics had claimed to have the Spirit. It was denied that prophets necessarily have an ecstatic character. A churchman at this time wrote a pamphlet to the effect that it is unnecessary for a prophet to speak in ecstasy. The church was unable to understand the prophetic Spirit any more. It was understandably afraid of the Spirit because in the name of the Spirit all kinds of disruptive elements entered into the church.

The other idea was that of the "end". After the expectation of Jesus and the apostles that the end was very imminent had been disappointed, the apostolic fathers began to establish themselves in the world. The disappointment that the end did not come caused great difficulties and led to the necessity of creating a worldly church, a church that is able to live in the world. Montanism was a reaction against this worldly church. But the Montanists experienced what the earlier Christians had experienced; the end they expected did not come. So they also had to establish themselves in the world; they also became a church. It was a church with a strict discipline, and to a certain extent it was an anticipation of the sectarian type of church which arose during the Reformation and in later Protestantism. The Montanists believed that they represented the period of the Paraclete, following the periods of the Father and the Son. The sectarian revolutionary movements in the church have generally made the same claim; they represent the age of the Spirit.

It happens, however, that when the attempt is made to fix the content of what the Spirit teaches, the result is extreme poverty. This happened, for example, to the Quakers after their initial ecstatic period. When the content is fixed it turns out that there is nothing new, or what is new is more or less some form of a rational moralism. This happened to George Fox and his followers, and to all ecstatic sects. In the second generation they become rational, moralistic, and legalistic; the ecstatic element disappears; not much remains that is creative compared to the classical period of apostolic Christianity. The Montanists fixed their poor contents in new books; they adopted the idea of a prophetic succession. Of course, this is self-contradictory, because succession is an organizational principle, whereas prophecy is an anti-organizational principle. The attempt to combine them was unsuccessful, and will always be unsuccessful.

The Christian Church excluded Montanism. However, its victory over Montanism also resulted in loss. This loss is visible in four ways: (1) The canon was victorious against the possibility of new revelations. The solution of the Fourth Gospel that there will be new insights, always standing under the criticism of the Christ, was at least reduced in power and meaning. (2) The traditional hierarchy was confirmed against the prophetic spirit. This meant that the prophetic spirit was more or less excluded from the organized church and had to flee into sectarian movements. (3) Eschatology became less significant than it had been in the apostolic age. The ecclesiastical establishment became much more important. The expectation of the end was reduced to an appeal to each individual to be prepared for his end which can come at any moment. The idea of an end of history was not important in the church after that. (4) The strict discipline of the Montanists was lost, giving way to a growing laxity in the church. Here again something happened which has frequently happened in the history of the church. Small groups arise with a strict discipline; they are regarded with suspicion by the church; they form themselves into larger churches; then they lose their original disciplinary power in themselves.

3. *God the Creator*

We must now deal with what the anti-gnostic fathers taught within the framework of the strict safeguards which they built up against gnosticism. The Gnostics had contrasted God the Father and God the Savior. Now the gnostic theory was called a *blasphemia creatoris*, a blasphemy of the Creator. This ought to be kept in mind by all neo-orthodox theologians today. There is much gnostic Marcionism in them, that is, a dualistic blasphemy of the Creator God. They put the Savior God in such opposition to the Creator God that, although they never fall into any real heresy, they implicitly blaspheme the divine creation by identifying it with the sinful state of reality. Against this tendency Irenaeus said that God is one; there is no duality in him. Law and gospel, creation and salvation, are derived from the same God.

This one God is known to us not speculatively but existentially. He expresses this in saying: "Without God, you cannot know God." God is never an object. In all knowledge it is he who knows in us and through us. Only he can know himself; we may participate in his knowledge of himself. But he is not an object whom we can know from the outside. God is unknown according to his greatness, his absoluteness, his unconditional character. He is known according to his love in which he comes to us. Therefore, in order to know God, you must be within God; you must participate in him. You can never look at him as an object outside yourself. This God has created the world out of nothing. This phrase "out of nothing" is not a description of the way God created, but a protective concept that is only negatively meaningful. It means that there is no prior resisting matter out of which God created the world, as in paganism. In creating the world God is not dependent on a matter which resisted the form which the demiurge, the world-builder, wanted to impose on it. The Christian idea is that everything is created directly by God without any resisting matter. God is the cause of everything. His purpose, the immanent *telos* of everything, is the salvation of mankind. The result is that the creation is good, and the Creator God is the same as the Savior God. We should see that the blasphemy of the Creator, new or old, is always based on a confusion of the created goodness of the world with its distortion.

This one God is a *trias*, a trinity. The word *trinitas* appears first in Tertullian. Although God is one, he is never alone. Irenaeus says: "There is always with him the word and the wisdom, the Son and the Spirit, through which he has made everything freely and spontaneously." God is always a living God and, therefore, never alone, never a dead identity with himself. He always has his word and his wisdom with himself. These are symbols of his spiritual life, his self-manifestation and his self-actualization. The motive of the doctrine of the trinity is to speak of God as living and to make understandable the presence of the divine as a living, creative ground. According to Irenaeus, these three are one God because they have one *dynamis*, one power of being, essence, or potentiality. "Potentiality" and "dynamics" are the Latin and Greek terms respectively for what we can best translate as "power of being".

Tertullian spoke of the one divine substance which develops itself in the triadic economy. "Economy" means "building-up". The divinity builds up eternally in a unity. Any polytheistic interpretation of the trinity is sharply rejected. On the other hand, God is established as a living God, not as a dead identity. Thus Tertullian used the formula *una substantia, tres personae* to speak of God.

Contrary to gnosticism, man is created good. He has fallen by his own freedom. Man who is mortal by nature was supposed to become immortal through obedience to God, remaining in paradise and participating in the food of the gods, in the tree of life. But he lost this power by disobedience to God. So it must be regained. Immortality, as we said before, is not a natural quality but something which must be received as a gift from the realm of the eternal. There is no other way to get it. Sin is spiritual as well as carnal. Adam has lost the possible *similitudo* (similitude) to God, namely, immortality, but he has not lost the natural image, because the natural image makes him human. Here we have Irenaeus' famous distinction between *similitudo* and *imago*. These two words are used in the Vulgate translation of Genesis 1:26, which states that God made man in his *image*, after his *likeness*. Irenaeus places a theological interpretation on these two words. Every man has the natural image of God; man as man, as a finite, rational being, is able to have a relationship to God. *Similitudo* means that man has the possibility of becoming similar to God. The main point in this similarity with God is eternal life. If someone gets eternal life, he overcomes his natural mortality and participates in the eternal life as a gift of God.

4. *The History of Salvation*

The history of salvation was described in three or four covenants. The first covenant is that which is given with creation.

This is the natural law which is ultimately the law of love innate in man. Secondly, the law is reinstated after it faded away when man lost his immediate innocent participation in it. The third stage is law as it is re-established in Christ, after Judaism distorted the law of Sinai. The law is the same throughout, namely, the law of love innate in man by nature. God does not give arbitrary commandments, but he restates those commandments which are identical with man's essential nature and which are, therefore, valid under all circumstances. Then, in Tertullian, we have a fourth covenant, because he became a Montanist. This is the covenant with the Paraclete, the divine Spirit, who gives the new law at the end of the days. This means that the history of salvation was understood as the education of mankind in terms of a law. This made it possible to understand why the Old Testament belongs to the Christian Scriptures and why philosophy belongs to Christianity. They are all stages in the one history of salvation. They are not negated but confirmed by the revelation in Christ. The problems connected with a dualism were solved in terms of a history of salvation in different covenants. There is not only one revelation. The biblical idea of *kairos* means that there is a revelation adapted to each new covenant situation, first, that of paradise, then that of the elected nation, then that of the followers of Christ, and, sometimes, that of the divine Spirit. In each case there is a different *kairos*, a different "right time". This kind of thinking liberates Christianity from a narrowness in which its own revelation is declared to be the only one and is not viewed within the whole context of the history of revelation. Such a narrowness leads, as in the case of Marcion and, partly at least, in the Barthian school, to an isolation of revelation over against the whole history of mankind.

Turning to christology, Irenaeus said: "The invisible of the Son is the Father; the visible of the Father is the Son." This is eternally so. There is always something which is potentially visible in God, and there is always something which remains as mystery and abyss in God. These are two sides which symbolically are distinguished as Father and Son. The Son who is eternally the visible of the Father becomes manifest in the personal appearance of Jesus as the Christ. The anti-gnostic fathers emphasized the monotheistic aspect in Christianity more strongly than the Apologists because they had to deal with Christian polytheistic tendencies. The Apologists, with their Logos doctrine, were drawn into a dangerous approximation to polytheistic thinking, or tritheistic, if the Spirit is handled in the same way as the Logos. In the line of thought which leads from John to Ignatius and Irenaeus, the Logos is not so much a lesser hypostasis, an inferior form or power of being in God, but is much more God himself as revealer, as his self-manifestation.

Irenaeus called salvation *anakephalaiōsis*, or *recapitulatio*, meaning recapitulation. He was pointing to Ephesians 1.10 which speaks of all things in heaven and earth being gathered up into Christ. Irenaeus built his idea of the history of salvation on these words in Ephesians. It means that the development which was broken in Adam is resumed by Christ and fulfilled in him. In Christ the new mankind has started. That which mankind was supposed to become, once disrupted by Adam, has finally reached its fulfillment in Christ. However, not only mankind but the whole cosmos finds its fulfillment in the appearance of the Christ. In order to accomplish this, Christ had to participate in the nature of Adam. Thus Christ is the beginning of the living as Adam is the beginning of the dead. Adam is fulfilled in Christ; this means that Christ is the essential man, the man Adam was to become but did not actually become. Adam was not in a state of fulfillment from the beginning; he lived in childish innocence. Here we have a profound doctrine of what I call a transcendent humanism, a humanism which says that Christ is the fulfillment of essential man, of the Adamic nature. Such a fulfillment became necessary because a break occurred in the development of man; Adam fell away from what he was to become. The childish innocence of Adam has been lost; but the second Adam can become what he was to become, fully human. And we can become fully human through participation in this full humanity which has appeared in Christ. This includes eternal life, similitude with God with respect to participation in infinity.

When I go into these matters, I am always surprised how much better the theology of the ancient church was than the popular theology which developed in the nineteenth century, how much profounder and more adequate to the paradox of Christianity, without becoming irrationalistic, nonsensical, or absurd. Of course, there were absurd elements on the borderline, on the edges, with respect to miracles, etc. But the central position was utterly profound, namely, the understanding of Christ, not as an accidental event or a transmutation of a highest being, but as fulfilled or essential humanity, therefore always related to Adam, to man's essential being and to his fallen state.

5. *Trinity and Christology*

Tertullian provided the fundamental formula for the trinity and christology. He used juristic language in a skillful way so that it became decisive for the future. The formulae of Tertullian entered the Latin creeds of the Roman Catholic Church. "Let us preserve the mystery of the divine economy which disposes the unity into trinity, the Father, the Son and the Holy Spirit, three not in essence but in grade, not in substance but in form." Here we have for the first time the word *trinitas*, introduced by Tertullian into ecclesiastical language. He also spoke of the unity in the trinity, denying any form of tritheistic tendencies. Instead, he speaks of "economy", an important word in ancient Christian theology. To speak of divine economy is to speak of God "building up" his manifestations in periods of history. In a living and dynamic way the trinity is built up in historical manifestations. But in this trinity there is but one divine essence. If we translate "essence" by "power of being", we have what this word meant. There is one divine power of being, and each of the three economic manifestations of the power of being participates in the full power of being.

God has eternally the *ratio* (reason) or *logos* in himself. It is an inner word. This is, of course, the characteristic of spiritual existence. If we say God is Spirit, we must also say he is trinitarian; he has the word within himself and has the unity with his self-objectivation. The word proceeds from God just as the beam proceeds from the sun. In the moment of creation the Son becomes a second person, and the Spirit a third person. The divine substance or essence, meaning power of being, is in all three persons. Tertullian's term "persona" does not mean the same as our word "person". You and I are persons because we are able to reason, to decide, to be responsible, etc. Such a concept of person was not applied to God at all, nor to the three *hypostases* in God. What then does *persona* mean? *Persona*, like the Greek word *prosōpon*, is the mask of the actor through which a special character is acted out. Thus we have three faces, three countenances, three characteristic expressions of the divine, in the process of divine self-explication. These are the classical formulae of trinitarian monotheism.

Tertullian also provided basic formulae with respect to christology. He said: "We see a double essence, not confused but united in one person, in God and the man Jesus." In this statement we have the formula of the doctrine of the two natures, or powers of being, in the one person of Christ. Here *persona* means one individual face or being of personal character, namely, Jesus. In this person two different powers of being are united, one divine and one human. Each of these powers is independent; neither is confused with the other; yet they are united in one person. If we ask how this is possible, we are anticipating the later discussions.

On the question whether the incarnation is a metamorphosis, that is, God *becoming* man, or the acceptance of a human essence, Tertullian decides for the latter. Like most of the theologians Tertullian is certain that God is ultimately unchangeable, and that the two powers of being must be preserved in their respective identities. Jesus as man is not a transformed God; he is a real man, true man. He can be true God also, but he is not a mixture of both. If the Logos were transfigured or transformed into something else, he would have changed his nature; but the Logos remains Logos in the man Jesus. So Tertullian thinks more in terms of the Logos adopting a human nature instead of the mythological idea of transmutation.

According to Irenaeus the saving power is the divine Spirit who dwells in the church and renews the members out of what is old into the newness in Christ. Christ gives them life (*zōē*) and light (*phōs*); he gives them the new reality. This is God's work in man, accepted by faith. Therefore, no law is needed since we love God and the neighbor. That is the Pauline element, but it is not strong enough to overcome the anti-Pauline elements. Ultimately, the new being is mystical and ethical. In this sense Irenaeus' conception is the highest form of early Catholicism, but it is not Protestant. In Protestantism the renewal takes place by justification through faith.

Irenaeus thinks of the process of salvation in terms of a mystical regeneration into immortality. In contrast to this, Tertullian speaks of a wholesome discipline as the content of the Christian life. He speaks of a process of education by the law, and the reality of obedience to it is eternal life. Here we have Tertullian, the Roman juristic mind, who likes the law, and at the same time the ascetic pietist, who became a Montanist. In Irenaeus we have mystical participation, in Tertullian subjection to the law. These are the two sides of early Catholicism. The second aspect, subjection to law, became decisive just before the Protestant breakthrough. But the Protestant movement denied also the Irenaean form, and returned to the other side of Paul, namely, justification through faith.

In Tertullian we have the Roman Catholic form of Jewish legalism. The relationship to God is legal. Christianity is merely the new law. Christianity returns to the religion of the law, but is prevented from becoming simply another Jewish system of laws and rules by the sacramental salvation. Therefore, he could say: "the *evangelium*, the Gospel, is our special law." Transgressing the law means that guilt is produced and punishment is required. "But if we do his will, he will make himself our debtor. Then we can gain merits." There are two classes of demands: precepts and counsels. In this way every man can acquire a treasury of holiness in which he returns to Christ what Christ has given him. The virtue of the Christian is crowned. The sacrifice of asceticism and martyrdom moves God to do good to us. "In the measure in which you do not spare yourselves, in this measure, believe me, God will spare you." Here at the end of the second century we meet many ideas that were to become important in later Roman Catholicism. Already we have the idea that while the precepts are for everybody, there are special counsels for monks; and we already have the idea of Christ as the new law. Roman Catholicism emerged quickly in Christianity. The reason for this is that Roman Catholicism was the form in which Christianity could be readily received, including all the Roman and Greek forms of thinking and living.

6. The Sacrament of Baptism

At this time baptism is still the most important sacrament. It removes past sins. Baptism has two meanings: it means the washing away of sins and the reception of the divine Spirit. This, of course, presupposed the baptismal confession of the creed, the consciousness of one's sins and the certainty of the Savior.

The practice of baptism had three characteristics: (1) One lays the hand on the candidate for baptism, and gives him sacred oil, the medium which makes the reception of the Spirit possible. (2) One rejects the devil, with all his pomp and angels. One leaves the demonic sphere; this meant the end of one's participation in paganism. This was not simply a moralistic formula; it went much deeper. It was breaking away from the demons which ruled the world, the rejection of polytheistic paganism. (3) The third element in baptism is the unity of forgiveness and regeneration. The pagan existence has come to an end, and the Christian existence begins. At baptism the preparatory stage of introduction into the church has come to an end. Those who are baptized are called the *teleioi*, the perfect ones. For they have reached the *telos*, the inner aim, of man's existence itself.

The theory of baptism in the anti-gnostic fathers was that the Spirit is united with the water, as it was in the gnostic mysteries. It was easy for Tertullian, with his Stoic background, to think of the Spirit as a material force in the water. This force somehow physically extinguishes the former sins and physically gives the Spirit. Here we see what has been called Tertullian's "materialism". This is important because it made infant baptism possible. If the water is the saving power, the child can be saved as much as the adult. It was not without some hesitation that Tertullian accepted this doctrine. But Christianity had to accept it as soon as it ceased to baptize individuals, one by one, called out of paganism, but baptized "all nations". Then the children cannot be excluded. However, if children are to be included, it is necessary to have a completely objective theory of baptism, because infants are not subjects who can decide.

The Lord's Supper was for Irenaeus the physical mediation of immortality. In it the union with heavenly and divine elements takes place.

These ideas are the making of the Roman Church; in the long run they were to become very influential. The Catholic Church was ready around the year A.D. 300. For this reason we cannot say that Protestantism is a restatement of the early centuries. The Catholic features were powerful very early. This is one of the reasons that the "middle way" of Anglicanism, which in itself would be an ideal solution to the schism of the churches, does not work. The so-called agreement of the first five centuries is by no means an agreement with the principles of the Reformation. Therefore, if someone says that we should unite by going back to the development which runs from Irenaeus to Dionysius the Areopagite, I would say that he had better become a Catholic, because Protestantism cannot do that. In these first centuries there are many elements which Protestantism cannot accept, for example, in the doctrine of the church, the system of authorities, the theory of the sacraments, not so much with respect to trinity and christology, although the implications are present there also.

E. Neo-Platonism

The end of Greek philosophy reached a state in which philosophy had become religion, and religion had become mystical philosophy. So when philosophers now became Christian, they could use a philosophy which was already half-religious. Philosophy at this time was not the philosophy taught today by empiricists, logical positivists, or naturalists. In the period of the New Testament philosophy itself included a religious attitude. This is why Christianity had to deal with philosophy, for it was a rival religion. The name of this religious philosophy was Neo-Platonism. In Neo-Platonism, Platonic, Stoic, and Aristotelian ideas were brought into a system which was philosophical and religious at the same time. Neo-Platonism expressed the longing of the ancient world for a new religion. It expressed the dissolution of all particular religions and at the same time the collapse of autonomous reason, the impossibility for reason to create by itself a new content of life. Therefore, these philosophers became mystics and, as mystics, they tried to create a new religion under the imperial protection of Julian the Apostate. In doing this they had to clash with Christianity. The great Alexandrian theologians, Clement and Origen, met the challenge of Neo-Platonism, and used its concepts to express Christianity.

Neo-Platonism is important not only because of its influence on Origen, who produced the first great theological system, but because through Dionysius the Areopagite it influenced all later forms of Christian mysticism and most forms of classical Christian theology, especially with respect to the doctrines of God, the world, and the soul. It is impossible to understand the further development of Christian theology without knowing something about Neo-Platonism, the last great attempt of paganism to express itself in terms of a philosophical theology, which was both science and life for the ancient mind.

Plotinus was the philosopher most responsible for the system of Neo-Platonism. There is not only a scientific and a religious side to it, but also a political aspect. The emperor, Julian the Apostate, tried to introduce the Neo-Platonic system against Christianity, which shows that he considered it not only as science or philosophy, but as an all-embracing system of religious elevation of the soul.

For Plotinus God is the transcendent One; he is the one who transcends every number, even the number "one" inasmuch as it is a number which includes 2, 3, 4, 5, etc. It is that which is beyond number, and for this he uses the word "one". Thus, whenever we hear the word "one" in mystical language, it is not to be understood as one number alongside others, but as that which transcends all numbers. The One points in particular to that which is beyond the basic cleavages of reality, the cleavage between subject and object, and between the self and the world. Therefore, the divine is the abyss of everything specific, the abyss in which everything definite disappears. But this abyss is not simply something negative; it is the most positive of all because it contains everything that is. When you read in mystical literature about "transcendent nothingness", do not interpret this as "nothing" but as "no-thing", that is, nothing definite, nothing finite, but the ground of everything finite and definite. Since it is without differentiation within itself, it is immovable, unchangeable, and eternal. Out of this eternal ground of everything, in which everything disappears, all things have their origin at the same time. The whole system is a description of the way in which the world and all its forms originate in the ultimate ground of being. The first thing which is originated, like the light which is radiated out of the sun, is what in Greek is called the *nous*, which can be translated as "mind" or "spirit". It is the second principle after the ultimate principle, after the ground of being from which it has emanated. This second principle, the *nous*, is that in which the first principle, the eternal ground, looks at itself. It is the principle of the self-intuition of the eternal. God is manifest to himself in the principle of the *nous*. This self-intuition of the divine in the *nous* is the source of all forms and structures, of all possibilities and of what Plato called "ideas". These "ideas" are the essential potentialities of being. Everything true and beautiful is contained in the *nous*, in the divine mind and his eternal self-intuition. Not only are the universal essences—treehood, redness, etc.—in the eternal mind, but also the essences of the individuals. In God is the form of each of us, independent of the changes in every moment of our lives, that form which a great painter would see and express in his portrait of us.

But there is a third principle which Plotinus called the "soul". The soul is the principle of life in all Greek thinking. It is not primarily an immortal substance, but the principle of movement. It is the principle which moves the stars, so the stars have souls; the principle which moves the animals and plants, so they also have souls; the principle which moves our bodies, so we have souls; the principle which moves the whole universe, so there is a world-soul. This soul-principle is midway between the *nous* and the bodily reality. It is the productive power of the existing world; it forms and controls matter, as our life-principle forms and controls every cell in our body. The soul of the world actualizes itself in many individual souls. Everything has an individual soul. These individual souls give movement and life to everything, but they all have their common principle in the world-soul.

This principle of soul, universally and individually, is the principle of ambiguity. Plotinus knew that life is ambiguous, that ambiguity is a definite characteristic of life. The soul is turned both toward the spirit (or *nous*) and toward matter. It looks in two directions, so to speak; it looks always to meaningful contents. In our language we call this man's spiritual life, expressed in knowledge, ethics, aesthetics, etc. At the same time it looks to our bodily existence and the whole world of material embodiment.

In this system of hierarchies, coming down from the ultimate to the mind and soul and matter, everything which is has a place. In this way Plotinus could place the whole mythological world into his system, after it was purified by philosophy. The gods of the pagans become limited powers of being which have their place in the whole of reality. This world is harmonious; it is directed by the principle of providence. This union of providence and harmony—the main principle of the Enlightenment and of the modern belief in progress—forms the basis of an optimistic world-view. This optimism immediately makes itself felt in another statement of Plotinus, namely, that the planetary forces, the demonic forces, are an illusion. They have no independent power; they are subjected to providence, just as Paul described it in Romans 8. The difference is that Plotinus derived this statement from his philosophy of cosmic harmony, while Paul derived it from the victorious triumph of Christ over the demons.

There are many different souls in the cosmos: mortal souls, such as plants, animals, and human beings, and immortal souls, such as the half-divine and divine beings of ancient mythology. These mythological gods are re-established in this system as powers of being. They do not contradict each other but have their definite place in this system of hierarchies.

The principle which orders this whole world, in terms of providence, is the logos. The logos is the rational side of the *nous* or mind. It is not another hierarchy but is only the dynamic side of the *nous*; it is the principle of reason which organizes everything providentially and gives it its place. To use a modern expression, it is the natural law to which everything is subjected, in physics and living bodies. The *nous* is not the logos; it is the source of all contents, but the logos gives order to them. The logos is the more dynamic principle, the providentially working power which directs the natural and moral laws.

Because of its ambiguity the soul is able to turn away from the *nous*, and with it from its eternal source in the abysmal One. It can separate itself from its eternal origin and turn to the lower realms. Nature is the realm of the unconscious; it stands between matter and the conscious soul. But nature has unconscious souls; in man alone the soul is completely conscious. This turning away of the soul from the *nous* toward matter, toward the bodily realm, is the source of evil. Evil is not a positive power; it is the negation of the spiritual. It is participation in matter, in non-being, in that which has no power of being by itself. Evil arises when the soul turns to non-being. Neither Greeks nor Christians could admit that evil is an ontological reality. The idea that there is a divine ground of evil, a divine being which produces evil, is the Manichaean heresy. Evil is non-being. When this statement is made, whether by Plotinus, Augustine, or myself, the charge is made that this means that sin is not taken seriously, that sin is nothing. The sound of the word "non-being" conveys the impression to some that sin is imaginary, not real. However, a distortion of something which has being is as real as the undistorted state of that being, only it is not ontologically real. If sin were ontologically real, this would mean that there is a creative principle of evil, as in Manichaeism; but this is what the Christian doctrine of creation denies. Augustine said, "*Esse qua esse bonum est*", being as being is good. Evil is the distortion of the good creation.

Plotinus described this non-being (*mē on*) as that which is matter and can become being. This non-being of which he speaks is that which as yet has no being and which resists against having being. He calls it that which lacks measure, limit, form. It is always in want, indefinite, hungry; it is the absolute poverty. In other words, evil is the presence of this non-being in our bodily existence. It is the absence of the power of being, the power of the good.

The soul turned toward this non-being because it believed that with its help it could stand upon itself. Thus, it separated itself from the ground and from the *nous* toward which it looked originally. But the soul looks back and yearns for the ground from which it came. Lovingly the soul ascends to that which is worth being loved, namely, the ground and origin of being itself. When the soul reaches the ultimate aim of its longing, it becomes like God. He who has the ultimate intuition of the divine has become one with God. But this way is hard. This way goes first through the virtues, next to the ascetic purification. The ultimate union with God cannot be reached either by morals or by asceticism in this life. It can only be reached by grace, that is, when the divine power of the transcendent One grasps the mind in ecstasy. This happens only rarely, only in great experiences which cannot be forced.

In the highest ecstasy there happens what Plotinus calls the flight of the one to the One, that is, of us who are individual ones to the ultimate One who is beyond number. What is the *telos*, the inner aim, the goal, the purpose, of man's being? Plato had already given the answer: *homoiōsis tou theou kata to dynaton*, that is, becoming similar to God as much as possible. This was also the aim of the mystery religions, in which the soul was supposed to participate in the eternal One. This is the Alexandrian scheme of thought. It is a circle which starts in the abysmal One, descending by emanation through the hierarchies until the ambiguous situation of the soul is reached, then through the soul falling into the power of the material world, which is determined by non-being. The circle continues then through the elevation of the soul, back through all these different grades up to the highest one, and in ecstasy this goal is reached. We must keep this system in mind, for we cannot understand the relationship of Christianity to mysticism and to Greek philosophy apart from it.

F. CLEMENT AND ORIGEN OF ALEXANDRIA

1. *Christianity and Philosophy*

The Neo-Platonic system was developed in Alexandria. Ammonius Saccas was the teacher of both Plotinus and Origen. Origen was the great theologian and philosopher of the school in Alexandria. This was a catechetical school, a kind of theological seminary. The first great teacher in this school was Clement of Alexandria. Clement used the Logos doctrine in a radical way. In this respect he was more dependent on Stoicism than on the Platonic school. God is the One who is beyond numbers. The Logos, however, is the mediator of everything in which the divine becomes manifest. The Logos, he said, is the man-loving organ of God, and therefore the educator of mankind in past and present. The Logos, as the self-manifestation of the divine, is always working in human minds. The Logos prepared the Jews by the law, and the Greeks by their philosophy. He has prepared all nations in some way. The Logos is never absent from people.

When Clement speaks of philosophy, he does not have in mind a particular philosophy, but that which is true in all philosophers. In his thought many elements from Greek philosophy are mixed with biblical materials. He quoted whole sections from Stoic sources. He introduced Christianity not only into philosophy but also into a philosophical way of life. *Philosophein* was defined by Clement as a striving for a perfect life. Living a philosophical life in the late Greek development was striving to become as near to God as possible. Clement's idea was to live according to the

Logos, a *logikon* life; perhaps we could translate this as a "meaningful life", a life in terms of objective meanings. Christians start first with faith, *pistis*. *Pistis* is not adequately translated by "faith". It is a state of being in faith. In this sense faith is a state of participation in the reality of the new being. It includes conversion, ascetic tendencies, passions, and hope. This is the presupposition of everything else in Christianity, and here Clement deviates from the Greek philosophers. Living according to the Logos means participation in the realm of faith and love, that is, in the realm of the church. The Alexandrian theologians were not independent philosophers, but members of the Christian Church. Therefore, they participated in the state of faith which is presupposed by all knowledge. However, the state of faith is insufficient since it is understood only as assent and obedience. A real participation demands something more, a drive toward knowledge or *gnōsis*. The Christian is the perfect "gnostic". *Gnōsis* is a cognitive faith, a faith which develops its contents cognitively. It is a scientific explanation of the traditions of faith. "Scientific" here is used not in the sense of the natural sciences but in the methodological sense. Everybody is on the way of this development, but only a few reach the aim. The perfect ones are only those who are, as Clement says, "gnostics according to the ecclesiastical canon". This means that philosophers are bound by the ecclesiastical tradition which they accepted when they entered the church. The highest good for these perfect gnostics is the knowledge of God. This knowledge is not a theoretical knowledge in terms of arguments and analyses, but a participation in God. It is not *epistēmē*, that is, scientific knowledge; it is *gnōsis*, that is, mystical or participating knowledge. It is not a *gnōsis* of free speculation but of participation in the congregation and in God. The tradition remains the canon, that is, the criterion, and the church is the mother without which *gnōsis* is unattainable.

Clement's thought is a great example of a synthesis of Christian thinking and Greek philosophy. Christianity had to cope with Neo-Platonism as a universal and extremely impressive system. All the values of the past were united in it. Christianity had to use it and conquer it at the same time. This was done by the school of Alexandria. Christianity was elevated to a state of highest education.

Porphyry was one of the most important Neo-Platonists. He

acknowledged the high educational standing of the Alexandrian school, especially of Origen. He expressed regrets, however, that Origen would live in a barbaric and irrational way as a Christian. Participation in the Christian congregation was incomprehensible to him as a Neo-Platonist. Porphyry acknowledged Origen's philosophical creativity; he said that Origen "hellenized" by interpreting the strange myths of the Bible by Greek thought. Clement and Origen were both Greek philosophers, and at the same time faithful and obedient members of the Christian Church. They had no doubt that it is possible to combine these two things.

Origen begins his system with the question of sources. He takes the sources much more seriously than Clement. The sources are the biblical writings and their summary in the ecclesiastical teaching and preaching. The ancient "rule of faith" provided the systematic scheme of his thought, but the Scriptures are the basis of its contents. The first step for the true theologian is the acceptance of the biblical message. Nobody can be a theologian who does not belong to the church. A free-soaring philosopher is not a Christian theologian. But more than this is required of the theologian. He must also try to understand things philosophically, and that means for Origen in terms of Neo-Platonic philosophy.

2. *The Allegorical Method*

The basic authority for Origen was Scripture. He introduced the famous distinction between three meanings of the Scripture. (1) The *somatic*, literal or philological sense. Everybody can understand the somatic sense (from *sōma*, meaning "body"); it is identical with the literal historical meaning. (2) The *psychic* or moral sense. The moral sense means the application of the biblical text to our situation, its existential application to ourselves. (3) The *pneumatic* or spiritual sense. It is understandable only to those who are perfect, not in the moral sense but in the mystical sense. There are some cases in which the biblical text has only a mystical meaning; then this coincides with the literal sense. Ordinarily, however, the mystical sense has to be distinguished from the literal meaning. The mystical sense is to be found through the allegorical method; this is a method of finding the hidden meaning behind the texts.

This doctrine of the allegorical method, or the idea of a mystical meaning in the texts, was strongly attacked by the sixteenth-century reformers, and it is alien to our realistic philological mind. What is the reason behind the allegorical method? This is easily understood. It arose in order to make a text that is absolutely authoritative applicable to the situation of the interpreter. It became necessary to find a meaning other than the literal one. Every sermon does this with the biblical texts. Today it is done by those interpreters of the Old Testament who find the christological pronouncements of the New Testament in it. It is almost inescapable; if you have a text that is an absolute authority, and its literal meaning does not say anything to you, then consciously or unconsciously you use a method which transfers the original meaning into an existential meaning. Of course, this can lead to a complete undercutting of the authority of the text. For this reason the Lutheran Reformation re-established the genuine, literal, philological text as the real authority. But when we examine the dogmatic statements and their proofs derived from the Bible that we find in orthodox or fundamentalist authors, we notice immediately that they do exactly what Origen did; they use a method which interprets the Bible beyond itself. Only if you are completely honest can you have the literal text, and then say, "This does not say anything to us," or "We must say something else; we recommend *beyond* the text, and we do not mean to express a hidden meaning in the text." I think this is the only consistent attitude. But think of another example—the American Constitution and its Amendments. They have absolute, legal validity, but in order to make them applicable, there is the Supreme Court which interprets them. Interpreting always means applying something to the present situation. The justices of the Supreme Court do not apply the allegorical method; instead they speak of the "spirit" of the law, and the spirit of the law may often contradict the letter of the law.

There are two classes of Christians: (1) The many simple ones, who accept on authority the biblical message and the teachings of the church without understanding them fully. They take the myths literally. As Origen said, they prefer the healing miracles to the story of Jesus going with his three apostles to the mount of transfiguration, which is an allegorical or metaphorical expression for those who go beyond the literal meaning to a transformed interpretation of it. Origen referred to the attitude of the primitive believers as "mere faith". This represents a lower degree of Christian perfection. All Christians begin at this level. (2) There are those to whom the charisma of *gnōsis*, the grace of knowledge, is given. In this way the converted, educated Greek becomes the perfect Christian, but he always does it on the basis of faith. This concept of faith is different from the meaning of faith in Protestantism. Here faith means the acceptance of doctrines, whereas in Protestantism faith is acceptance of the re-uniting grace of God. For Origen the first step is the acceptance of authority; the second is the autonomous rational understanding of the biblical message. The second step does not do away with the first step, but is possible only on the basis of it.

3. *The Doctrine of God*

The first doctrine in Origen's system was the doctrine of God. God is being-itself, and therefore beyond everything that is. He is beyond knowledge, because knowledge presupposes the cleavage between subject and object. He is beyond change and passion. He is the source of everything. But he has his *Logos*, his inner word, his self-manifestation. This *Logos* makes God manifest first to himself and then to the world. The Logos is the creative power of being; all powers of being are united in him. The whole spiritual world is united in the Logos. It is the universal principle of everything in particular, of anything that has being. This divine Logos radiates eternally from the ground of being, from the divine abyss, as splendor radiates from the source of light. Therefore, one is not supposed to say: "There was a time when the Son did not exist." To say this is to deny the eternity of the Logos. There never was a time in which the Son, the eternal Logos, did not exist.

The eternal Logos is eternally generated out of the divine substance. He is not created "out of nothing"; he is not finite. He has the same substance with the Father. Here the formula *homoousios tō patri* (being of one substance with the Father) first arises. In spite of the eternity of the Logos, however, the Logos is less than the Father. Only the Father is without origin; he is not even generated. He is *auto theos*, God by himself, whereas the Son is God by the Father. The Son is the picture of the goodness or essence or nature of God, but not God himself.

Thus, we have two trends in this Origenistic thinking. First, the Son is co-eternal with the Father; secondly, the Son has a kind of lesser validity and power of being than the Father. The Son is the highest of all generated realities, but he is less than the Father. The same thing is true of the Spirit, who is working in the souls of the saints. Although the religious tradition of the congregations demands that the *trias* (the three) be the object of adoration, the Spirit is called less than the Son and the Son less than the Father. And sometimes the highest spiritual beings are even called gods. This means that two principles are in conflict in Origen's thought. The one is the divinity of the Savior; he must be divine in order to be able to save. The other is the scheme of emanation. There are degrees of emanation from the absolute, the Father, down to the lowest levels. The line of division between the highest three (Father, Son and Spirit) and the rest of spiritual beings is somewhat arbitrary.

The rational natures, or spirits, which are eternal were originally equal and free, but they fell away from their unity with God in different degrees of distance. As result of their revolt in heaven against God, they may have fallen into material bodies. This is their punishment and at the same time the way of their purification. The human soul is the mediation between these fallen spirits and the human body. The human soul is the spirit which has become cold. That is, the intensive fire, which is the symbol for the divine Spirit, is reduced to a life process. The fall is a transcendent fall. It precedes our existence in time and space. And it is a free fall; it is decided in freedom. The freedom is not lost by the fall, but it is actual and present in all concrete actions. In these concrete actions the transcendent fall becomes historical reality. We could say that the individual act represents the eternal nature of the fall. In other words, our individual existence in time and space has a prelude in heaven. The decisive thing about us has already happened when we appear on earth. This has particular reference to sin. Sin is based on the transcendent fall. This doctrine of the transcendent fall is difficult to understand for people who have grown up in nominalistic thinking. It is understandable only if one realizes that transcendent powers are realities and not individual things. There is a profound meaning in this doctrine which makes it necessary as a symbol in Christian theology. It means that our human existence and the existence of reality as a whole are considered not only as creation but also as guilt and judgment. When we look at the world, we see that it is universally fallen. Its fallenness penetrates through everything, even through nature outside of man. If we ask: Where did it come from? Why is the fall universal? Why are there no exceptions? Then the answer is: Because the fall precedes the creation, just as the fall follows the creation. Origen has two myths of the fall. The one is transcendent; mythologically speaking, it is not in space. It is the eternal transition from union with God to separation from God. The other is the immanent, inner-historical fall. The transcendent fall becomes actual through special acts on the historical plane. Sin is spiritual, but the bodily and social existence strengthens sin. It is transcendent and a destiny which, like every destiny, is united with freedom.

As in Plotinus, sin for Origen is a turning away from God. It is not something positive. Being evil means being without goodness. Sin, therefore, has a double relation to creation. With respect to the creation of the free and equal spirits, creation precedes the fall; with respect to the bodily world, creation follows the fall and follows the freedom of the spirits. On account of the freedom of the spirits, it is possible for the fall to happen again even in eternity. The end of the world process is not necessarily the end of history. The fall may repeat itself, and then the whole process starts over again. In these ideas we see the cyclical thinking of Greek philosophy with respect to history. This way of thinking was not overcome by Origen, as it was done later by Augustine.

4. *Christology*

The most difficult part of Origen's thought has to do with his christology. The Logos unites itself with the soul of Jesus, who is an eternal spirit as everyone else is. He is pre-existent as all souls are. But the Logos unites himself with just this soul. The soul of the man Jesus has received the Logos completely. The soul of Jesus has merged into the power and the light of the Logos. This is a mystical union which can be emulated in all saints. The soul mediates between the Logos of God and the body of man. In this way there are two sharply separated natures united in Jesus. The statement of the Fourth Gospel that the *Logos became flesh* is a literal way of speaking. The truth is that the Logos took on flesh so much that it could be said that he had become it. This is more like adoptionistic thinking. Popular feeling in the East, on the other hand, wanted to have a God on earth who walks with us, not a divine transcendent power who merely takes on flesh, and then returns after he has taken it on. But for Origen this idea was unacceptable because the Logos can never cease to be also outside of Jesus. The Logos is the form of everything that has form. After the incarnation the Logos ceased to be a man, but this is somehow the case with all spiritual beings, who for this reason are called gods. But if they are gods, where does the dividing line come between them and the third person of the trinity? This problem was not solved, and could not be solved on the basis of the doctrine of emanation. In the doctrine of emanation there is a continuous going down and returning. Christianity, however, belonged to monotheism. How can monotheism be maintained if there are two emanations which are lower than God and at the same time divine?

When men follow the example of the Logos, they themselves become *logikoi*, that is, determined by meaning, reason, and creative power. They are led back to deification. However, Jesus had to do something else to make this possible for men. He had to give his body as a sacrifice. To whom did he give it? To Satan, as a ransom! Satan demands such a price for letting the others go free; but Satan was betrayed. Satan was unable to keep Jesus, because Jesus was pure and therefore not within the pale of Satan's power. This idea of the betrayal of Satan was not only a theological notion in Origen but was also to be found in popular piety. The Middle Ages was full of stories of how the peasants, especially their wives, betrayed the devil when he came, so he had to leave them alone. To us this seems to be a grotesque mythological idea, and it certainly is if taken literally. But it contains a profound religious insight, namely, that the negative element can never ultimately prevail; it cannot prevail because it lives from the positive. When Satan takes Jesus into his power, he cannot keep in his power that from which he himself lives, namely, the divine nature. This shows the ultimate futility of sin. It cannot indefinitely keep in its control the positive power of being, because this power of being is derived from the good. The good and the power of being are one and the same thing. So the meaning of Origen's doctrine is that it is impossible for Satan to prevail ultimately, because he lives from that against which he strives to prevail.

Origen's interpretation of the Song of Songs in terms of the mystical love of the soul with Christ introduced into practical piety an idea which had a tremendous effect on later church history. The human soul is the bride of the Logos; this is the meaning of this love song. The soul receives the bridegroom in herself; she is sometimes visited by the Logos. That is, the divine Spirit is sometimes experienced by us, sometimes the soul is left alone, and no one visits her from the eternal. This is the first mystical interpretation of the Song of Songs that is directly related to the individual. In Judaism it was interpreted in terms of the relation between God and the synagogue. Here we see an example of the necessity for allegorical interpretation. The Song of Songs itself is nothing more than a Jewish love song, perhaps a wedding song which was performed at weddings or festivals. Yet it is in the canon and has divine authority. What can be done with it? The answer of the Jews was that it concerns the relationship between God and the nation. And in my old Luther Bible, which I love dearly because I received it for my baptism, there is something that is said in the superscription of the Song of Songs about the relationship between God and the church. But Origen interpreted it in terms of the mystical marriage between Christ and the soul. This is, of course, an example of mysticism, but it is a transformation of non-Christian mysticism. It is concrete mysticism. The soul, being grasped by the Spirit of God, does not go beyond itself into the abyss of the divine, but the Logos, the concreteness of the divine, comes into the soul. This is the first step in what I call the "baptizing" of mysticism. Mysticism could be introduced into the church by becoming concrete. If Origen, and later on Bernard of Clairvaux, speaks of the mystical marriage between the Logos and the soul, the centered personality is not destroyed. It is preserved, as in a marriage there is a complete union in which the persons are not destroyed.

5. *Eschatology*

The last point in Origen's theology is the doctrine of the final end of history and the world. He interprets this end spiritualistically. The primitive imagery is interpreted in spiritual terms.

The second coming of Christ is the spiritual appearance of Christ in the souls of the pious. He comes back to earth again and again, not in a dramatic appearance in physical terms, but into our souls. The pious people are fulfilled in a spiritual experience. The "spiritual body" of which Paul speaks is the essence or the idea of the material body. It is that which is painted by a great portrait painter. This is what partcipation of the body in the eternal means.

The punishment for sin is hell. Hell is the fire which burns in our conscience, the fire of despair because of our separation from God. This, however, is a temporary state of purging our souls. At the end everyone and everything will become spiritualized; the bodily existence will vanish. This famous doctrine of Origen is called *apokatastasis tōn pantōn*, the restitution of all things. Because freedom is never cancelled out, there is the possibility that the whole process could start over again. Origen was a thoroughgoing philosopher of freedom, and this is what distinguishes him from Augustine.

This spiritualization of eschatology was at least part of the reason that Origen became a heretic in the Christian Church, although he was its greatest theologian. The simple ones revolted against this great system of scientific theology. Monks and others did not want to yield their literalism with respect to the future life, the final catastrophe, the eternal judgment, etc. The motives of the simple ones were mixed. Partly this reaction to Origen's doctrine was due to a Jewish type of realism of bodily existence, against a Greek dualism, and partly it was motivated by the idea of revenge against those who were better off on earth. So they fought for a very realistic and literalistic idea of judgment, final catastrophe, and heaven. The church took their side and condemned the heretical side of Origen.

G. Dynamic and Modalistic Monarchianism

The simple ones revolted also against Origen's Logos christology which he had received from the Apologists. The laymen, the simple ones, were not interested in the cosmological speculations of the Logos concept. They wanted to have God himself on earth in Christ. This group was called the Monarchians, from *monarchia*, meaning "one man's rule". They wanted to have only one ruler,

one God not three, as they felt was entailed by the Logos christology. Against the Logos as a second God, they stressed the
"monarchy" of the Father. This movement was a monotheistic
reaction against the tritheistic danger of the Logos doctrine. The
Logos doctrine hypostasized the Son beside God, and the Spirit
beside both of them.

A man named Theodotus, a craftsman from Rome, thought that
Jesus was a man on whom the divine Spirit descended in baptism, giving him the power of his messianic vocation. But this
did not make him God. People of this type of thinking were most
interested in those passages in the Gospels which deal with Jesus
as a man. There is perhaps a connection between Theodotus and
a group in Asia Minor called the *Alogoi,* so called because they
denied the doctrine of the Logos. And since the Logos idea
appeared in the Fourth Gospel, they rejected it. They tried to
establish the true text and to stress its literal interpretation against
allegorizing. They were in a sense predecessors of many later
movements in church history which emphasized the humanity
of Jesus, from the school of Antioch through medieval adop-
tionism to modern liberal theology, over against the Logos as
God becoming man. This is called the adoptionistic or dynamic
christology. The man Jesus is adopted; he is filled by the Logos or
the Spirit, but he is not God himself. This is the one wing of the
monarchic, monotheistic reaction against the Logos Christology.

1. *Paul of Samosata*

Paul of Samosata, a bishop of Antioch, was in the line of thinking we have just presented. He said that the Logos and Spirit are
qualities of God, but not persons. They are eternal powers or
potentialities in God, but not persons in the sense of independent
beings. Jesus is a man who was inspired by this power from
above. The power of the Logos inhabited Jesus as in a vessel, or
as we live in houses. The unity that Jesus has with God is the
unity of will and love; it is not a unity of nature, because nature
has no meaning with respect to God. The more that Jesus
developed in his own being, the more he received of the Spirit.
Finally he achieved eternal union with God, and then he became
the judge and received the status of God. He became God, but
somehow he had to deserve to become God. Such an idea is, of

course, the negation of the divine nature of the Savior. This denial is what made him a heretic, although many people of his time and even today would prefer to follow his way of thinking.

The Monarchian movement itself was split. The one side followed the adoptionist christology. It says that God, or the Logos, or the Spirit, adopted a fully human individual, made him into Christ, and gave him the possibility of becoming fully divine in his resurrection. In the West we find this way of thinking in Theodotus of Rome and in the East in Paul of Samosata. This christology started with human existence, then it emphasized those biblical statements which refer to the humanity of Christ, and finally it showed that Jesus was driven by the Spirit while on earth and in the end elevated into the divine sphere. The other side of Monarchianism is called modalistic Monarchianism; it was more in line with the basic feeling of the masses of Christians. "Modalism" means that God himself appears in different modes, in different ways. It was also called *Patripassianism*, which means that the Father himself suffered in Christ. Another name for this movement is Sabellianism, from its leading representative, Sabellius. This became a widespread movement in the East and the West, and was a real danger to the Logos christology.

In the West there was a man named Praxeas with whom Tertullian was fighting. His idea was that God the Father himself was born through the Virgin Mary, that God the Father himself, the only God, suffered and died. To be God means to be the universal Father of everything. If we say that God was in Jesus, this means that the Father was in him. Therefore, Praxeas and his followers attacked the so-called *ditheoi*, those who believed in two Gods, and the *tritheoi*, those who believed in three Gods. They fought for the monarchy of God and for the full divinity of Christ in whom the Father himself appeared. Both notions had great popular support because the popular mind wanted to have God himself present on earth, a God who is with us, who participates in our fate, and whom we can see and hear when we see and hear Jesus.

2. Sabellius

Sabellius was the leader of the modalistic Monarchians. He said: "The same is the Father, the same is the Son, the same is the

Holy Spirit. They are three names, but names for the same reality. Do we have one or three Gods?" Father, Son, and Spirit are names, they are *prosōpa* (countenances, faces), but they are not independent beings. They are effective in consecutive energies; one follows the other, but the same God appears in different faces. It is the same God acting in history in three countenances. The *prosōpon* (countenance) of the Father appears in his work as creator and law-giver. The *prosōpon* of the Son appears from the birth to the ascension of Jesus. Since the ascension of Jesus the countenance of the Spirit appears as the life-giver. Through all appearances it is the same monarchic Father-God. Therefore, it is not adequate to speak of a *trias* in heaven. There is no transcendent, heavenly trinity. Instead of being transcendent, the trinity is historical or "economically", in the sense of *oikonomia*, building a house. The trinity is built up in history.

When Sabellius says that the same God is essentially in the Father, Son, and the Spirit, that there are only differences of faces, appearances, or manifestations, he is saying that they are all *homoousios*. That is, they all have the same essence, the same divine power of being. They are not three beings, but they have the same power of being in three manifestations. Although this trend of thinking was condemned, it has never disappeared. It reappeared as a strong monotheistic trend in Augustine and through him in Western theology in general. This modalistic thinking was in opposition to the Logos christology. If you are able to distinguish these two basic trends, you have an insight into what was involved in these seemingly incomprehensible struggles over an iota in *homoousios* and *homoiousios*. This was not a fight over abstract concepts, but it was a conflict between a monotheistic trend and the attempt to establish divine hierarchies between God and man. The East in general, dependent as it was on Plato, Plotinus, and Origen, was interested in hierarchical essences between God and man. This, of course, would make of Christ a demi-god, as we shall see. The West, and some groups in the East, were interested in the divine monarchy, on the one side, and in the humanity of Jesus, on the other. For us as Westerners, the problem of hierarchies is an abstract one, not a problem of living realities.

H. The Trinitarian Controversy

First we must see how the trinitarian problem developed after Origen. Origen was so powerful in his constructive thinking that he conquered all rivals, also the Monarchian and Sabellian theologians. And his christology was so impregnated with mystical piety that his statements could become formulae of a creed. We must not forget that when the Greek thinkers produced a confession or creed, it may seem like abstract philosophy to us, but to them it was the mystical intuition of essences, of powers of being. For instance, in Caesarea a creed was used in baptism which had added mystical formulae from Origen: "We believe in Jesus Christ, the Logos of God, God from God, Light from Light, Life from Life, first-born of all creatures, generated out of the Father before all generations." This is both philosophy and mysticism. It is Hellenistic and not classical Greek philosophy. Hellenistic philosophy was united with the mystical traditions of the East. Therefore, seemingly abstract philosophical concepts could become mystical confessions.

This combination of mystical philosophy with a Christian confession was endangered when the emanation system of Origen was called into question from the point of view of Christian conformism. For example, the eternity and the pre-existence of all spirits, the idea of the transcendent fall, the spiritual body-less resurrection, and the spiritualized eschatology, were all questioned. The place of the Logos was also questioned. Common-sense conformism, supported by the Monarchian reaction, demanded nothing less than God on earth. The theory of emanation by degrees, in hierarchies of powers of being, demanded something less than that which is ultimately transcendent, the One which is beyond everything given.

Out of this conflict a division occurred in the school of Origen between a left wing and a right wing of Origenistic thinking. The right wing said: Nothing is created or subordinate in the *trias*; nothing has been added which is not in the trinity from the beginning. The Son is not inferior to the Father, nor the Spirit to the Son. Representatives of this position wanted what is today called a "high christology". The Son in Jesus is not less than the Father himself.

The left wing opposed the traditionalism of the right wing; it was "scientific" and modernistic. This position held that the Son is essentially strange to the Father; he was a created being; he had no being before he was generated. This means that the Logos christology is developed in hierarchical terms. First, there is God the Father, the highest hierarchy, the eternal One beyond everything; then there is the Logos, the second hierarchy and inferior to the first; the Spirit is the third hierarchy, and inferior to the second. The immortal spirits form the fourth hierarchy, lower than the three others. These are the two wings involved in a great struggle which almost ruined the Christian Church.

Besides theological differences politics became involved in the trinitarian controversy. The attempt was made to find a practical way to solve the problem without going into its theoretical depths. This was the way of Roman eclecticism, something like our American pragmatism. Rome provided the direction for a practical solution which avoided the depths of Greek thinking. Dionysius, the pope in Rome, declared: "Two things must be preserved: the divine *trias* and the holy message of monarchy." These were the two main terms of the two wings, the one affirming the holy message of the monarchy, which stood against the Logos christology, the other affirming the divine *trias*, which expressed the Logos christology. So the pope took the main formulae of both groups and said they must both be preserved. But he did not say how that was possible. This was practical church politics, an approach which finally prevailed, as we shall see. But it prevailed only after a tremendous conflict of almost eighty years. This conflict, which we call the Arian controversy, had a lasting effect on the church, and the decision which was finally reached became valid for all periods of Christianity.

1. *Arianism*

The Arian controversy was a unique and classical struggle which was caused by many motives. The politics of the emperors was involved in it. They needed a unity in the church because Christianity had by this time become the favored religion of the Roman Empire. This threatening division in the church would split the whole empire into pieces, it was feared. Personal feuds between bishops and theologians were involved. There was also a conflict between a narrow traditionalism and an unrestrained speculation. A strong emphasis on theoretical solutions to problems collided with popular monastic fanaticism. But that is not the whole story. The really decisive issue, its basic meaning and permanent significance, had to do with the question: How is salvation possible in a world of darkness and mortality? This has been the central question ever since the apostolic fathers, and it was the question involved in the great trinitarian and christological controversies.

Athanasius, the great foe of Arius, answered that salvation was possible only on one condition, namely, that the Son of God was made man in Jesus so that we might become God. This is possible only if the Logos is eternal, if it is really God who has appeared to us in Jesus. God is Father only because he is the Father of the Son. Thus, the Son is without beginning; eternally the Father has the Son. The Son is the eternal Son of the Father; and the Father is the eternal Father of the Son. Only if they are co-eternal can Jesus, in whom the Logos is present, give us eternity. He can make us like God, which always means to make us immortal, and to give us eternal knowledge, the knowledge of eternal life. Not even the highest of all created spirits can give us a real salvation. A created spirit, even the highest, is less than God. But we are separated from God. We are dependent on God and must return to him. So God himself must save us.

According to Arius, a presbyter from Alexandria, only God the Father is eternal and unoriginated. The Logos, the pre-existent Christ, is a creature. He is created out of nothing; there was a time when he was not. Origen had made the statement that there was no time in which he was not. Against this the left-wing Origenistic theology said that there was a time in which he was not. This time was prior to our temporal existence, but it was not eternity. The Logos is not eternal. The power of God at work in Jesus is not the eternal divine power itself, but is a limited and lower hierarchy. This Logos is strange to the divine nature and dissimilar in every respect from the Father's essence. The Logos can neither see nor know the Father completely and exactly. He becomes God only in the way in which every saint may become deified. This deification happened, as it happens in every saint, through his freedom. The Logos had the freedom to turn away from God, but he did not do that. This Logos, a half-divine power, is the soul of Jesus. This means that Jesus is not fully man with a natural human soul. Mary gives birth to this half-God, who is neither fully God nor fully man. This solution of Arius is in line with the hero cults of the ancient world. This world is full of half-gods, gods who even in heaven (i.e., Olympus) are not fully gods but derived forms of God. Jesus is one of these gods, but he is not God himself.

2. *The Council of Nicaea*

Arius' christology was rejected at the Council of Nicaea, A.D. 325. The Nicene Creed begins: "We believe in one God, the Father Almighty, Maker of all things visible and invisible." These are important words. The word "invisible" has reference to the Platonic "ideas". God is the creator not only of the things on earth, but of the "essences" as they appear in Plato's philosophy. The Creed continues: "And in one Lord, Jesus Christ, the Son of God, begotten of the Father, the only-begotten of the essence of the Father, God of God, and Light of Light, true God of true God, begotten not made, being of one substance [*homoousios*] with the Father, by whom all things were made in heaven and on earth, who for us men and our salvation came down and was incarnate and was made man. He suffered and the third day he rose again, ascended into heaven. From thence he comes to judge the quick and the dead. And in the Holy Ghost." Then it goes on to say: "And those who say there was a time when he was not, or he was not before he was made, and he was made out of nothing, and out of another substance or thing, or the Son of God is created or changeable, or alterable, they are condemned by the Catholic Church." This is the fundamental Christian confession. The central phrase is "of one substance with the Father". Nothing like this is said of the Holy Ghost. And this was the reason for further struggles and decisions. The condemnations are interesting; the all-embracing one is directed against the Arians: "Those who say there was a time when he was not . . . are condemned by the Catholic Church."

Now we will present the significance of the decision of Nicaea for world history and the history of the church:

(1) The most serious Christian heresy was overcome. Christ is not one of the many half-gods; he is not a hero. He is God

himself appearing in divine essence within a historical person. It meant a definite negation of paganism. In Arius paganism again raised its head after it had been defeated in the anti-gnostic struggle. The victory of Arianism would have made Christianity only one of many possible religions.

(2) The confession of Nicaea was expressed in terms more pleasing to Rome and the West than to the East. The East did not like the *homoousios*; instead it wanted a ladder of hierarchies. Rome and her allies in the East insisted on the *homoousios*. For this reason the decision of Nicaea was immediately attacked. A sixty-year struggle ensued until in A.D. 381 a settlement was reached more satisfying to the East.

(3) The decisive statement is: "Being of one substance with the Father." This is not in the scheme of emanation but in the scheme of Monarchianism. Consequently it was accused of being Sabellian; and so were the main defenders, Athanasius and Marcellus.

(4) The negative character of the decision is especially evident in the condemnations. The creatureliness of Christ is negated. He has no other *ousia* than the Father; but what the *homoousios* is was not explained. It was not decided whether the three *prosōpa* are really differences in God, and if so whether they are eternal or historical. And no doctrine of the Spirit was given. Only one thing was determined: Jesus Christ is not an incarnated half-god; he is not a creature above all others; he is God. And God is creator and unconditioned. This negative decision is the truth and the greatness of the Council of Nicaea.

(5) There were some other implications. The statements were made in philosophical, non-biblical terms. Some Greek concepts were taken into the dogma, not so much as classical philosophy but as mystical philosophy of religion.

(6) From now on the unity of the church is identical with the majority of the bishops. A conciliarism had developed in hierarchical terms; the majority of the bishops replace all other authorities. Only much later did the claim of the Roman bishop to a special status among the bishops become dominant, until finally the authority of the majority of the bishops was abolished.

(7) The church had become a state church. This was the price which had to be paid for unity. The emperor did not command the content of the dogma, but he exercised pressure. When there were revolts against the dogma, the emperors after Constantine

had to exert even more pressure. This means that a new development in church history, indeed, of world history, had begun.

3. *Athanasius and Marcellus*

The chief defender of the decision of Nicaea was Athanasius.
He was primarily a great religious personality. His basic religious
conviction was unalterable, and therefore he was able to use a
variety of scientific means and political ways to advance his cause.
His style was clear; he was consistent and cautious, although at
times he could be compromising in his terminology. Several times
he was expelled from his episcopal see in Alexandria. He was
persecuted, but in the end he was victorious over heretics and
emperors. Athanasius saved the decision of Nicaea, but in order
to do so he had to compromise with a more Origenistic interpretation of the Nicene formulae.

For Athanasius sin is overcome by forgiveness, and death,
which is the curse of sin, is overcome by the new life. Both are
given by Christ. The new life includes communion with God,
moral renewal, and eternal life as a present possession. Positively
speaking, eternal life is deification, becoming like God as much as
possible. Thus, two things are needed, a victory over finitude
and a victory over sin. There must be both participation in the
infinity of God and participation in the holiness of God. How
can this be provided? Only by Christ who, as true man, suffers
the curse of sin and, as true God, overcomes death. No half-god,
no hero, no limited and relative power of being can do that. Only
as historical man could God change history, and only as divine
could he give eternity. There is no such thing as a half-forgive-
ness or half-eternity. If our sins are forgiven, they must be fully
forgiven; if we are eternal, we must be fully eternal. No half-god
could be the Savior. Salvation is the problem of christology.

The Christ who performs this work of salvation is not understandable to the human mind except through the divine Spirit.
Only through the Spirit can we come into unity with the Christ.
This implies that the Spirit of Christ must be as divine as Christ
himself. Groups arose after the Nicene decision to deny the
divinity of the Spirit. Athanasius fought against them too, and
said: They are wrong, for they want to make the Spirit into a
creature. But if the Spirit of Christ is a creature, then Christ also

is a creature. The Spirit of Christ is not the human spirit of the man Jesus; the Spirit of Christ is not a psychological function. The Spirit of Christ is God himself in Jesus and through him in us. In this way the trinitarian formula which remained unfinished at Nicaea was finally completed. In order to be able to unite us with Christ, the Spirit must be as divine as Christ himself, not half-divine, but fully God.

One of Athanasius' supporters was Marcellus, by whom the Monarchian tradition entered the discussion. Although he was an intimate friend of Athanasius, Marcellus was condemned by the more Origenistic theologians who did not like his Monarchian tendencies. Marcellus' emphasis was on monotheism. Before the creation God was a *monas*, a unity without differentiation. His Logos was in him, but only as a potential power for creation, but not yet as an actual power. Only with the creation does the Logos proceed and become the acting energy of God in all things, through whom all things have been made. At the moment of creation the divine *monas* has become a *dyas*, the unity has become a duality. In the incarnation, the act in which the Logos took on flesh, the second "economy" is performed. An actual separation occurs between Father and Son, in spite of the remaining potential unity, so that now it is possible for the "eyes of faith" to see the Father in the Son. Then a further broadening of the *monas* and of the *dyas* occurs, when after the resurrection of Christ the Spirit becomes a relatively independent power in the Christian Church. But these separations are only preliminary; the independence of the Spirit and of the Son is not final. The Son and the Spirit will finally return into the unity with the Father, and then the flesh of Jesus will wither away. The potential or eternal Logos should not be called the Son; he becomes the Son only through the incarnation and the resurrection. In Jesus a new man, a new manhood, appears, united with the Logos by love.

What we have described is a dynamic Monarchian system. The trinity is dynamized, is put into movement, approaches history, and has lost the static character it has in genuine Origenistic thinking. But this system was rejected. It was accused of being Sabellian, of representing that kind of Monarchianism in which God the Father himself appears on earth. The Origenistic system of degrees and hierarchies triumphed against Marcellus.

But the struggle continued. The Origenistic protest against the *homoousios* led not only to conflict with people like Athanasius or Marcellus, but also against the Nicaenum itself. This happened in the East, of course. The Origenists who had been overwhelmed by the pressure of the emperor at Nicaea gathered their forces again and insisted, against the Nicaenum, on three substances in the trinity. This was, so to speak, a pluralistic interpretation of the trinity, in the scheme of emanation, of hierarchies and powers of being. The trinity is seen in degrees, but only the Father is unconditioned and unlimited. He alone is the source of everything eternal and temporal. This was the mood of the Eastern theologians and the popular piety in the East. This mood prevailed again and again, in some cases with strong support of the emperor, who defied the decision of his predecessor Constantine and tried to press the supporters of Nicaea against the Nicaenum.

There was, however, a shortcoming in Eastern theology; it was united only negatively and not on a positive decision. So it was easy to split it and reduce its power of resistance against the Nicaenum. There were some in the East who practically returned to Arius; they were called the *anomoioi* (Anomoeans), which means "the Son is unlike the Father in all things". He is completely a creature. There were still others who mediated between the Nicaenum and the mood of the East. They were called the *homoiousianoi*, for they accepted the *homoiousios*, but not the *homoousios*. *Homoiousios* is derived from *homoios* which means "similar". This means that the Son is similar in essence to the Father. So now we have the struggle between the *homoousios* and the *homoiousios*. The hostile pagans in Alexandria cracked jokes about this fight going on in the streets, barbershops, and stores, in which Christians were arguing over an iota, the smallest letter in the alphabet, the only letter that distinguishes *homoiousios* from *homoousios*. But this was more than a fight over an iota; a different piety lay behind it. For the *homoiousianoi* the Father and Son are equal in every respect, but they do not have the identical substance. This group interpreted the Nicene formula *homoousios*, which they could not remove any more, in the sense of *homoiousios*. And even Athanasius and the West finally agreed that this could be done, if only the formula itself were accepted. The West in turn accepted the eternal generation of the Son, a formula which derived from Origen and which the

West did not like, and with it the West accepted the inner-divine, eternal trinity, which is a non-historical (non-economic) view of the trinity. The East, on the other hand, accepted the *homoousios* after it was possible to interpret it in the light of the *homoiousios*. And under these same conditions the East also accepted the *homoousia* of the Spirit.

This means that theological formulae were discovered which were able to resolve the struggle, but theological terms are never able to overcome the religious difference itself. We shall see how this worked itself out in the later developments of the Eastern and Western churches, in the coming fights and struggles and in the final separation. But for the time being the Synod of Constantinople, A.D. 381, was able to make a decision in which both East and West agreed, in which the *homoousios* and the *homoiousios* could come together. Before this was possible, however, new theological developments had to occur. These developments are represented by the three great Cappadocian theologians.

4. *The Cappadocian Theologians*

The three Cappadocian theologians were Basil the Great, Gregory of Nyssa, his brother, and Gregory of Nazianzus. Basil the Great was the bishop of Caesarea; he was many things, a churchman, bishop, the great reformer of monasticism, a preacher, and a moralist. He fought against the old and neo- and semi-Arians, against everything which followed the idea that Christ is a half-god and a half-man. Basil died, however, before the favorable decision of Constantinople was reached.

Basil's younger brother, Gregory of Nyssa, was called "the theologian". He continued the Origenistic tradition and its "scientific" methods. After Christianity became victorious under Constantine and after the Nicene dogma became fixed, it was possible now again for theology to attempt a union of Greek philosophy and Christian dogma. But this theology no longer had the freshness of the first great attempts made by the Apologists and Origen. It was much more determined by the ecclesiastical situation and the Creed of Nicaea; thus, it was more a matter of formulae than of material creativity. Gregory of Nazianzus created the definitive formulae for the doctrine of the trinity. He had become an intimate friend of Basil when both of them were students in Athens. They were united not only in their common theological convictions but also in their common asceticism. Gregory of Nazianzus became bishop and was president of the synod of Constantinople for a certain period.

These Cappadocian Fathers, especially Gregory of Nazianzus, made sharper distinctions between the concepts that were used in the trinitarian dogma. Two series of concepts were used: the first is one divinity, one essence (*ousia*), one nature (*physis*); the second series is three substances (*hypostaseis*), three properties (*idiōtētes*), three persons (*prosōpa, personae*). The divinity is one essence or nature in three forms, three independent realities. All three have the same will, the same nature and essence. Nevertheless, the number three is real; each of the three has its special characteristics or properties. The Father has the property of being ungenerated; he is from eternity to eternity. The Son has the characteristic of being generated. The Spirit has the characteristic of proceeding from the Father and the Son. But these characteristics are not differences in the divine essence, but only in their relations to each other. This is complex and abstract philosophy, but it offered the formula which made the reunion of the church possible. The Council of Constantinople removed the condemnations which had been added to the Creed of Nicaea, because they did not apply to the new terminology any more. It also said something about the Holy Spirit which was not included at Nicaea: "And in the Holy Spirit, the Lord and Giver of life, who proceedeth from the Father, who with the Father and the Son together is worshipped and glorified." These phrases have mystical power and could be used liturgically.

This decision ends the trinitarian struggle. Arius and Sabellius and their many followers were excluded. The negative side of this decision is clear, but its positive implications for developing the doctrine of the trinity pose extreme difficulties. I shall point out four of them.

(1) On the one hand, the Father is the ground of divinity; on the other hand, he is a special *persona*, a particular *hypostasis*. Now, if these two points of view are taken together, it is possible to speak of a quaternity instead of a trinity. It is possible to speak of the divine substance as the one divine ground, and of the three persons, Father, Son, and Spirit, as the manifestations of the ground. Then we have a quaternity rather than a trinity. There

was always an inclination in this direction, and Thomas Aquinas still had to fight against it. As a rule theology said: The Father is both the source of all divinity and of each of the manifestations.

(2) The distinctions in the eternal trinity are empty. The doctrine of the trinity was created in order to understand the historical Jesus. As long as this was kept in mind, the difference between God and Jesus was evident. But how can differences be maintained in the realm of a transcendent trinity? Distinctions are made by words like non-generated, generated, and proceeding. And what do such words mean? They are words without content, because there is no perception of any kind which can confirm their meaning. To anticipate a bit, Augustine said these differences are *not* expressed because something is said by them, but in order not to remain silent. This means that if the motives for the doctrine of the trinity are forgotten, the formulae become empty.

(3) The Holy Spirit even now remains an abstraction. The Spirit can be brought in concretely only if he is defined as the Spirit of Christ, of Jesus as the Christ; but if he is placed into the transcendent trinity, he is more an abstraction than a person. For this reason the Spirit was never very important for Christian piety. In the moment in which he was deified in the same sense that Christ was considered divine, the Spirit was replaced in actual piety by the Holy Virgin. The Virgin who gave birth to God acquired divinity herself to a certain extent, at least for popular piety.

(4) The idea of three *hypostaseis*, three different *personae*, could lead to tritheism. This danger became much more real when the philosophy of Aristotle replaced that of Plato. Plato's philosophy was always the background of mystical realism in the Middle Ages. In this philosophy the universals are more real than their individual exemplars. In Aristotle the matter is quite different. Aristotle called the individual thing the *telos*, the inner aim, of all natural development. If this is the case, the three powers of being in God become three independent realities, or more exactly, the three manifestations of God become independent powers of being, independent persons. Those who are nominalists by education have a great difficulty in understanding the trinitarian dogma. For nominalism everything which is must be a definite thing, limited and separated from all other things.

For mystical realism, as we have it in Plato, Origen, and the Middle Ages, the power of being in a *universal* can be something quite superior to and different from the power of being in the individuals. Therefore, the danger of tritheism was very minimal as long as the trinitarian dogma was interpreted in terms of the Platonic philosophy. Tritheism became a danger as soon as the Aristotelian categories came to predominate, and with it the nominalistic trend which placed great emphasis on the individual realities. Then the Son and the Spirit could become, so to speak, special individual beings; then we are in the realm of tritheism.

The great theologian in the East, John of Damascus, protested against this consequence. He emphasized the unity of action and being among the three manifestations of God. However, something else happened. For practical piety the trinitarian dogma became just the opposite of what it was originally supposed to be. It was supposed to be an interpretation of Jesus as the Christ; it was supposed to mediate this understanding to the Greeks with the help of the Logos doctrine. But the consequences of the Logos doctrine had become so dangerous in Arius, in particular, that traditional theology reacted against it. When it was still used, its philosophical meaning had been broken. In this way the trinitarian dogma became a sacred mystery. The sacred mystery was placed on the altar, so to speak, and adored. It was introduced into the icons, the pictures which are so important for the cult in the Eastern church, into liturgical formulae and hymns, and there the mystery has lived ever since. However, it lost its power to interpret the meaning of the living God.

I. The Christological Problem

The christological problem is historically a consequence of the trinitarian controversy. In principle, however, it is the other way around. The trinity is the answer to the christological problem. It is an answer whose final formulae seem to deny the basis on which it arose. The question was: If the Son is of one substance with the Father, how can the historical Jesus be understood? This was the purpose of the whole trinitarian dogma. But with the trinitarian dogma formulated as it was at Nicaea, is it still possible to make Jesus understandable? How can he who is of divine nature, without any restriction, be a real man at the same time? The christological controversy, which lasted for several centuries and brought the church once again to the edge of self-destruction, was an attempt to answer this question.

There were always two main types of christological thought: Either God as Father (or as Logos or Spirit) used the man Jesus of Nazareth, begetting, inspiring, and adopting him as his Son, or a divine being (the Logos or eternal Son) *became* man in an act of transformation. The Creed of Nicaea, with its *homoousios* and its Monarchian tendency, favors the former solution. And so does the Roman theology. The emphasis on the divinity of the eternal Son makes the emphasis on the humanity of the historical Son much easier. A half-god can be transformed into man; God himself can only adopt man. But this former solution was not in the line of Origenism. In Origen the eternal Logos is inferior to the Father and has, by his union with the soul of Jesus, in eternity the traits of the historical Jesus. Therefore, he can easily be transformed into Jesus with the help of the body, and a transformation christology can result. No sharp distinction between these two possibilities was made. The *homoousios* could be interpreted closer to Sabellius or to Arius. This means that the christological interpretations that followed Nicaea could be either in the sense of adoption or in the sense of transformation. This uncertainty was soon discovered by some theologians. It became a matter of controversy when a man arose to do what Arius had done in the trinitarian struggle, namely, to draw out the consequences of the Origenistic position, but now in the sphere of christology. This man was Apollinarius of Laodicea.[1]

1. *The Antiochean Theology*

The West never followed the Alexandrian line, of which Apollinarius was the most radical expression. The religious interest of the Alexandrians really had to do with the problem of salvation. How is salvation possible unless the humanity of Jesus is more or less swallowed up into the divinity, so that we can adore him as a whole, so that his mind is identical with the divine

[1] Editor's note: At this point in Tillich's lectures, Father Georges Florovsky delivered two lectures on Apollinarius and on Cyril of Alexandria. For this reason Tillich did not himself deal with their positions at any length.

Logos? The answer is: It would be impossible. Therefore, the general trend moves in the direction of what was later called Monophysitism. According to Monophysitism there is only one nature; the divine nature has swallowed up the human nature.

The West and the school of Antioch protested against this tendency in Alexandrian theology. One of the first theologians of this school was Theodore of Mopsuestia. The Antiochean school has definite characteristics which distinguish it from the school of Alexandria, and which make this school the predecessor of the emphasis on the historical Jesus in modern theology.

(1) The school of Antioch had a strong philological interest and wanted an exact interpretation and emphasis on the historical picture of Christ. In this way it anticipated the historical criticism developed in the modern period.

(2) The school had a rational tendency—just as liberal theology also had—in the sense of Alexandrian philosophy.

(3) The Antiochean theologians also had strong ethical-personalistic—instead of mystical-ontological—interests, just as Rome and the Stoics had.

Rome and the West were not always on the side of Antiochean theology, but on the whole Antioch represented the main trends of the West. In alliance with Antioch in the East, it was possible for Rome, with its emphasis on history and personality, to become victorious over the mystical ontological interest of the East. Popular religion, however, was on the whole on the side of Alexandria and against Antioch. Antioch could not prevail for a number of reasons. The basic structure of the dogma was against it, coming as it did from Origen and being much more in line with Alexandrian thinking. Politics was against it and there was also a lack of moral resistance against the superstitions which had developed widely in Christianity at that time. The personalities were not great enough to resist the demands of the people for a magically working God who walks on earth and whose human nature is only a gown for his divine nature. Nevertheless, Antioch, in alliance with Rome, saved the human picture of Christ in its religious significance. Without Antioch the church would probably have lost entirely the human picture, and the historical consciousness of the West would not have been able to develop.

Antioch defended the church against the Monophysites for whom the human character of Christ was swallowed up in divinity and who also gave rise to numerous magical and superstitious ideas. Thus, Antioch paved the way for the christological emphasis of the West. It is perhaps impossible for someone from the West fully to understand the religious meaning of the East. This is even more difficult for Americans than for Europeans, because Europe is much closer to the East, not only geographically but historically. The mystical-ontological elements permeate the whole of Western culture in Europe. This is not the case in the United States. Your heritage is indebted to the Antiochean school and to Rome which, in alliance with this school, saved the kind of attitude which is natural to you.

Theodore of Mopsuestia emphasized against Apollinarius that in Christ there is a perfect nature of man in union with the perfect nature of God. He said: "A complete man, in his nature, is Christ, consisting of a rational soul and human flesh; complete is the human person; complete also the person of the divinity in him. It is wrong to call one of them impersonal." It was common in the East, in Monophysitism, to hold that only one nature is personal, the divine nature and not the human. Therefore, Theodore said: "One should not say that the Logos *became* flesh." For Theodore this was a vague, metaphorical way of speaking and should not be used as a precise formula. Instead, one should say: "He took on humanity." The Logos was not transformed into flesh. This idea of transformation, or transmutation, was felt by him to be pagan, so he rejected it. The pagan spirit of superstition wanted to have a transformed God walking on earth. But then Theodore was confronted by a difficult problem. If the human and divine sides of Christ are themselves persons, is he not then a being with two personal centers? Is he not a combination of two sons, a monster with two heads, as Theodore's enemies put it? Theodore tried to show the unity of the two persons. He rejected the unity in essence or nature. In essence they are absolutely different because the divine nature cannot be confined to an individual man. The Logos is universally present. Even when Jesus lived, the flowers were blooming, animals were living, men were walking, and culture was going on. The Logos was active in all this. He said that it is impossible for the Logos to be only the man Jesus. He spoke, therefore, of a unity by the Holy Spirit, which is a unity of grace and will. In this way he established in Jesus an analogy with the prophets, who were driven by the Spirit. How-

ever, this is a unique event in Jesus, for in the prophets the
Spirit was limited, whereas in Jesus the Spirit was unlimited.

The union of the two natures started in the womb of Mary. In
it the Logos connected himself with a perfect man in a mysterious
way. This Logos directed the development, the inner growth, of
Jesus, but never by coercion. As every man Jesus had grace, even
unlimited grace. Grace never works through coercion but through
the personal center. By the grace of God Jesus increased in
perfection. In this way, he said, there is one person in Jesus, but
the natures are not mixed. He denied that he spoke of two sons;
instead, he said, he affirmed two natures. The divine nature does
not change the human nature in its essence. Jesus had a human
nature which by grace could follow the divine nature. Thus, one
could speak of Mary giving birth to God. This was the decisive
formula. It was against the tradition of the Antiocheans, but they
could not deny the phrase *theotokos* (Mother of God). He justified
the acceptance of this phrase by saying that Mary also gave birth
to a man. This is a direct and adequate way of speaking; the
other, that Mary gave birth to God, is only indirectly adequate,
because the body of Jesus was united with the Logos of God.

In the same way Theodore agreed that the human nature must
be adored and, conversely, that God had suffered. These things
can be said only of the unity of the person. Of this unity one can
say these things because what can be said of the unity can be
said of the whole being. But he rejected the idea of a transformation of the Logos into a human being. The Western theologians
said that the oneness of nature is reached only when Christ is
elevated to the throne of God at the resurrection, with the body
and the human soul being glorified and transformed. This event
of the human side being swallowed up is a transcendent event
which happens in heaven, not on earth. So Theodore said that
only the flesh, that is, the historical person, suffered and died,
not the divine nature in him. It is blasphemy to say that divinity
and flesh belong to one nature. Ambrose said that though Christ
had two natures, he suffered only in his human nature. The same
grace which accepted the human nature in Christ and made him
the Son of God also justified us before God and made us his children.

Thus we see here two allies: Rome, with her empirical, personal, and historical interest; Antioch, having the same interest,

but using it for philological studies and philosophical considera-
tions. This alliance of Rome and Antioch might have led perhaps
to a full victory of the Antiocheans over the Alexandrians. But
this did not happen. For Rome had more of a political than a
theological interest. Rome was the great center of the church and
as such it did not want to surrender Christianity on account of a
theological formula.

Nestorius was one of the leaders of the Antiochean school. In
A.D. 429 he preached against the doctrine of *theotokos*, that the
Virgin Mary gave birth to God. Nestorius taught that Mary gave
birth to a man who became the organ of divinity. Not the divinity
but the humanity of Christ suffered. Thus, one could say that
Mary is *christotokos*. Later Nestorius admitted that indirectly one
could speak of Mary as *theotokos* in the sense that God the Logos
came down and united himself with the man to whom Mary gave
birth. But this was not a divine being coming down to become
a man in terms of a transmutation myth.

The two natures of Christ preserve their qualities in the personal union. They are connected without being mixed in the
humanity of Jesus. The term "man" describes the one nature in
him, the term "God" or "Logos" the other nature. These ideas
brought the charge of heresy against Nestorius. They were
generally present in the Antiochean tradition, but with Nestorius
they became suspect and finally repudiated. If we say that
Nestorius became a heretic, we could say that he was the most
innocent of all heretics. Actually he was a victim of the struggle
between Byzantium and Alexandria.

2. *The Alexandrian Theology*

There were other developments which supported the Alexandrian cause.

(1) For a long time the Mary-legend, for which there is little
basis in the Bible, had grown out of the pious imagination. The
figure of Mary attracted the novelistic mind.

(2) The second reason for the predominance of Alexandria over
Antioch was the high valuation placed on virginity strengthening
the trend toward asceticism.

(3) There was also a spiritual vacuum in the religious life of
that period. The empty space which wanted to be filled was the

desire to have a female element in the center of religion. Egypt had such an element in its myth of Isis and Osiris, the goddess and her son, but Christianity did not. In this it followed Judaism, which discarded every female element. The Spirit was not able to replace the female element. First of all, the Spirit appears, in the stories of Jesus' birth, as the male factor. Secondly, the Spirit is an abstract concept. Thus, in the popular mind the Spirit could never replace the different forms of male-centered religion which came from the Old Testament.

(4) The transformation christology of Alexandria had a popular appeal. Imagine a simple-minded human being who wants to have God. If you tell her: "There is God, on the altar; go and have him there", then she will go. But how is this possible? Because of the incarnation, for in the incarnation God *became* something which we can have, whom we can see, with whom we can walk, etc. This is popular feeling, and this feeling became decisive against the Antiocheans.

Cyril of Alexandria wanted to show that the human nature was taken into the unity of the Logos, who remained what he was. So he could say that the Logos himself experienced death, since he received into himself the body of Jesus. In his formula, "out of two natures, one", he accepted the abstract distinction of the natures, but in actuality there is no difference between the two natures. This made it possible for him to be the protagonist in the fight for the *theotokos*. His religious motive was this: It is not a man who has become King over us, but God himself who appeared in the form of a man. If Nestorius were right, then only a man, and not the Logos, would have died for us; if he were right, then in the Lord's Supper we eat the flesh of a man. What the people wanted was the physical presence of the divine.

At first it seemed that the Antiocheans and the Alexandrians could be united. Then, however, the Alexandrians reacted so vigorously and victoriously that Rome took the side of Antioch. Rome put a condition to the Antiocheans; they had to remove Nestorius because he was under too much suspicion. After a compromise was worked out at the Council of Ephesus (A.D. 431) and a number of other synods, including the famous *Latrocinium* of Ephesus (the synod of robbers), a final settlement was reached at the Council of Chalcedon (A.D. 451). Here the alliance of Rome and Antioch proved its strength. They were helped by the fact that one from the opposition, Eutyches, a monk in Constantinople, put forth such a radically Monophysitic position that he was condemned. This was both a condemnation of Alexandria and a victory for Antioch.

3. *The Council of Chalcedon*

Pope Leo I wrote a letter which became decisive for the outcome at Chalcedon. It said that the properties of each nature and substance were preserved entire, and came together to form one person. Humility was assumed by majesty, weakness by strength, mortality by eternity. There was one true God in the entire and perfect nature of true man. The Son of God therefore came down from his throne, from heaven, without withdrawing from his Father's glory, and entered this lower world, because of the unity of the person in each nature, which can be understood that the Son of Man came from heaven, and conversely that the Son of God has been crucified and buried. Here we have the same phenomenon as in the theology of Antioch. A radical statement is combined rather easily with traditional ideas. The decision of Chalcedon was made on this basis. In significance it was not surpassed by Nicaea, and together with Nicaea it surpasses all other synodal decisions. No one can study systematic theology today without knowing something about this decision at Chalcedon. The substance of it was expressed in paradoxical formulae.

(1) "Therefore, following the holy Fathers, we all with one consent teach men to confess one and the same Son, our Lord Jesus Christ, the same complete in Godhead and also complete in manhood."

(2) "True God, and at the same time true man, of a reasonable soul and body."

(3) He is "consubstantial with the Father, according to his Godhead, and consubstantial with us according to his manhood; in all things like unto us, apart from sin."

(4) He is "begotten before all ages of the Father according to the Godhead, and in these latter days, for us and for our salvation, born of the Virgin Mary, the God-bearer (*theotokos*), according to the manhood."

(5) "One and the same Jesus Christ, Son, Lord, Only-begotten, in two natures. These two natures must not be confused, and they

are natures without any change, without division, without separation."

(6) "The distinction of natures being by no means annulled by the union, but rather the characteristic of each being preserved and coming together to form one person and one substance. He is not parted or divided into two persons but one and the same Son and Only-begotten, God the Word, the Lord Jesus Christ."

In this document, as in similar ones, we see how readily philosophical terms could have a transition into liturgical and poetic language. The negative side of these statements is clear. The positive side is more doubtful. The position of Rome was victorious, but different interpretations were possible. The East was disappointed by the decision; the delegates from Alexandria did not subscribe. If they had subscribed to something so contrary to popular demand back home, they would have been beaten to death by the fanatic monks on their return. The reaction of the East against Chalcedon, in its radical aspects, was strong enough to divide the East from Rome to such a degree that it became an easy prey to the Islamic puritan reaction. This is especially true of the Monophysitic churches of Egypt and neighboring countries. They were all swallowed up by the reaction of Islam, which I would call a puritan reaction, that is, a reaction against the sacramental superstitious form into which Christianity had fallen more and more. I have a thesis—I do not know whether Father Florovsky would agree with it—that the attacks of Islam would never have been successful if Eastern Christianity had taken into itself the elements of personality and history. Instead, Christianity in this region fell deeper and deeper into popular superstition, and so became vulnerable to the Islamic type of reaction.

The decision of Chalcedon was partly denied, partly set aside. From A.D. 482–519 the first schism occurred between the East and the West. Chalcedon was maintained by the West; the East either rejected it or veered toward a Monophysitic interpretation of it. After the reunion under Emperor Justin (519), Monophysitism became victorious in Alexandria. It was a radical return to Cyril and his emphasis on the unity of the natures. After the union in the incarnation only one nature is present. Christ is one, according to his composite nature, according to his person, according to his will. After the union there is no duality of natures

or energies. The more radical Monophysites said that Chalcedon
and Pope Leo, who asserted two natures and two energies,
should be condemned. These Monophysites taught that with the
conception in Mary the flesh of Christ became progressively
deified. That really made Mary a goddess. The radicals said their
enemies adored something mortal. They wanted nothing less
than God on earth, without human relativity.

4. *Leontius of Byzantium*

Emperor Justinian wanted a reunion of the Chalcedonians and
the Monophysites. He was aided in this by the teaching of a
monastic theologian, Leontius of Byzantium. By combining Cyril
and Leo with a new scholastic idea he found a solution to the
christological problem which endured in the East for a long time.
Leontius said that the human nature in Christ does not have its
own *hypostasis*; it is *anhypostasis* (without *hypostasis*). Here
hypostasis means being an "independent being". Instead, the
human nature is *enhypostasis*, which means that the human
nature is *in* the *hypostasis* of the divine Logos. Here we have
reached scholasticism. When it comes to the formula *enhypostasis*,
we do not really know what that means. But the reason it was
invented is clear. The question was: Can two natures exist without an independent head, an *hypostasis*? The answer was, they
cannot. Therefore, Christ has one *hypostasis* representing the two
natures.

The being of the human nature is in the Logos. This meant that
the theology of Antioch had to be condemned, including Theodore. The religious meaning of this Byzantine theology became
visible in the fight about the suffering of God which was expressed in liturgical and theological formulae. The *treis-hagion* (thrice
holy) was also enlarged to the formula: "Holy God ... Almighty
... immortal, who for us was crucified, have mercy upon us." One
of the holy *trias* has suffered in the flesh. This was carried through
and dogmatized in A.D. 553, at the Fifth Ecumenical Council in
Constantinople, in spite of protests from Rome. The Council
expressed itself in fourteen anathemas. The two natures are distinguished only in theory, not in practice. The person of the
Logos has become the personal center of a man. The human
nature has no personal characteristics of its own. This was the

decisive point, because if this is the case, how can he help us? The Crucified is the true God and Lord of glory, and one of the trinity. The identification of Jesus Christ with the Logos is complete. As in the icons in which Christ appears in gold-ground setting, the human personality has disappeared.

But the West could not be so easily conquered. A new reaction of the West occurred. The question arose whether the one person of Jesus Christ has one or two wills. This time the fight was between the *Monothelites* and the *Dyothelites*. This time the West prevailed. Christ who has two natures also has two wills. The human nature is not swallowed up by the divine. This whole development can be grasped only if we realize that the key to it is the problem of how salvation is related to the individual, to history, and to personal life. On this point the West was clear, the East was not.

The last controversy in the East had to do with the icons. *Eikōn* means "image". Icons were the images of the fathers and saints in the churches. The icons deserve veneration and not adoration. However, if one asks what this distinction actually means, we must say that in popular understanding veneration always develops into adoration.

We have been surveying the rise and further fate of the christological doctrine as formulated at the Council of Chalcedon. Through all this there has probably been a hidden protest against this emphasis on the Eastern church. This is understandable because it does not have the same vital significance to you as, let us say, the Reformation or modern theology. However, the situation is such that if you know the fundamentals of the early development, and really understand it, everything else becomes comparatively easy. If, on the other hand, you know only the contemporary situation, and not the foundations, then everything is in the air. It is like a house built from the roof rather than from the foundations. I believe that the developments in ancient Christian theology are really foundations, foundations that must be considered immediately after the biblical foundations.

The doctrine of Chalcedon, whatever we think of the use of Greek terms in Christian theology, saved the human side of the picture of Jesus for our Western theology, and even for the East. The human side was on the verge of being completely swallowed up by the divine nature, so that succeeding developments in the

West, including the Reformation, would not have been possible. This is the importance of the Council of Chalcedon and its decision, which the East never really accepted, but transformed it and let it become swallowed up in its sacramental way of thinking and acting.

To understand the steps in the christological doctrine, always keep in mind two pictures: (1) The being with the two heads, God and man, where there is no unity; (2) The being in which one head has disappeared, but also humanity has disappeared. The one remaining head is the head of the Logos, of God himself, so that when Jesus acts, it is not the unity of something divine and something human, but it is the Logos who is acting. Thus, all the struggles, the uncertainties, the despair and loneliness, which the Gospels present, were only seemingly experienced by Jesus, but not really. They are inconsequential. This was the danger in the Eastern development. The fact that this danger was overcome is due to the decision of Chalcedon. We must be grateful to the Eastern church that it was able to do this against its own basic feeling. The power of the Old Testament and the power of the full picture of the human side of Jesus prevented the East from failing in this respect.

J. PSEUDO-DIONYSIUS THE AREOPAGITE

Dionysius the Areopagite is the classic Christian mystic, one of the most interesting figures in Eastern church history. He was also of extreme importance to the West. In Acts 17.34 we read of a man called Dionysius who followed Paul after he had preached in the Areopagus. His name was used by a writer who lived around A.D. 500. In the tradition this man was accepted as the real Dionysius who talked with Paul. He wrote his books under the name of Dionysius. What seems to us now a falsification was a custom in ancient writing. It was not a betrayal in any technical or moral sense to launch one's books under famous names. Not until the fifteenth century was this falsification historically established. It is an established historical fact that the man who wrote these books wrote around A.D. 500 and used the name of Paul's companion in Athens in order to lend authority to his books. He was translated into Latin by John Scotus Eriugena, a great theologian of the West, around 840. This Latin translation was used throughout the Middle Ages and had many scholastic commentators. Dionysius represents the main characteristics of the Byzantine end of the Greek development. He is the mediator of Neo-Platonism and Christianity, and the father of most of Christian mysticism. His concepts underlie most Christian mysticism in the East as well as the West. Some of his concepts, such as that of hierarchy, entered the ordinary language and helped greatly to form the Western hierarchical system of Rome.

We have two basic works of his, *On the Divine Names* and *On the Hierarchies*. The latter book is divided into the heavenly and the ecclesiastical hierarchies. The word "hierarchy" was probably created by him; at least we do not know whether anyone else had used it before. The word is derived from *hieros*, meaning "holy, sacred" and *archē*, meaning "principle, power, beginning". Thus, hierarchy is defined by Dionysius as a "holy system of degrees with respect to knowledge and efficacy". This characterizes all Catholic thinking to a great extent; it is not only ontological, but also epistemological; there are degrees not only in being, but also in knowledge. The system of holy degrees is taken from Neo-Platonism, where it was first fully developed after Aristotle and Plato (*Symposium*). The man who is most important is Proclus, a Neo-Platonic philosopher who has often been compared with Hegel. He has the same kind of triadic thinking—thesis, antithesis, and synthesis—and brings all reality into such a system of holy degrees.

The surprising thing about Dionysius is that this system, which was the end of the Greek world and summarized everything Greek wisdom had to say about life, was introduced into Christianity and used by it. A short time before, this system had been used by Julian the Apostate in order to combat Christianity. Thus, Julian and the Christian theologians who fought against each other in a life-and-death struggle were united in a Greek Christian mystic and theologian, Pseudo-Dionysius.

The other book is *On the Divine Names*. The term "Divine Names" is also a Neo-Platonic term, which the Neo-Platonists used when they brought all the gods of the pagans into their system. How could they do this? Because they followed the philosophical criticism in terms of which no educated Greek of that time believed literally in the pagan gods. Still there was the tradition, there was popular religion, and so something had to be done about these divine names. They tried to show that the qualities of the divine were expressed in these names. These names express different degrees and powers in the divine ground and divine emanation. They point to principles of power, of love, of energy, and other virtues, but they cannot be taken as names for special beings. This means that they discovered, in present-day terminology, the symbolic character of all our speaking about God. Writings on the divine names can be found throughout the medieval period. The theologians wrote on the symbolic meaning of everything we say about God. They did not use the word "symbol" at that time, but they spoke of "name" as an expression of a characteristic or quality. If we follow the insight of classical theology in this respect, we will not say, as is often done, that our speaking of God is *only* symbolic. This "only" is very wrong! The wrong is on our side when we fall into a literalism, against which also the Reformers, especially Calvin, fought.

The symbolic interpretation of everything we say about God corresponds to the idea of God which Dionysius developed. How can we know about God? Dionysius answered: There are two ways of recognizing God. First, there is the way of positive or affirmative theology. All names, so far as they are positive, must be attributed to God because he is the ground of everything. So he is designated by everything; everything points to him. God must be named with all names. Secondly, however, there is the way of negative theology which denies that he can be named by anything whatsoever. God is beyond even the highest names which theology has given to him. He is beyond spirit, beyond the good. God is, as Dionysius says, super-essential. He is beyond the Platonic ideas, the essences, beyond all the superlatives. He is not the highest being but beyond any possible highest being. He is supra-divinity, beyond God, if we speak of God as a divine being. Therefore, he is "unspeakable darkness". By this combination of words he denies that God, in view of his nature, can be either spoken of or seen. Thus, all the names must disappear after they have been attributed to God, even the holy name "God" itself. Perhaps this is the source—unconsciously—of what I said at the end of my book, *The Courage to Be*, about the "God above God", namely, the God above God who is the real ground of everything that is, who is above any special name we can give to even the highest being.

It is important that the positive and the negative ways lead to the same end. In both cases the forms of the word are negated. If you say everything about God, you can just as well say that you say nothing about him, that is, not anything special. This is the first thing, of course, which must be said about God, because it is this which makes him God, namely, that which transcends everything finite. In this sense even the problem of unity and trinity disappears in the abyss of God. Since that which is super-essential, beyond the Platonic ideas, is also beyond all numbers, it is even beyond the number "one"—so that there is no difference between three or one or many in this respect. Whenever it is said that God is One, translate this to mean that God is beyond all numbers, even the number "one". Only on this basis can we then speak of "trinity", and of the infinite self-expression in the world.

From this abysmal One, which is the source and substance of all being, the light emanates, and the light is the good in all things. Light is a symbol not only for knowing but also for being. It is as the Greek philosopher Parmenides said, that where there is being there is also the *logos* of being. This light, which is the power of being and knowledge, is identical with itself; it is un-shaken and everlasting. There is a way downward and a way upward. We have this already in Heraclitus who said that in everything there is a trend from earth over water over fire to air, and an opposite trend from the air to earth. That is, there is a fundamental tension in every living being, a tension of the creative power of being going down, and the saving power of being going up. The three stages of the way upward are purgation, illumination, and union. Purgation is purification in the ethical-ascetic realm; illumination is in the realm of mystical understanding; union is the state of perfection, the return into unity with God. In this last stage something takes place which Dionysius called the mystical ignorance. The same thing was mediated to the modern world through Nicholas of Cusa in his idea of learned ignorance (*docta ignorantia*). These two men say that this is the only ultimate true knowledge. This word "ignorance" says that we do not know anything special any more when we have penetrated into the ground of everything that is. And since everything special is changing, it cannot be ultimate reality and truth. If you penetrate from everything changing to the ultimate, you reach the rock of eternity; you have the truth which can rest on this rock alone.

This fundamental reality is represented in degrees called hierarchies. The line from above to below is the line of emanation. The line from below to above is the line of salvation. The hierarchies represent both ways. They are the way in which the divine abyss emanates. At the same time, they are the revelations of the divine abyss, so far as it can be revealed, in the upward way of saving union with God. From the point of view of the way upward, the hierarchies have the purpose to create the greatest possible similarity and union of all beings with God. The old Platonic formula, "being equal to God as much as possible", was used also by the Areopagite—coming nearer and nearer to God and finally uniting with him.

Every hierarchy receives its light from the higher one and passes it down to the lower one. In this way each hierarchy is active and passive at the same time. It receives the divine power of being and gives it in a restrictive way to those which are lower than it. However, this system of degrees is ultimately dualistic. There are two fundamentally different hierarchies, the heavenly and the earthly. The heavenly hierarchies are the Platonic essences or ideas above which there is God. These are the first emanations from God, which Dionysius interpreted as hierarchies of angels. This is a development which had already occurred in later Judaism (the inter-testamental period). The concept of angels—which is a symbolic personalistic concept—amalgamates with the concept of hypostatized essences or powers of being. They become one and the same being and represent the heavenly hierarchies. If you want to interpret the concept of angels in a meaningful way today, interpret them as the Platonic essences, as the powers of being, not as special beings. If you interpret them in the latter way, it all becomes crude mythology. On the other hand, if you interpret them as emanations of the divine power of being in essences, in powers of being, the concept of angels becomes meaningful and perhaps important. The sentimental picture of angels as winged babies has nothing to do with the great concept of divine emanations in terms of powers of being.

The ecclesiastical hierarchy on earth is an image of the heavenly hierarchy. The angels are the spiritual mirrors of the divine abyss. They always look at him and are the immediate recipients of his power of being. They are always longing to become equal with him and to return to him. With respect to us, they are the first revealers. If we understand the matter in this way, we can understand what it means that they are the essences in which the divine ground expresses itself first. There are three times three orders of angels—which is, of course, a scholastic play—making it possible to give a kind of analogy to the earthly hierarchies. The earthly hierarchies are powers of spiritual being. Here we can learn something about medieval realism. The earthly hierarchies are:

(1) The three sacraments: baptism, the Lord's Supper, confirmation;

(2) The three degrees of the clergy: deacons, priests, bishops;

(3) The three degrees of non-clergy: the imperfect, who are not even members of the congregation, the laymen, and the monks, who have a special function.

These nine earthly hierarchies mediate the return of the soul to God. They are all equally necessary and are all equally powers of being. As children of nominalism, you will immediately ask: What does it mean that sacraments are equal with people (clergy, laity) as hierarchies? This can be understood only if you realize that the people here function as bearers of sacramental power, as bearers of the power of being. The same is true of the sacraments. This is what makes it possible for Dionysius to call all nine of them hierarchies. They are all sacred powers of being, some of them embodied in persons, some in sacraments, and some in persons who only have the functions of being believers in the congregation.

This brings the earthly world into a hierarchical system, because earthly things such as sounds, colors, forms, stone, etc. are used, especially in the sacraments, to express the ecclesiastical hierarchy. All reality belongs to the ecclesiastical reality, because the ecclesiastical reality is the hierarchical reality as expressed in the different degrees of being and knowledge of God. In the mystery of the church all things are interpreted in terms of their symbolic power to express the abyss of divinity. They express it and they guide everything back to it. The ecclesiastical mysteries penetrate into the interior divinity, into the divine ground of all things. Thus, a system of symbols in which everything is potentially included is established. This is the principle of

Byzantine culture, namely, to transform reality into something which points to the eternal, not to *change* reality as in the Western world.

Hence, hierarchical thinking in the East is much more in the vertical line, interpreting reality by penetrating into its depths, whereas the kingdom of God concept, as in Protestantism, belongs to a horizontal theology. Looking at the situation in terms of East and West, the East lacked the ability to work in the historical line of transforming reality, and therefore became first the victim of the Islamic attack, and then a victim of the Marxist attack. On the other hand, when we look at our culture we can say without much doubt that we have lost the vertical dimension to a great extent. We always go ahead; we never have time to stand somewhere and to look above and below.

To understand what I mean by making everything transparent for the divine ground, we should look for a moment at art. We have the most translucent religious art in the Byzantine mosaics. These mosaics have no tendency at all to describe anything which happens in the horizontal line. They want to express the presence of the divine through everything which appears on the horizontal level of reality, on the place of time and space, by making everything a symbol pointing to its own depths. This is the greatness of the mosaics. There are a few examples of them in the New York Metropolitan Museum of Art. There you have the expression of divine transcendence, even when the subjects are completely earthly—animals, trees, men of politics, women of the court. Every expression has its ultimate symbolic meaning. The last great controversy in the Byzantine church had to do with icons, or pictures, because the Byzantine culture believed in the power of pictures to express the divine ground of things. The danger was very great that popular belief would confuse the transparency of the pictures with the power of the divine itself, which is effective through the pictures but is never identical with them. The whole conflict was over the meaning of the transparent power of the pictures. For the East this was essential; therefore, most of the great art came from there, and then conquered the West. The danger then became so great in the West that after Rome had partly capitulated, it finally was attacked again by Protestantism, especially Reformed Protestantism, in a way which removed the pictures from the churches altogether. Thus, in

Calvinism natural objects lost their transparency. This is the meaning of all iconoclastic (image-destroying) movements. This is understandable as a reaction to the superstitious way in which many Catholics prayed *to* their pictures, etc. When we realize, however, that by the same act all natural objects lost their transparency, one cannot be so sure about it. Things become merely objects of technical activity, nature becomes dedivinized, and its function to represent the divine becomes lost. We can say that what the Byzantine culture effected was the spiritualization of all reality. That is not to be confused with idealization, which is something quite different. Hofmann's picture of Jesus is an idealization. A Byzantine picture of Jesus has transparency, but it is not an idealized picture. The divine majesty is visible throughout, not a nice human being with ideal, manly handsomeness. So I would say that the Eastern church represents something which we have lost. Therefore, I am especially happy that Eastern Orthodox churches could be taken into the World Council of Churches, thus making communication with them possible again. We should not imagine that we have nothing to learn from them. It may happen that with centuries of more intimate contact, the dimension of depth may again enter Western thinking.

The system of Dionysius was received by the West. There were two things which made this possible, which Christianized or baptized this mysticism. First, the emanation was understood not in a natural but in a personal picture. God has given existence to all beings because of his benevolence. This goes beyond pagan thinking. Here the personalistic element comes in and the Neo-Platonic dualism is removed. Secondly, the system of hierarchies was built around Christ and around the church. All things have their power of illuminating and uniting only in relationship to the church and to the Christ. Christ is not one hierarchy alongside others. This was prevented by Nicaea. But Christ is God manifest, who appears in every hierarchy and works through each one. In this way the system of pagan deities and mysteries, which lived in Neo-Platonism, was overcome, and in this way the Western church could receive the system of hierarchies and mysteries. As a result medieval mysticism was not in opposition to the ecclesiastical hierarchy. They worked together; only much later did conflicts arise.

K. TERTULLIAN AND CYPRIAN

The two men in the West with whom we must deal first are Tertullian and Cyprian. We already discussed Tertullian to some extent in connection with the Montanist movement of radical spiritualism and radical eschatology. He was its greatest theological representative. We also spoke of him in terms of his ability to create those trinitarian and christological formulae which, under pressure from Rome, finally conquered all the other suggestions made by the East. Further, we saw that he was a Stoic philosopher, and as such he used reason to develop his rational system in a radical way. The same Tertullian, however, was also aware of the fact that in Christianity there is also the element of paradox. He who said that the human soul is naturally Christian (*anima naturaliter christiana*) is the same one who is supposed to have said—though he did not actually say it—"I believe because it is absurd" (*credo quia absurdum est*). What Tertullian actually said was: "The son of God died: it is by all means to be believed, because it is absurd. And he was buried, and rose again; the fact is certain, because it is impossible." This *paradoxa* is a mixture of two factors: first, it expresses the surprising, unexpected reality of the appearance of God under the conditions of existence; secondly, it is a rhetorical expression of this idea in the way in which Roman orators used the Latin language. It must not be taken as a literal expression, but by means of a paradox a pointing to the incredible reality of the appearance of Christ. Now, people added to this the formula, *credo quia absurdum est*, but Tertullian himself never said this. With such a view he never would have been able to present such clear dogmatic formulae and, as a Stoic, believe in the ruling power of the Logos.

In Tertullian there also appeared an emphasis on sin, which was to become important in the West later. He spoke of the *vicium originis*, the original vice, and identified it with sexuality. In this way he anticipated a long development in Roman Christianity, the depreciation of sex and the idea of the universality of sinfulness.

For Tertullian the Spirit is a kind of fine substance, as it was also in Stoic philosophy. The fine substance is called Spirit, or grace or love. They are actually the same thing in Catholic theology. Thus,

Roman Catholic theology can speak of *gratia infusa,* infused grace, infused like a liquid, a very fine substance, into the soul of man and transforming it . This is the non-personalistic element in Roman Catholic sacramental thought. This grace can be infused sacramentally into the oil of extreme unction, into the water of baptism, into the bread of the Lord's Supper, and thus into the soul. This is one of the sources of this kind of "spiritual materialism", so to speak, which played such a great role in the Roman Church.

Finally, Tertullian represented the idea that asceticism, the self-denial of the vital reality of oneself, is the way to receive this substantial grace of God. He used the juristic term "compensation" for sin; asceticism is the compensation for the negative character of sin. And he used the term "satisfaction". By good works we can "satisfy" God. And he spoke of "self-punishment". To the degree that we will punish ourselves, God will not punish us. All of this is legalistic thinking, although Tertullian was not himself a jurist. But every Roman orator and philosopher used the legal categories. This was in general a fundamental characteristic of the West and it became decisive for the later development of the Roman Church.

Cyprian, bishop of North Africa, had his greatest influence on the doctrine of the church. The problem of the church which Cyprian discussed was a very existential one. There were the persecutions as a result of which there were those who were called the *lapsi,* those who fell away either by recanting the faith or by surrendering books to the searching servants of the pagan authorities or by denouncing fellow Christians in a trial. This was a matter of great concern to the church. These people wanted to return to the church and overcome the weakness which had caused them to fall. Who should be readmitted to the church? The church could not accept those who had fallen out of sheer malignancy. Who should make the decision as to who is eligible to return? The ordinary teaching was that it shall be done by those who were "spirituals", that is, those who had become martyrs or in some other way had proved that they were fully responsible Christians. This method, however, was a sort of remnant from the past in which the "spirit" was still dominant over the "office". But now the office wanted to set aside this remnant of the past and to take over this decision too. The bishop, who is the church, must make the decision on the *lapsi*. And he should decide in a very liberal way; he should accept those who fell even more than once, in the same way that other mortal sinners are received.

On the other hand, the teaching was still powerful that the Spirit must decide whether or not someone can belong to the church. So Cyprian said that the bishops are the spirituals, those who have the Spirit, namely, the Spirit of succession from the early apostles, apostolic succession. In this way the Spirit became the qualification of the office. This was the greatest triumph of the office, that now the Spirit is bound to the office, and the Spirit is called the Spirit of succession. This was a transition to the idea that the clergy are endowed with the graces by virtue of ordination, and that the highest of all clergy, the pope himself, embodies the grace of God on earth.

Another existential problem was what to do with people who are baptized by heretics and schismatics. I hope the difference is clear. Heretics are those who have a different faith, those who have deviated from the doctrinal order of the Christian Church. Schismatics are those who follow a special line of church-political development, those who split away from the church, motivated perhaps by a conflict between bishops or by an unwillingness to accept the bishop of Rome. Hence, the separation of the Eastern and Western churches is called a schism. The Eastern church is considered by Rome not as a heretical church but as a schismatic church. Protestantism is considered by Rome as a heretical movement, because the very foundations of faith are at stake and not only the refusal to acknowledge the bishop of Rome.

Now the question arose as to how it was possible to receive into one's own congregation persons who had been baptized by one of these groups. The answer that was given was in terms of the objective character of baptism. The validity of baptism does not depend on the person who performed it. We shall see how Augustine carried this through. Cyprian's idea of the church stood behind all this.

(1) "He who does not have the church as Mother cannot have God as Father." "There is no salvation outside the church" (*extra ecclesiam nulla salus*). The church is the institution in which salvation is attained. This represents a change from the early

Christian period in which the church was a community of saints and not an institution for salvation. Of course, in this period too salvation was happening in the church; people who were being saved from paganism and from the demons gathered in the church. But the church itself was not considered as an institution of salvation but as a community of the saints. This emphasis in Cyprian is very consistent with the legal thinking of the West.

(2) The church is built on the episcopate. This is according to divine law and is, therefore, an object of faith. "Therefore you must know that the bishop is in the church and the church is in the bishop, and that if somebody is not with the bishop, he is not in the church." This is the purest form of episcopalianism, although somewhat different from what that word means today.

(3) The unity of the church is correspondingly rooted in the unity of the episcopate. All bishops represent this unity. However, in spite of the equality of all of them, there is one representative of this unity; that is Peter and his See. The See of Peter is the church "from which the priestly unity has arisen, the womb and the root of the Catholic Church." This is said prior to Augustine. The consequence of this, although not yet in Cyprian's mind, was unavoidably the principate of Rome in a much more radical way than he expressed it.

(4) The bishop is *sacerdos*—the Latin word for "priest". The main function of the priest is sacrificial. The priest sacrifices the elements in the Lord's Supper and thus repeats the sacrifice on Golgotha. "He imitates what Christ did; he offers a true and perfect sacrifice to God the Father within the church." Here again this is not yet the same thing as the Catholic Mass, but it would unavoidably lead to it, the more so in the primitive nations, with their realistic thinking and their tendency to take as real what is symbolic. Many of the fundamentals of the Roman Church existed as early as about A.D. 250, when Cyprian lived. Whatever we say against the Roman Church, we should not forget that the early developments in Christianity led this way. And when today one speaks of the agreement of the first five centuries, this is entirely misleading. Of course, Protestants, Catholics, and Orthodox agree on the major synodal decisions, but this is only an apparent agreement, because the living meaning of these things was absolutely different from what the Reformers built up as Protestant

doctrine. If you look at a man like Cyprian, you can see the difference. No Protestant can accept any of these points.

Let me sum up some of the points of the Occidental tradition.

(1) One could mention first the general practical, activistic tendency in the West, the legal relations between God and man, the much stronger ethical impulses for the average Christian, not with respect to himself but with respect to the world. And we can include in this point the eschatological interest, without mystagogical and mystical emphasis. In short, we could say that law more than participation characterizes the West from the very beginning.

(2) The idea of sin, even original sin, is almost exclusively Occidental. The main concerns of the East dealt with death and immortality, error and truth. The main focus of the West was on sin and salvation. In St. Ambrose, for example, the apostle Paul, the main teacher on sin and salvation, is held in high esteem. Ambrose has been called the *doctor gentium*, the teacher of the nations. Paul has the keys of knowledge; Peter has the keys of power. Throughout the history of the Middle Ages there continued a struggle between Peter and Paul, so to speak, between the keys of knowledge which finally prevailed in the Reformation, and the keys of power which always prevailed in the Roman Church. Therefore, according to St. Ambrose grace is primarily understood as the forgiveness of sins and not as deification, as we have it in the Platonic attitude in the East.

(3) The latter point has the following consequences: Western Christianity emphasizes the historical humanity of Christ, his humility and not his glory. For example, on the door of St. Sabina in Rome, before which I stood with great awe, you find in woodcut relief the first picture or sculpture of the crucifixion. The door is world-famous, coming from the fourth century. Here the West shows that it deviates from the Christ of glory which you find in all mosaics; this is more symptomatic of the difference between East and West than many theological formulae. Of course, the same thing is also expressed in theological formulae. What we said when we dealt with Chalcedon can now be illustrated by contrasting a mosaic in, let us say, Ravenna, which was under Byzantine influence at that time, with the door in St. Sabina. There you find the two christologies clearly expressed in picture. In the one you have the tremendously powerful Lord

of the universe, the Judge of the world in all glory, or as the risen One, in his majesty surrounded by angels, men, animals, and inorganic parts of nature, all of which participate in his glory. In the other you have this wonderful—from another aspect, poor—presentation of the suffering Christ. The former is Alexandrian christology, which portrays a Christ whose bodily existence is swallowed up by the divine form. The latter is Antiochean, Roman christology, which emphasizes the humanity of Christ more than anything else, including his suffering humanity. This gives an example of the difference in feeling. Thus, we have in the whole history of painting in the West the most wonderful, the most cruel, and the most destructive representations of the crucifixion. The early Gothic crucifixes, of which there are many, are such that perhaps trustees of a modern church would not permit them to be hung; they are so ugly. As if the crucifixion were a beautiful thing! It was ugly—and that is what the West accepted and could understand.

(4) The idea of the church is emphasized much more in the West than in the East. Somehow the church is built according to the legal structure of the Roman state, with the principle of authority, with the double law—the canonic and the civil law. The hierarchical power is centralized in the pope; and everyone personally participates, even the monks, in the sacrament of penance.

L. The Life and Thought of Augustine

Now we come to the man who is more than anyone else the representative of the West; he is the foundation of everything the West had to say. Augustine lived from A.D. 354 to 430. His influence overshadows not only the next thousand years but all periods ever since. In the Middle Ages his influence was such that even those who struggled against him in theological terminology and method—the Dominicans, with the help of Aristotle—quoted him often. Thomas Aquinas, who was the great opponent of Augustinianism in the Middle Ages, quoted him affirmatively most frequently.

In Augustine we also have the man to whom all the Reformers referred in their fight with the Roman Church. He influenced modern philosophy in a profound way insofar as it was Platonic, for example, Descartes and his school, including Spinoza. He has influenced modern theology as well. I would say, almost unambiguously, that I myself, and my whole theology, stand much more in the line of the Augustinian than in the Thomistic tradition. We can trace a line of thought from Augustine to the Franciscans in the Middle Ages, to the Reformers, to the philosophers of the seventeenth and eighteenth centuries, to the German classical philosophers, including Hegel, to the present-day philosophy of religion, to the extent it is not empirical philosophy of religion, which I think is a contradiction in terms, but a philosophy of religion which is based on the immediacy of the truth in every human being.

1. *The Development of Augustine*

To understand Augustine we must trace his development in seven different steps, and then an eighth step which is a negative one with respect to content.

(a) The first of these seven steps, which may help us to understand the immense influence of this greatest of all church fathers, is Augustine's dependence on the piety of his mother. This means, at the same time, that he is dependent on the Christian tradition. This reminds us of Plato's situation. When Plato wrote, he also wrote out of a tradition, the aristocratic tradition of the Athenian gentry to which he belonged. However, this tradition had come to an end in the self-destructive Peloponnesian War; the masses took over, and then, as always, followed the tyrants. The aristocracy was killed, not only as human beings, but as the principle of aristocracy itself. So what Plato saw in his mind was an ideal form of political and philosophical existence; it was a vision which had no reality any more. Therefore, I must warn you about a mistake! The name of Plato overshadows everything else in Greek thought, even Aristotle. However, do not imagine that Plato was the most influential man in the later ancient world. To be sure, he did have some influence and his book, *Timaeus*, was almost the "bible" of the later ancient world. But he could not exercise real influence because everything he developed was in the realm of pure essences, and no longer had historical foundations. Here I am thinking in terms of pure economic materialism. If the social and economic conditions no longer exist, if a civilization has reached a certain state, it cannot be influenced, much less transformed, by the ideal form of ideas which come from the past. There is a parallel to this in our day in the longing for the Middle Ages; the increasing power of the Roman Church has something to do with this situation. But it cannot succeed. We cannot go back to the Middle Ages, although this is the hope of every Catholic. Thus, when Plato wrote his *Republic* and later on his *Laws*, implying in these writings all elements of his philosophical thought—which included at the same time his social, psychological, and religious thought—he was acting in some sense as a reactionary. By reactionary we mean that he was driving toward something which was a matter of the past, and could not be re-established any more in the period of the Roman Empire. This produced again a kind of emptiness in which the Cynics, Skeptics, and Stoics were much more important than Plato, because they were adequate to the situation. Stoicism, not Platonism, governed the later ancient world. Plato, however, returned in the Middle Ages.

Augustine was in quite the opposite situation. Whereas in Plato a great aristocratic tradition came to an end, a new tradition started in Augustine. He had a pagan father and a Christian mother. The pagan father made it possible for him to participate in what was greatest in paganism at that time, and his Christian mother made it possible for him to enter into another tradition, a new archaism.

(b) Augustine discovered the problem of truth. This second step is connected with the fact that he read Cicero's book, *Hortensius*. In it Cicero dealt with the question of truth. For Cicero this meant choosing between existing ways of truth, between the different philosophies. Cicero, a great Roman statesman, answered in terms of a kind of eclectic philosophy, as I believe every American statesman would do if he were to write a book on truth. He would choose those elements in philosophy which are most relevant to the political situation in which he found himself. Likewise, Cicero was interested in truth from a practical point of view. He was not an original philosopher. After the catastrophe of Greek philosophy this was impossible. Hence, from a pragmatic point of view he held that what enhances good citizenship in the Roman Empire is of philosophical value. The ideas which enhance are providence, God, freedom, immortality, rewards, etc. Augustine was in the same situation, only for him it was the City of God, not the *civitas terrena*, which he had in mind. So he developed a pragmatic philosophy, with Platonic and other elements, on the basis of the need of the Christian life, not on the basis of Roman citizenship. The basic form was pragmatic and eclectic, as in Cicero. Augustine also was not an original philosopher in the sense in which Plato or the Stoics were. He was a philosopher in whom the great synthesis between the Old Testament idea of Yahweh and the Parmenidean idea of being was achieved. More than anyone else in the history of the church Augustine was responsible for the communion of Jerusalem with Athens.

(c) The third point was his Manichaeism. The Persian religion was dualistic and in the Hellenistic period produced a movement called Manichaeism, named after its leader Mani. It was a Hellenized Parsism, dualistic in character. We can consider it a mixture between the prophecy of Zoroaster, the prophet of the Persian religion, and Platonism in the form of the gnostic thinking in the late ancient world.

The Manichaeans were for a long time the main competitors of Christianity. They asserted that they represented the truly scientific theology of their time. Augustine was attracted to it for this reason, and also because the dualism of the Manichaeans made it possible to explain sin rationally. This is the reason that the Manichaeans have always had some influence in the history of Christianity. In the Middle Ages there were always some sects influenced by Manichaean ideas, and there are many Manichaean ideas around today without our knowing them as such. Whenever sin is explained in terms of two ultimate principles, that is Manichaean; the evil principle is as positive as the good. For ten years Augustine was attracted to Manichaeism. There were reasons for this. First of all, for this group truth was not a merely theoretical issue, a matter of logical analysis, but it was a religious issue, a matter of practical or existential concern. Secondly, truth was saving truth. Manichaeism was a system of salvation. The elements of the good, which are captivated by the evil principle, are saved from it. Thirdly, truth lies in the struggle between good and bad, which gives one the possibility of interpreting history.

Augustine always remained under the influence of Manichaeism. He left the group and fought against it, but his thinking and even more his feeling were colored by its profound pessimism about reality. His doctrine of sin is probably not understandable apart from his Manichaean period. Augustine left Manichaeism under the influence of astronomy. Astronomy showed him the perfect motion of the stars, that is, the fundamental elements in the structure of the universe. This made any dualistic principle impossible. If the universe has a structure of regular mathematical forms which can be calculated and which are harmonious, where can you find the effect of the demonic creation in the world? The world as created in its basic structure is good; this is what he derived from astronomy. This means that he used the Greek Pythagorean idea of the cosmos. He used the principles of form and harmony as expressed in mathematics.

This Greek European principle overcame for Augustine the Asiatic dualism and negativity. Thus, the separation of Augustine from the Manichaean philosophy was a symbolic event. It meant the liberation of modern natural science, mathematics, and technology from the Asiatic dualistic pessimism and negation of reality. This was extremely important for the future of Europe. The later medieval Augustinian philosophers and theologians were always men who emphasized astronomy and mathematics more than anything else. Modern natural science is born, as are Platonism and Augustinianism, on the basis of a belief in a harmonious cosmos determined by mathematical rules. This was also the world-view of the Renaissance. If we look deeper into the movements of thought, we can see that this anecdote about Augustine leaving the Manichaeans because of astronomy, after he had joined them because of its explanation of sin and evil, becomes a world-historical symbol for the relationship of the Asiatic East and the European West.

(d) After Augustine left the Manichaean group, he fell into skepticism, as often happens if you are disillusioned about a system of truth. You may fall into doubt about every possibility of truth. At this time the mood of skepticism was widespread. Even in the later Academy, the Platonic school, skepticism about knowledge existed in what was called probabilism. Only probable statements are possible; no certainty is possible. All of Augustine's earlier philosophical writings deal with the problem of certainty. He wanted to overcome the skeptical philosophy; he wanted certainty. This is an important element in his thinking because it presupposed the negative end of the Greek development. The heroic Greek attempt to build a world on the basis of philosophical reason came to a catastrophic end in skepticism. The attempt to create a new world in terms of a doctrine of essences ended in skepticism. It is on this basis that the emphasis on revelation must be understood. Skepticism, the end of Greek philosophy, was the negative presupposition of the way in which Christianity received the idea of revelation. Skepticism is very often the basis for a doctrine of revelation. Those people who emphasize revelation in the most absurd supernaturalistic terms are those who enjoy being skeptical about everything. Skepticism and dogmatism about revelation are correlated. The way that Christianity emphasized revelation up to the Renaissance is related to the tremendous shock Western mankind experienced when all the attempts of the Greek philosophers to bring certainty proved to be in vain.

Skepticism also gave rise to a new doctrine of knowledge, a new epistemology, which Augustine created. It starts with the *inner* man instead of the experience of the external world. Skepticism, which was the end of all attempts to build a world in the objective realm, in the realm of things and objects, had the effect of throwing Augustine upon himself to find therein the place of truth. Thus, we have two consequences of his participation in skepticism: the one is that he accepted revelation, the other that to find certainty as a philosopher he looked into the innermost center of his soul, in the subject himself. Augustine stood between skepticism and the new authority, that of the church, just as Plato stood between the old authority and the beginning of skepticism. Here again we have the end of the archaic period in Plato and the beginning of a new archaic period in Augustine.

(e) Augustine's liberation from skepticism in the philosophical realm was brought about by his Neo-Platonic period. While skepticism was at one end of Greek thinking, Neo-Platonism was at the other. Skepticism was the negative, Neo-Platonism the mystical, way that Greek philosophy came to its finish. Augustine became a Neo-Platonic philosopher and used this philosophy as the basis for a new certainty, the immediate certainty of God. In Neo-Platonism you have the immediacy of truth in the inner soul, and from this he got his new certainty of the divine.

Neo-Platonism also gave Augustine the basis for his interpretation of the relationship of God and the world; God is the creative ground of the world in terms of *amor* (love). Then, from a psychological point of view it gave him an entrance into himself, although this had to be supported by his Christian experience. But now Augustine did something which later on all Renaissance philosophers also did—he turned the meaning of Neo-Platonism into its opposite. Neo-Platonism was a negative philosophy, a philosophy of escape from the world. The elevation of the soul out of the material world into the ultimate is the meaning of Neo-Platonism. Augustine changed this emphasis; he dropped the idea of degrees, and instead used Neo-Platonism for the immediate experience of the divine in everything, but especially in his soul.

(f) Augustine overcame skepticism not only philosophically with the help of the Neo-Platonists, but also with the help of the authority of the church. This happened under the influence of St. Ambrose, bishop of Milan, in whom the authority of the church was represented. The principle of authority was a form in which the new archaism, or the new archaic period which starts with the church tradition, became conscious of itself. The catastrophe of skepticism drove Augustine more and more to authority, to the authority of revelation, concretely given to him by the authority of the church.

The entire medieval development had an underlying anxiety of skepticism, the anxiety of meaninglessness, as we would call it, over against which the acceptance of revelation and authority stood. Authority for Augustine meant the impressive, imposing, overwhelming power of the church and its great representatives. The phenomenon of authority was not a problem of heteronomy, as it is for us, that is, subjection to what someone else tells us to accept. For Augustine it was the answer to the question implied in ancient skepticism. Therefore, he did not experience it as heteronomy but as theonomy, and somehow rightly so at that time.

(g) Another thing which impressed Augustine profoundly was Christian asceticism, as represented by monks and saints. He experienced the tension between the mystical ideal and his own sensual nature. In Augustine's time the sphere of sexuality was profanized in a terrible way. Neither Stoic reason nor Neo-Platonism was able to overcome this profanation on a large scale. The natural forms of love, sanctified by tradition and faith in the archaic periods of Greece and the other countries, had been destroyed. An unrestrained naturalism of sex prevailed.

None of the preaching of the Stoics, Cynics, or Skeptics was able to help against this, because they preached the law, and the law is powerless against a naturalistically distorted libido. Augustine found a new principle of sanctification which proved the solution for himself and for others in this realm. It had the same tension in itself as we met in the Christian Neo-Platonism in Dionysius, that is, both affirmation and negation of the world. Christianity affirms creation and sanctifies existence through the historical appearance of the divine in Christ. Neo-Platonism negates creation; in fact, it has no real creation. And it negates the historical appearance of God, or makes it a universal event which always is happening. Augustine was divided; insofar as he was a Christian, with his roots in the Old Testament, he valued family and sex, to the extent that sex was kept within the family. Being influenced by Neo-Platonism and the ancient negativity toward the world, he denied sex and praised asceticism. This conflict went on through the whole history of the church. We find it even in the Reformers, although the Reformation was basically on the positive side of Augustine, affirming the body in dependence on Old Testament prophetism. On the other hand, the suspicion of libido was so deeply rooted in the Christian tradition that in spite of their radicalism, the Reformers were unable to eradicate the remnants of Neo-Platonic asceticism, and were suspicious of everything sexual. This is still true of Protestants in countries under Calvinist influence.

(h) It is important not only to understand these seven steps in the development of Augustine, but also to notice what is missing among these major influences on him. Aristotle is missing, not entirely, of course, because Plotinus had taken much of Aristotle into his system. Yet, Aristotle was not directly important for Augustine. This means that Augustine did not include in his philosophy and theology the concern for Greek science. Not only Greek natural science, but also political science was not really implied in his thinking. This is significant for the further development in the Middle Ages.

(1) What Aristotle did was to construct a system of mediation, not a system of dualism, as we have in Plato and Plotinus. The system of mediation could not be used by Augustine because for him the dualistic world-view seemed to be the adequate expression of Christianity.

(2) The emphasis in Aristotle on the importance of the individual provides a basis for tendencies which are far removed from Augustine, who wanted the *community* of the church.

(3) Aristotle speaks about the middle way between the extremes. He denies anything like the erotic and ascetic ecstasies of Augustine. Again, it is a quasi-bourgeois attitude. The consequences of this later on become very explicit in Protestantism.

(4) Aristotle represents the special sciences which deal with things in their rational and horizontal relationship. Augustine denies the importance of such things. What is important is the knowledge of God and the soul, not knowledge of the natural things.

(5) Aristotle was a logician. Augustine had no particular interest in logic. The intuitive and voluntaristic character of his thinking made him disinterested in the abstractions of pure logic.

(6) Aristotle was an inductive thinker, an empiricist. He started from the given reality in time and space and went up from there to the highest abstractions. Augustine, following Plato, was an intuitive thinker; he started from above and went down to the empirical realities.

Now, these two different attitudes were due to clash as soon as Aristotle was rediscovered in the thirteenth century. For this reason this is the greatest century of Christian theology; it is completely determined by the tension between Aristotle and Augustine. This tension continues through all the succeeding centuries. If anyone wishes to place a label on me, he can call me an "Augustianian", and in this sense "anti-Aristotelian" and "anti-Thomistic". I am in basic agreement with Augustine with respect to the philosophy of religion, but not necessarily in other things. For example, as a *Gestalt* theologian or philosopher I am closer to Aristotle than to Augustine or Plato, because the idea of the living structure of an organism is Aristotelian, whereas the atomistic, mechanical, mathematical science is Augustinian and Platonic.

2. *Augustine's Epistemology*

The purpose and the way of knowledge are expressed in Augustine's famous words: "I wish to know God and the soul." "Nothing else?" "Nothing at all." God and the soul! This means that the soul is the place where God appears to man. He wants to know the soul because only there can he know God, and in no other place. This implies, of course, that God is not an object beside other objects. God is seen in the soul. He is in the center of man, before the split into subjectivity and objectivity. He is not a strange being whose existence or non-existence one might discuss. Rather, he is our own *a priori*; he precedes ourselves in dignity, reality, and logical validity. In him the split between the subject and object, and the desire of the subject to know the object, are overcome. There is no such gap. God is given to the subject as nearer to itself than it is to itself.

In the Augustianian tradition the source of all philosophy of religion is the immediacy of the presence of God in the soul or, as I prefer to say it, the experience of the unconditional, of the ultimate, in terms of an ultimate or unconditional concern. This is the *prius* of everything. This is not a matter of discussing whether or not somebody exists. Augustine connects this with the problem of certainty. He says that we have immediate evidence of two things, first, the logical form—because even the question of evidence presupposes the logical form—and secondly, the immediate sense experience, which should really be called "sense impression" because "experience" is too ambiguous. What he means is this: I now say that I see blue. Objectively the color may be not blue but green—sometimes I confuse these two, especially in ladies' dresses, to the horror of Mrs. Tillich. In any case, the sense impression I have is blue. This is absolutely certain, even if the dress is not blue. This is what he means with immediacy. I may see a man, but as I come nearer, it is in reality a tree. This often happens when you are walking in a fog. This means there is no certainty about the objective element in it; but there is absolute certainty about the impression I have as such. There is skepticism about everything real. Logical forms are not real; they are structures which make questions possible. Therefore, they are immediate and necessary. And sense experiences are not real, except insofar as I have them. Whether they are more than this, I do not know. Thus, these two evidences—of the logic and of the perception—do not overcome skepticism.

How then can doubt about reality be overcome? First, we must start with the general doubt; we must doubt about everything. It was not Descartes who first said this. It was said even before

Augustine. But Augustine also said it. Is there a point of certainty somewhere? He said: "You know that you are thinking."
"Do not go outside; go into yourself," namely, where you are
thinking. "The truth dwells in the interior of man, for a mind
knows nothing except what is present to the mind. But nothing is
more present to the mind than the mind itself." That is to say, the
immediate self-consciousness of the asking skeptic is the fixed
point. The truth which was lost in the exterior world, where
everything fell under skepticism, is found again in the interior
world. The soul is the inner realm, in contrast to Greek philosophy
in which it is the power of life. The discovery of soul in this
sense is one of the most important consequences of Christianity.
It includes the world as the sum of all appearances. In contrast to
the Greeks, where the soul is a part of all things, the world now
becomes an object. The world is an appearance for the soul,
which is the only real thing.

Now these ideas—go into your inner reality and there you will
find truth—sound very much like Descartes' *cogito ergo sum* (I
think, therefore I am). The difference is that in Descartes the
self-certainty of the ego is the principle of mathematical evidence
—he derives from this his rational system of nature—whereas for
Augustine the inner evidence is the immediacy of having God. So
Augustine says: After going into your soul, transcend yourself.
This means that in your soul there is something which transcends
your soul, something immutable, namely, the divine ground. He
refers here to the immediate awareness of that which is unconditional. This is certainly not an argument for the existence of
God, but a way of showing that God is presupposed in the situation of doubt about him. "While not seeing what we believe, we
see the belief in ourselves." That is, we see the situation of being
grasped by something unconditional.

There were people whom Augustine met who said: Why truth
at all? Truth as such is not necessary. Why not stick to probabilities? Why not restrict oneself to pragmatic answers, answers
which work? Augustine replied that this is not sufficient, because
it leads to a complete emptiness of life. Without something unconditional or ultimate, the preliminary meanings lose their significance. This cannot be counteracted by saying that the human
situation is not one of *having* truth but of searching for truth.
Augustine replies that searching for truth is no answer to the

question of truth, because if we are searching for truth, we must at least have some intuition of truth, we must know when we approach truth that we are approaching it. In order to know that we are approaching truth, we must already have some criterion, namely, truth itself. He is saying that in every relativism, however radical it may be, an absolute norm is presupposed, even if it cannot be expressed in propositions. Since truth is something which we can find only in the interior of the human soul, physics is useless for ultimate truth. It does not contribute to the knowledge of God. He says that while angels have knowledge of divine things, the lower demons recognize the world of bodies. A knowledge of the bodily world involves participation in it. Knowledge is union; union implies love; and he who deals cognitively with the bodies loves them and participates in them. This means that he is distracted from the highest, divine knowledge; it means that he is in untruth. The natural sciences have meaning only insofar as they show the divine causes in nature and show the traces of the trinity in flowers and animals; they have no meaning in themselves. The consequence of this is that for the greater part of the Middle Ages the natural sciences were reduced in significance and were not really furthered at all. The technical relation to nature is of no interest to Augustine, nor the analytic character of controlling knowledge. This makes the attitude of the Middle Ages to the natural sciences understandable. If the people of the Middle Ages loved nature, it was because they could see it as an embodiment of the trinity. This, of course, gave them the possibility of artistic production, which is much higher than most of what we produce under the power of controlling knowledge. Go to the Cloisters (Museum) and look at the carpets on the walls there; what you see there is not a representation of nature in terms of natural science. None of the flowers or animals is naturalistically exact; but they are all painted in order to show the traces of the trinity, that is, the movement of life to separation and reunion in the natural objects. They try to show the divine ground in nature, and that gives them their beauty. To understand these creations, you must see their *intentio*, that which is really meant.

Augustine said that the Neo-Platonists and Plato himself were nearest to Christianity. He saw trinitarian elements in their thought, especially the Logos doctrine. Then he says—an important statement for revealing the relationship of theology and philosophy—that one thing which philosophy could not affirm is that the Logos has become flesh. Philosophy makes it possible for theologians to speak of the Logos, but when theology says the Logos became flesh, this is a theological statement based on a religious message that distinguished Christianity from classical philosophy. The statement about the Logos becoming flesh is a matter of revelation, not philosophy. The Logos as the universal principle of the cosmos appears in historical form. This is a unique, incomparable historical event.

3. *The Idea of God*

Augustine's idea of love is the power which unites the mystical and ethical elements in his idea of God. Let us first deal with his idea of love before taking up the problem of God. Anders Nygren, the Swedish theologian who wrote *Agape and Eros*, criticized Augustine, as he did Christian theology in general, for combining *erōs* and *agapē* in a synthesis. Nygren is right that in Augustine there are both elements. *Agapē* is the element of love in the New Testament sense of the personal, forgiving character of God. *Erōs* represents the longing of all creatures for God as the highest good, the desire to be united with it, to fulfill itself by intuiting eternally the divine abundance. The *agapē* element is emphasized when we speak of God moving down to man in *caritas*—I prefer the Latin word to the much distorted word "charity"—of becoming humble in Christ, exercising grace and mercy, participating in the lowest and elevating it to the highest. *Erōs*, on the other side, drives from below to above; it is a longing, striving, being moved by the highest, being grasped by it in its fullness and abundance. The Logos becoming flesh, that is *agapē*. But all flesh (all natural and historical reality) is desirous for God; this is *erōs*. In my *Systematic Theology* I have shown that if you remove *erōs*, you cannot speak of love toward God any more, because this is love toward that which is the highest power of being in which we are fulfilled.

God is *summa essentia*, ultimate being, beyond all categories, beyond all temporal and spatial things. Even the categories of substance cannot be used. Essence and existence, being and quality, functions and acts, these cannot be distinguished in this side of God. The negative theology which we found in Dionysius is present also here; both were dependent on Neo-Platonism. On the other hand, there is the positive way. God is the unity of all forms; he is the principle of all beauty. Unity is the form of all beauty and God is the unity of all forms. All ideas, all essences, or power, or principles of things, are in the mind of God. Individual things come to pass and return to God through the ideas.

Here we have the two elements in the idea of God. Insofar as God is beyond any difference, he is beyond subject and object. Love is not a subjective feeling directed toward an object. It is not that objects are ultimately loved, but through our love toward them love itself is loved. *Amor amatur,* love is loved; this means that the divine ground of being is love. Love is beyond the separation of subject and object. It is the pure essence, blessedness, which is the divine ground in all things. If we love things in the right way, including ourselves, we love the divine substance in them. If we love things for their own sake, in separation from the divine ground in them, we love them in the wrong way; then we are separated from God. There is thus for Augustine a right kind of self-love; this is to love yourself as loved by God, or to love God, the divine ground of everything, through yourself.

Augustine is also in the personalistic tradition of the Old and New Testaments and the early church. This is more important for him than for the Eastern theologians, like Origen. He sides completely with the West in the trinitarian discussion. He is more interested in the unity of God than in the different *hypostaseis,* the three *personae,* in God. He expresses this in terms which make it clear he is one of those responsible for our present-day inclination to apply the term *persona* to God, instead of applying it individually to the Father, Son, and Spirit. Of course, Augustine never became heterodox in this respect, although he leaned, as did the West generally, toward a Monarchian view. That he was inclined in this direction is evident by the analogy he sees between the trinity and the personal life of man. He says: "Father, Son, and Spirit are analogous to *amans* (he who loves), *quod amatur* (that which is loved), and *amor* (the power of love)." Or: "The trinity is analogous to memory, intelligence, and will." This means that he uses the trinity in order to give analogically a description of God as person. Since God is a person, and that means a unity, all acts of God toward the outside (*ad extra*) are always acts of the whole trinity, even the act of the incarnation. None of the three *personae* or *hypostaseis* acts for himself. Since the substance of all things is love, in its threefold appearance as *amans, quod amatur,* and *amor,* everything which is created by the divine ground bears the traces of the trinity. This gives a theonomous character to the immediate world. The forms of life are not denied or broken but theonomously filled with divine substance.

On the relation of God to the world, Augustine expressed very clearly the doctrine of creation out of nothing. There is no matter which precedes creation; creation is done without an independent substance. This means there is a continuous threat of finitude. I believe that when our modern existentialist thinkers, including myself, say that finitude is the mixture of being and non-being, or that non-being is present in everything finite, this has something to do with Augustine's statement that everything is in danger of the fathomless abyss of nothingness. The world is created in every moment by the divine will, which is the will of love. Therefore, Augustine concluded—and the Reformers followed him—that the creation and preservation are the same thing; the world is at no moment independent of God. The forms, laws, and structures of reality do not make it an independent reality. God is the supporting power of being, which has the character of love. This makes every deistic fixation of the two realities—God and the world—impossible. God is the continuous, carrying ground of the world.

All of this is in agreement with Augustine's famous doctrine of time. Philosophically speaking, this is his greatest achievement, because here he really starts a new era of thinking about the concept of time. (Cf. his prayer, Book II of the *Confessions.*) Time is not an objective reality in the sense in which a thing is. Therefore it is not valid for God. The question how time was before creation is meaningless. Time is created *with* the world; it is the form of the world. Time is the form of the finitude of things, as is space also. Both world and space/time have eternity only insofar as they are subjects of the eternal will to creation. That means they are potentially present in the divine life, but they are not eternal as real; as real they are finite; they have a beginning and an end. According to Augustine there is only one world process.

This is the decisive statement by which he denies the Greek concept, held by Aristotle and the Stoics, that the world is cyclical, that there are cycles of birth and rebirth which repeat themselves infinitely. For Augustine there is a definite beginning and a definite end; only eternity is before and after this beginning and end. For the Greeks space was finite and time was infinite, or better, endless. For Augustine neither time nor space is infinite. He agrees with the Greeks on the finitude of space. They could not understand the infinity of space because they were all potential sculptors; their world-view was plastic; they wanted to see bodies in space. The infinity of space would have disrupted the plastic form of reality, expressed in mathematical forms by the Pythagoreans. Augustine, however, said time was finite. This finitude of time is necessary if time is to have an ultimate meaning. In Greek thought it does not; instead it is the form of decay and repetition. Time has no meaning of itself in creative terms. The endlessly recurring times of nature are meaningless. Meaningful time is historical time, and historical time is not a matter of quantity. The six thousand years of world history about which Augustine speaks *are* the meaning of time. And if, instead, there were one hundred thousand years or even a few billion years, this could not take away the meaning of time. Meaning is a qualitative, not a quantitative, concept. The measure of time is not clock time. Clock time is physical time; it tends to repeat itself. But the meaning of time is the *kairos*, the historical moment, which is the qualitative characteristic of time.

There is one world whose center is the earth, and one history whose center is the Christ. This one process is eternally intended by God, but eternity is not time before time, nor is it timelessness. It is something beyond all these categories. However, although the world is intended eternally, it is neither eternal nor infinite; it is finite and meaningful. Infinite meaning is actualized in the finite moment. This feeling of finitude makes the Middle Ages understandable to us. People then felt that they lived in one process which has a definitely known beginning with the days of creation a few thousand years before our time and which will have a definite end with the days of judgment a few years or a few thousand years ahead of us. We live within this period, and what we are doing in it is extremely important—it is the meaning of the whole world process. We are in the center of everything that happens, and Christ is in the center of everything that we are. This was the medieval world-view. You can imagine how far we are removed from it if you realize what this means not in terms of words but in terms of a feeling toward reality, an awareness of one's existence.

4. *The Doctrine of Man*

Augustine said that the decisive function in man is the will. It is present in memory and in intellect, and has the quality of love, namely, the desire toward reunion. This predominance of will was another of the great ideas by which the West overcame the East, and which produced the great medieval struggle between voluntarism and intellectualism. The two basic activities of the soul—knowledge and love, or will, which is the same—have an ambiguous character. They are directed partly toward themselves and partly beyond themselves. They are directed toward one's self in self-knowledge and self-love. "We are, we know that we are, and we love this our being and knowing." This means we are self-related and self-affirming. We affirm ourselves in knowledge and in will.

On the other hand, love and knowledge transcend ourselves and go to the other beings. Love participates in the eternal; this is its own eternity. The soul has transtemporal dimensions. This participation is not what is usually called immortality, but it is the participation in the divine life, in the divine loving ground of being. However, this idea is in tension with another in Augustine. One could say that this mystical element is in tension with an educational element. The souls are not only eternal in their essence, but also immortal in the technical sense of continuation in time. As a result those who are excluded from eternity because they are separated from God are still immortal; this immortality means their punishment and damnation. They are excluded from God; this means they are excluded from love—love is the ground of being—and they deserve no pity. There is no unity of love between them and the others. If this is the case, however, one must ask how there can then be unity of being, if being is love. Here we see one of those conflicts between mystical-ontological thinking and ethical-educational thinking. We saw the same conflict in Origen when he spoke about the *apokatastasis tōn pantōn*, the return of everything to God, the final salvation of every-thing that has being, a teaching which the church rejected. In this sort of conflict esoteric theology, philosophy, or mysticism always chooses the one side, specifically the side of the eternal and the union with God in eternity. Ecclesiastical, educational or ethical thinking always chooses the other side, namely, the per-sonal possibility of being eternally condemned and punished. Logically this is impossible to hold, because the very concept of the eternal excludes continuation in time, and the ontological concept of love, which is so strong in Augustine, excludes being which is not in unity with love. The educational view exercises a continual threat over everyone. Therefore, the church has always maintained it, accepting the logical contradiction in order to produce the threat of the eternal (i.e., endless) condemnation. Ontological mysticism and educational moralism contradict each other on such matters.

I am reminded here of another problem which is perhaps much more concrete in our time. Anybody who seriously reflects on it, or at least carries on his reflection within the Christian or exis-tentialist tradition, will no doubt agree that the idea is utopian that at a certain time the kingdom of God, or the classless society, will be established on earth, without power or compul-sion. Utopian means literally (from *ou-topos*, no place) that there is "no place" for this in time and space. But if this is admitted, then we diminish the fanatical will toward political revolution and the transformation of society. Some will tell you they know this is utopian, but if they tell the people, they will no longer fight for the transformation of society. They can fight only if they believe the final stage is at hand, if the kingdom of God is at hand. Only this conviction releases the power to act. What are we to answer? Here we have the same problem. The ethical, in this case the social-educational, point of view contradicts the insight into the relation of time and eternity. So many say, we know this is utopianism, but we must affirm it, otherwise people will not act. Others say, and I belong to this latter group, the disappointment which follows utopianism always and necessarily makes it impos-sible to speak like this to people, if you know better, because the disappointment is worse than the weakening of fanaticism. This would be my decision, and yet it is a very questionable one.

In Augustine even the unbaptized children are not condemned

to hell but to the *limbus infantium* where they are excluded from the eternal blessedness, from the divine love. Such an idea might have had a tremendous educational and ecclesiastical value in certain periods of history, but not for us any more. Very often it produces—this is especially true of the personal fear of condemnation—neurotic stages, and therefore we cannot say that it is superior.

5. *Philosophy of History*

Augustine's philosophy of history is based—as philosophy of history usually is—on a dualism, not an ontological dualism, of course, which is impossible, but a dualism in history. On the one hand, there is the city of God, on the other the city of earth or the devil. The city of God is the actualization of love. It is present in the church, but the church is a *corpus mixtum*, a mixed body, with some people who belong to it essentially and spiritually and others who do not. Then there is a mediation between these two characteristics of the church, the one wherein it represents the kingdom of God and the other wherein it is a mixed body, and this is the hierarchy. The hierarchy, those who have the consecrations, mediates between the two. In them Christ rules the church and Christ is present. Thus, the Catholic Church could use Augustine in both ways. It could identify the kingdom of God with the church to such a degree that the church became absolutized; this was the one development which actually happened. On the other hand, the difference could be made very clear, and this is what the sectarian movements and the Protestants did. There is a dialectical relationship between the kingdom of God and the church in Augustine. It was ambiguous enough to be useful for different points of view. But one thing was clear for him: there is no thousand-year stage in world history, no third age. Chiliasm or millennialism was denied by him. Christ rules the church in this present time; these are the thousand years. There is no stage of history beyond the one in which we are living. The kingdom of God rules through the hierarchy, and the chiliasts are wrong. We should not look beyond the present period in which the kingdom of God is present in terms of history.

The kingdom of the earth has the same ambiguity. On the one hand, it is the state of power, compulsion, arbitrariness, tyranny;

Augustine called it the "gangster state". It possesses all the imperialistic characteristics that we see in all states. On the other hand, there is the unity which overcomes the split of reality, and from this point of view it is a work of love. If this is understood by the emperor, he can become a Christian ruler. Here again we have the ambiguous valuation: the state is partly identical with the kingdom of the devil and it is partly different from it because it restricts the devilish powers.

History has three periods: that before the law, that under the law, and that after the law. In this way we have a fully developed interpretation of history. We are in the last period, in the third stage; it is a sectarian heresy to say that another state must still be expected. The medieval sects, of course, expressed this heresy. In this light the struggle becomes visible between the revolutionary attempts of the sectarian movements and the conservatism of Augustine's philosophy of history.

6. *The Pelagian Controversy*

We touched on Augustine's doctrine of man when speaking of the voluntaristic character of his thinking, his idea that the center of man is not the intellect but the will. In this he began a development which goes through the whole Western world, represented by theologians and philosophers for whom the will is the center of man. When we come to the medieval philosophers and theologians, and to the modern ones, we will see how this influence was continually maintained in creative tension with the tendencies coming from Aristotle. The tension between Augustine and Aristotle is the decisive power which moves the medieval history of thought; almost everything can be seen in relation to this tension.

So far this has been only a description of man in his essential relationship. If man is seen in his essential relationship to God, to himself, and to others, then he is seen by Augustine as a will whose substance is love. This love is the creative ground of everything that is. This is an idea of love in which *agapē* and *erōs* are united. However, this essential nature of man is not his existential nature; it is not actual in time and space. On the contrary, this essential nature of man is distorted by what Augustine calls sin, especially original sin, in line with the tradition of the New Testament and the church. His doctrine of sin, the center of his doctrine of man, was developed in his controversy with Pelagius.

Augustine's conflict with Pelagius is one of the great struggles in church history, comparable to the trinitarian and christological controversies. It is one which repeats itself again and again in the history of the church. Already in the New Testament there was the tension between Paul and the writers of the "catholic" Letters; we have it between Augustine and Pelagius, somehow also between Thomas Aquinas and the Franciscans, and finally between Karl Barth and the present-day liberals. One point is always decisive. Usually it is discussed in terms of the concept of freedom, but this is misleading because freedom has so many connotations not relevant for this question. The decisive point is the relationship of religion and ethics. The question is whether the moral imperative is dependent on the divine grace for its actualization, or whether divine grace is dependent on the fulfillment of the moral imperative.

Pelagius was not an isolated heretic. He represented the ordinary doctrine of people who were educated in Greek thinking, especially in Stoic traditions, and for whom freedom is the essential nature of man. Man is a rational being, and a rational being has freedom of deliberation and decision. This alone would not have made him a heretic, because most of the Eastern church had exactly the same idea of freedom. But Pelagius developed this concept in a way which brought him into conflict with Augustine. When this conflict was resolved, Augustine was at least partly victorious and Pelagius was an arch-heretic, whose name still stands for one of the classic Christian heresies.

For Pelagius death is a natural event, not a result of the fall. Since death belongs to finitude, it would have happened even if Adam had not fallen into sin. The same idea, we have already seen, was expressed in Ignatius and Irenaeus, namely, that man is naturally finite and destined to die as everything natural. However, according to the story of paradise it is possible for man to overcome his essential finitude through participation in the food of the divine. What Pelagius does is to leave out the second possibility and to affirm only the first as true and in accord with the Christian tradition.

The sin of Adam belongs to him alone and not to the human race as such. In this sense original sin does not exist. Original sin would make sin into a natural category, but man is a moral being. Therefore, the contradiction of the moral demand must be an event of freedom and not a natural event. Everybody must sin in order to be a sinner. The simple dependence on Adam does not make anyone a sinner. Here again Pelagius is saying something that is universally Christian, that there is no sin without personal participation in sin. On the other hand, he does not see that Christianity also stresses the tragic universality of sin, thus making it a destiny of the human race. The relationship to Adam as the one presupposed as the first man is, of course, mythological, but in this myth the Christian Church—whether it took it literally or not—has preserved the tragic element which we also find in the Greek world-view. Pelagius had a point, but he did not see the profundity of the Christian description of the human situation.

When children are born they are in the state of Adam before the fall; they are innocent. Of course, Pelagius could not close his eyes to the fact that the evil surroundings and customs distort their innocence. This is akin to the modern psychoanalytic theory of the relationship to the parents or their representatives which determines the complexes and other negativities in the depths of the soul. Today there is even another theory, the biological theory that the distortion is inherited and cannot be avoided even if you place the child in the best possible surroundings. There is some distortion in its very nature from birth. However, Pelagius wanted to avoid the idea of hereditary sin. Sin is not a universally tragic necessity, but a matter of freedom. America is very much in favor of this Pelagian idea that every individual can always make a new beginning, that he is able by his individual freedom to make decisions for or against the divine. The tragic element, on the other hand, is very much known in Europe, and is not so near to the heart of Americans. In Europe the negative side of Augustinianism—we could call it existentialism—has emphasized the tragic element and has reduced the ethical zeal and impact that Pelagianism can have.

The function of Christ under these circumstances is a double one: to provide the forgiveness of sins in baptism to those who believe, and to give an example of a sinless life not only by avoiding sins but also by avoiding the occasions of sins through asceticism. Jesus was an example of asceticism, a kind of first monk; Pelagius himself was a monk. Grace is identical with the general remission of sins in baptism. Grace has no meaning after this because then man is able to do everything himself. Only in the situation of baptism does man receive the grace of forgiveness.

We can say that Pelagianism has a strong ethical emphasis with many ascetic elements, but the tragic aspect of life has been entirely lost. Do not take him lightly; take him seriously. I do not say that we are all born Pelagians—as I say about nominalism—but I would say that Pelagianism is very near to all of us, especially in those countries which are dependent on sectarian movements, as America so strongly is. It is always effective in us when we try to force God down to ourselves. This is what we usually call "moralism", a much abused term. Pelagius said that good and evil are performed by us; they are not given. If this is true, then religion is in danger of being transformed into morality.

Against these views of Pelagius we have Augustine's doctrine of sin. Augustine agreed with Pelagius that freedom is the original, essential quality of man, so that Adam was free when he fell. Originally man's freedom was directed toward the good, and the good is the love with which God loves himself. In this sense everybody is free. But this freedom is dangerous, so dangerous that man could change his direction toward God and direct himself instead toward particular things in time and space. Augustine saw that the danger of freedom was so great that he created the famous doctrine of *adjutorium gratiae*, the helping power of grace, which was given to Adam before he fell. He was not in pure nature (*in puris naturalibus*). The assisting power of grace made it possible for Adam to continue indefinitely in directing his will toward God. It made it *possible* for him. This, however, was a point on which the Reformers disagreed with Augustine. This *adjutorium gratiae*, this assisting power of grace, implied indirectly that nature in itself cannot be good; it must be fulfilled by supernature. It implied that man *in puris naturalibus*, in his purely natural state, is so endangered that actually he must fall, unless supernature helps him. The Reformers placed such an emphasis on human nature—very similar to the Renaissance at this point—that they declined this idea of a *donum superadditum*, a gift of grace that is added to man's nature. This is a very profound distinction, and behind this seemingly Scholastic terminology there is hidden the question of the valuation of creation. In the doctrine of the *donum superadditum* there is something of the Greek valuation of matter as the resisting power. An element of the Greek tragic feeling enters here in contrast to the Jewish and Protestant affirmation of nature as good in itself.

Augustine held that the first man, Adam, had the freedom not to fall, not to die, not to turn away from the good. In this state he was at peace with himself—a profound remark in view of our modern depth psychology; he was at peace with all things and all men. There was no cupidity, no desire, not even in sexual life. There was no pain in this state, not even in the event of childbirth. It was easy for Adam not to fall; there was no real reason for it. Yet, astonishingly, he did fall. And since there was no external reason for his fall, it started in his inner life. Sin, according to Augustine, is in its very inception spiritual sin. Man wanted to be in himself; he had all the good possibilities; there was nothing for him to endure from which he would have to turn away; he had everything he needed. However, he wanted to have all this by himself; he wanted to stay in himself. Therefore he turned away from God and fell. This is what Reinhold Niebuhr calls "pride" and what I prefer to call *hybris*, self-elevation. In this way man lost the assistance of grace and was left alone. Man wanted to be autonomous and to stand upon himself. This meant a wrong love of himself which cut off the proper love toward God. Augustine said: "The beginning of all sin is pride; the beginning of pride is man's turning away from God." If you say *hybris* instead of pride, it is profounder because pride often has the connotation of a special psychological attitude. But that is not what is meant here. The most humble people in a psychological sense can have the greatest pride.

Now these statements show first of all that Augustine was aware that sin is something which happens in the spiritual realm —turning away from the ground of being to whom one belongs. It is not a naturalistic doctrine of sin. Even more important than this, Augustine shows clearly the religious character of sin. Sin for him is not moral failure; it is not even disobedience. Disobedience is a consequence, not the cause of sin. The cause is turning away from God, from God as the highest good, as the love with which God loves himself through us. Since this is the nature of sin, it ought to be kept distinct from "sins", which refer to moral acts. Sin is primarily and basically the power of turning away from God. For this reason no moral remedy is possible. Only one remedy is adequate—a return to God. This, of course, is possible only in the power of God, a power which man under the conditions of existence has lost.

The immediate consequence of man's turning away from his highest good is the loss of this good. This loss is the essential punishment of man. Punishments in terms of educational or juristic terminology are secondary. For Augustine the basic punishment is ontological. If God is everything positive, the ultimate good, or the power of being overcoming non-being, the only real punishment that is possible is the intrinsic one of losing this power of being, of not participating any more in the ultimate good. Augustine described it thus: "The soul died when it was left alone by God, as a body will die when it is left by the soul." The soul which is dead, religiously speaking, has lost its control over the body. When this happened, the other side of sin became actual. The beginning is pride, *hybris*, turning to oneself, becoming separate from God. The consequence is concupiscence, the infinite endless desire. The word *concupiscentia*, desire or libido (in the ways in which modern psychology uses it) has two meanings in Augustine: the universal meaning, the turning toward the movable goods, those goods which change and disappear, and the narrower meaning of natural, sexual desire, which is accompanied by shame. This ambiguity of the term "concupiscence" is to be found also in Freud's concept of libido. Both terms are meant universally, the desire to fulfill one's own being with the abundance of reality, and both have the meaning of sexual desire. Innumerable consequences followed from this ambiguity. For example, in Freud there followed his puritanism, his depreciation of sex, his bourgeois suppression, and on the other hand, the revelation of this situation. But Freud never found a solution to this problem, either by suppressing or getting rid of the desire. And since you cannot get rid of it, you have, according to Freud, the desire unto death, the death instinct, as he calls it, which is the necessary answer to the endlessness of desire. In Protestantism, as in all of Catholicism earlier, the ambiguity of the term "concupiscence" had all sorts of ascetic consequences, including the most extreme and disgusting forms. The Reformers tried to reestablish the dignity of the sexual, but they succeeded only in a limited way. They never completely followed through on their own principles against the Roman Church. Therefore, anyone who knows anything about the history of moral behavior and the history of ethical theory in Protestantism will see that Christianity has been very uncertain on this point and has produced no satisfactory answer to this question implied in human existence.

Adam's sin is original sin for two reasons. We all existed potentially in Adam, in his procreative power, and in this way we participated in his free decision and thus are guilty. This is myth, of course, and a very questionable one. Secondly, Adam introduced libido, desire, into the process of sexual generation, and this element was passed on by heredity to all posterity. Everyone is born out of the evil of sexual desire. Original sin is primarily spiritual, sin of the soul, in Adam as in everyone else. But it is also bodily sin. Augustine had great difficulty in uniting the spiritual character of sin in everybody with the hereditary character of sin which derives from Adam.

Because of original, hereditary sin, everybody belongs to a "mass of perdition", to a unity of negativity. The most striking consequence of this is that even infants who die early are lost. Since everyone belongs to the mass of perdition, nobody can be saved except by a special act of God. This is the most powerful emphasis on the solidarity of mankind in the tragedy of sin. Thus, he denies most radically—almost in a Manichaean sense—the freedom in the individual personality. The all-embracing unity of mankind makes us what we are. Now, in the light of our modern research into depth psychology and sociology we are probably able to understand better than our fathers what Augustine meant, namely, the inescapable participation of everyone in human existence, in a social structure, and in an individual psychological structure, whether neurotic or otherwise. The question which arises, however, is: What about the participation of the individual in guilt? There is no answer to this in the context of Augustine.

Man has lost his possibility to turn toward the ultimate good because of his universal sinfulness. We are under the law of servitude, the bondage of the will. Therefore, grace is first of all *gratia data*, grace given without merit. It is given by God to a certain number of people who cannot be augmented or diminished; they belong to him eternally. The rest of the people are left to the damnation which they deserve. There is no reason in man for the predestination of the one group or the rejection of the other. The reason is in God alone; it is a mystery. Thus, one cannot speak of prescience, of foreseeing what man would do, as is often done in the doctrine of freedom. This is impossible since God's willing and knowing are identical. God can never look at something as though it were not carried by his power of being, that is, his will. God always wills what he knows. "He has elected us not because we would be holy, but in order to have us become holy." There is no reason in man for predestination. God does both the willing and the fulfilling.

Augustine was nevertheless not a determinist in the technical psychological sense. Predestination does not exclude man's will. The psychological will of man is preserved and distinguished from external forces, or from compulsory elements in man. But the direction of the will toward God is dependent on God's predestination, and his predestinating will cannot be explored. Grace is given to everybody who becomes a Christian. The forgiveness of sins, which is given first, happens in baptism and is received by faith. Here Augustine continues the general tradition. But beyond this, forgiving is a real participation in the ultimate good. This ultimate good has appeared in Jesus as the Christ, without which neither good thinking nor good acting nor loving is possible. He describes this side of grace as the inspiration of the good will, or he speaks of the inspiration of love, primarily the love toward God. "The Spirit helps", he says, "by inspiring in the place of bad concupiscence, good concupiscence, that is, diffusing *caritas* (*agapē*) within our hearts." Justification, therefore, is an inspiration of love. Faith is the means to receive it. But faith by that time already had the deteriorated sense— which makes Christian preaching about faith almost impossible today—of an acceptance of doctrines which are unbelievable. So Augustine distinguished between two forms of faith. The one form of faith he called *credere deo aut christo*, believing directed toward God or Christ, that is, accepting their words and commands; the other is *credere in deum aut christum*, believing *into* God and *into* Christ. The first is an intellectual acknowledgment, without hope and love. The second is a personal communion which is created by grace, or by the Holy Spirit, or by love.

This alone is the faith which justifies, because it makes him who is justified just.

Those who are predestined are not able to fall away again. They receive the gift of perseverance, the gift of not losing the grace which they have received. None of this depends on any merit, not even on the merit of not resisting grace, since grace for Augustine is irresistible when it comes to you.

With these ideas Augustine attacked Pelagius. In all respects it is the opposite of Pelagius' teachings. Augustine's doctrine, however, was never completely accepted by the church, although he was considered the greatest teacher of the church. Pelagianism was rejected, and even semi-Pelagianism, which cropped up later, was condemned a hundred years later. Yet, this rejection did not prevent it from creeping back into the church. Historians sometimes refer to this as crypto-semi-Pelagianism. It cannot be denied that especially in the Augustinian school, in the later Franciscans, semi-Pelagianism was very much alive. It was, of course, out of the question to repeat Pelagius' teachings in the official church. But semi-Pelagianism, which denied the irresistibility of grace and stressed the necessity to work to keep grace, crept back into the church to make Augustine's doctrine educationally possible. We spoke about this problem before. You cannot have such a doctrine as Augustine's in an institution of education, and the Christian Church was the only institution of education for a thousand years. In such a situation you must appeal to the free will of those to be educated. An extreme doctrine cannot be presented in a direct way to most people. Thus, the ultimate tragic element was not lost entirely, but it was to a certain extent restricted for the sake of the educational needs. This was the situation when the Reformers came upon the scene. In their time the tragic element had been reduced almost to nothing by the educational, ethical, and ascetic emphases which were dominant in the church. The churches with only some exceptions are usually very suspicious of any doctrine of predestination—at least the Catholic Church was—because that makes the ultimate relation to God independent of the church, or at least it tends to do so. So here again we have one of those tensions of which I spoke in connection with Origen and other theologians, the tension between the ultimate theological and the penultimate educational points of view. You always have these two elements in tension in religious instruction, in counseling, as well as in preaching. The great struggle between Augustine and Pelagius is perhaps the classic example of the problem in the Christian Church.

7. *The Doctrine of the Church*

Augustine's doctrine of the church has had a great influence on all Christian churches, not only the Roman, and therefore we must deal with it. We have already shown that in Cyprian the church is defined as an institution of salvation, largely replacing the concept of the church as the communion of saints (*communio sanctorum*). The consequence of regarding the church as an institution was a change in the idea of the holiness of the church. In this situation Augustine entered into conflict with the Donatist movement. Originally there was an emphasis on the sanctification of the individual members and the group as a whole. This emphasis gave way to the sacramental reality of the church. Now the holiness of the church is identical with the sacramental gifts, especially with the sacramental power of the clergy. The idea of *sanctus* (holy, saint) no longer refers to someone who is personally sanctified, but to one who has the sacramental power. This represents a fundamental change in meaning from the subjective to the objective element, from personal holiness to institutional holiness.

There were people in North Africa where Augustine was a bishop who did not go along with this development and who were interested in the actual sanctification of the church and its members, especially of the clergy. The issues which were involved were the following:

(1) the discipline in the act of penance;

(2) the question whether baptism is valid if performed by heretics;

(3) the question whether ordination is valid if performed by *traditores*, traitors, who either delivered over holy books during the persecutions, or denied they were Christians.

Are the objective graces valid if they are mediated by persons who are not subjectively holy? The Donatists excluded them and did not allow them to become ministers because for them the holiness of the church is the personal holiness of its representatives. The consequence of this would be to make individual

Christians dependent on the moral and religious status of the clergy. They would be dependent on the inner holiness of the ministers. Now, Augustine was clear about the fact that it is impossible to make a judgment of this kind, that any attempt to do so would lead to terrible consequences—to assume the role of God who alone can look into the hearts of people. He wanted to save the objectivity of the church in face of the demand for subjective holiness of its representatives. Here he followed the lead of Cyprian. To do this he introduced the distinction between faith (including hope) and love. Faith and hope are possible outside the church because they are determined by their content. You may live among heretics, you may even be one yourself, but if you satisfy the formula of baptism in the right way, then the content is decisive and not your personally heretical or morally unworthy status. The formulae are the same as they are in the Catholic Church. Thus, if the heretical churches use these same formulae, their objective contents make their sacramental actions valid.

Love, on the other hand, is something which cannot be found where there is not the right faith. Love is the principle which unites the church. This is not a simple moral goodness, which can be found everywhere, but it is the agapeic relationship of individuals to each other. This spirit of love, which is embodied in the church as the unity of peace, as the re-establishment of the original divine unity which is disrupted in the state of existence, is something that can be found only in the church. For this reason there is salvation only in the church. Salvation is impossible without the inpouring of *agapē*, that grace given like a fluid into the hearts of men. Although there may be valid sacraments outside the church, salvation can only be had within it.

This distinction between faith and love is of extreme importance and makes the church the only place of salvation for Catholics. From this there follows the distinction between the validity and the effectiveness of the sacraments. The sacraments of the heretics are valid if they are performed in terms of the orthodox tradition. This means nobody has to be rebaptized. On the other hand, the sacraments have no effectiveness within the heretical groups, but only within the church. For example, baptism always gives a *character indelebilis*, as the technical term stated; it is a quality coming from God, which one has throughout one's life whatever one does. This was very important because it enabled the medieval church to treat the pagans and Jews differently from the baptized Christians. The baptized Christians were subjected to the laws of heresy, while pagans and Jews were not. Even though baptized Christians should try to become Jews or pagans or Muslims, they could not because the very act of baptism conferred an indelible character upon them, no matter who performed the act, whether orthodox or heretical.

In the same way ordination is always valid. Priests who are fallen and excommunicated are forbidden to administer the sacraments, but if they should do it, the sacraments are valid. If in prison a medieval priest who happens to be excommunicated should marry a couple, the marriage is valid in spite of the fact that he was forbidden to do so. And no re-ordination is needed if the priest is absolved and rejoins the clergy, because ordination is and remains valid.

All of this made the people in the church completely independent of the quality of the priest. Nobody can know this quality for sure anyway. Of course, priests who committed mortal sins that were publicly visible were excommunicated and forbidden to perform sacramental acts, but this is different. What he does is valid in any case. What we have here is the hierarchical institution of salvation, which as an institution is independent of the character of those who function in its behalf, and within this institution there is the spiritual community of the faithful. According to Catholic doctrine the first is the condition of the second; according to sectarian beliefs the second, if anything, is the condition of the first. These two concepts of the church have been in conflict throughout the history of the church.

CHAPTER III

Trends in the Middle Ages

FIRST we shall present a survey of the main ideas and trends of the Middle Ages from beginning to end, and only after that take up a few of the leading figures.

The basic problem of the Middle Ages, one which we find in all its periods, is that of a transcendent reality, manifest and embodied in a special institution, in a special sacred society, leading the culture and interpreting the nature. If you keep this in mind, you can understand everything going on in the Middle Ages. Without it you cannot understand anything, because then you would measure the Middle Ages by your own standards of today. The Middle Ages do not permit this. If you consider the distorted pictures of the Middle Ages, a common judgment is that they were the "Dark Ages"; the implication is that we live in the age of illumination, so we look back upon this period of terrible superstition with a kind of contempt. But nothing of this sort is true. The Middle Ages were one form in which the great problem of human existence in the light of the eternal was solved. The people who lived during this thousand-year period did not live worse than we live in many respects, and in other respects they lived better than we do. There is no reason to look back upon the Middle Ages with any form of contempt. On the other hand, I am not a romanticist; I do not want to measure our own situation by standards taken from the Middle Ages as romanticism does.

The Middle Ages were not so uniform as our ignorance about them allows us to believe. They were very much differentiated. We can distinguish the following periods:

(1) The period of transition, A.D. 600–1000. The year 600 marks the papacy of Gregory the Great, a man in whom the ancient

tradition was still alive, but in whom the Middle Ages had already begun. During this period we have the years of preservation—as much as could be was preserved, which was comparatively little—and of reception; the tribes which ruled Europe, the Germanic-Romanic tribes, were taken in. It was the period of transition from the ancient to the medieval world, a transitional period which is sometimes called the "Dark Ages", particularly the ninth and tenth centuries. But they were not so dark as they seem. Great things happened then which prepared a new world out of which we all have come, even though we have forgotten it.

(2) The early Middle Ages, A.D. 1000–1200. During this time new and original forms developed which were decisively different from the ancient world. This is a creative and profound period, represented by Romanesque art.

(3) The high Middle Ages, A.D. 1200–1300. Here all the basic motifs are elaborated and brought into the great systems of the scholastics, of Gothic art, and of feudal life.

(4) The late Middle Ages, A.D. 1300–1450. From 1300 on we enter the period in which the Middle Ages disintegrate. But if we speak of "disintegration" we do not wish to depreciate the tremendous surge of new motifs which developed during this period and which made both the Renaissance and the Reformation possible.

A. Scholasticism, Mysticism, Biblicism

The first series of problems we shall discuss are the main cognitive attitudes, or the main theological attitudes. There were three of them that were always present and influential: scholasticism, mysticism, and biblicism.

Scholasticism was the determinative cognitive attitude of the whole Middle Ages. It is the methodological explanation of Christian doctrine. This term is derived from "school" and means "school philosophy"—philosophy as it was treated in the school. Today "school" has connotations of separation from life and "scholasticism" even more so. When we hear this word we think of lifeless systems—"as heavy as a horse", as was said by one of the scholastics. No one can read them, since they have nothing to do with reality. Scholasticism became distorted in the late Middle Ages; but the real intention of scholasticism was the theological interpretation of all problems of life. We have an extremely rich scholastic literature that had a tremendous influence on the spiritual life of the Middle Ages.

There was one limit to this: a scholastic education was given only to a small upper class. All the scholastic books were written in Latin, a language which only the educated of that time knew. Of course, the masses could not even read or write. So the question was how to bring the message discussed in these scholastic systems to the people. There were two ways: participation in the church services, the liturgies, pictures, hearing the music, and receiving other sense impressions, which do not require much intellectual activity but give the feeling of the numinous and some kind of moral guidance. However, this does not mean that these objective things were really personal experiences. This is what mysticism meant in the Middle Ages; it introduced personal experience into the religious life.

The meaning of mysticism has been misinterpreted by Protestant theology which began with Ritschl and is still alive in Barthian theology. It is misleading when people identify this mysticism with either Asiatic mysticism of the Vedanta type, or with Neo-Platonic mysticism (Plotinus). Forget about this when you approach the Middle Ages. Every medieval scholastic was a mystic; that is, he experienced what he was talking about as personal experience. This is what mysticism originally meant in the realm of scholasticism. There was no opposition between mysticism and scholasticism. Mysticism was the experience of the scholastic message. The basis of the dogma was unity with the divine in devotion, prayer, contemplation, and ascetic practices. If you know this, it may be hoped that you will not fall into the trap of removing mysticism from Christianity, which would mean to reduce the latter to an intellectualized faith and a moralized love. This is what has happened since the Ritschlian school became dominant in Protestantism. Do not make the mistake of identifying this type of mysticism with the absolute or abstract mysticism in which the individual disappears in the abyss of the divine. Mysticism—the Protestant Orthodox theologians called it *unio mystica*—is the immediate union with God in his presence. Even for the people of Orthodoxy this was the highest form of the relationship to God. In the Middle Ages mysticism and scholasticism belonged together.

The third attitude besides scholasticism and mysticism is biblicism. Biblicism is strong in the later Middle Ages and helps to prepare the way for the Reformation. Biblicism is not something exclusively Protestant, for there were always biblicistic reactions during the Middle Ages. These reactions were sometimes very critical of the scholastic systems and also of mysticism. Usually, however, these biblicistic reactions were united with mysticism, and often also with scholasticism. Biblicism was an attempt to use the Bible as the basis for a practical Christianity, especially a lay Christianity. Biblicism in the later Middle Ages was predominant and made it possible for many laymen even to read the Bible before the Reformation.

These three attitudes, scholasticism, mysticism, and biblicism, were in most cases united in the same person. They could also stand in tension with each other. For example, scholasticism and mysticism were in tension in the conflict between Bernard of Clairvaux and Abelard. But neither of these attitudes prevailed. Both gave what they had to give to the medieval church. And the biblicistic criticisms were simply appropriated as the biblical foundation of the scholastic system and the mystical experiences. Scholasticism was the theology of that time; mysticism was the personal experiential piety, and biblicism was the continuous critical reaction coming from the biblical tradition and entering the two other attitudes, finally overcoming both of them in the Reformation.

B. THE SCHOLASTIC METHOD

Scholasticism had one basic problem, that of authority and reason. What was the medieval authority? It was the substantive tradition on which medieval life was based. Authority was first of all the tradition of the church as it was expressed in the acknowledged church fathers, in the creeds and councils, and in the Bible. When we hear of "authority" today, we tend to think of it in terms of a tyrant, be it a father, a king, a dictator, or even a teacher. We should not read this meaning into the word *auctoritas* (authority) when we see it in the medieval sources; nor should we identify it with the pope at that time, which is a much later development, toward the end of the Middle Ages. In the earlier and high Middle Ages authority is the living tradition. The question arose: What was the relation of reason to the living tradition of the church in which everyone was living? There was no other tradition. This living tradition was as natural to them as the air we breathe is to us. This analogy may help us understand what living tradition meant in the Middle Ages.

The tradition, however, was composed of many elements, not all of which said the same thing. Upon inquiry into them, it became necessary to choose from among them. The Middle Ages experienced this first of all in the realm of practical decisions, that is, of canon law. Canon law was the basis of medieval life; the dogma was one of the canon laws, and this gave it its legal authority within the church. Thus, practical needs created a class of people whose task it was to harmonize the different authorities on the meaning of the canon laws, as they appear in the many collections of canon law. This harmonizing method was a dialectical method, the method of "yes and no", as it was called. Reason in the Middle Ages was the tool for this purpose. Reason combines and harmonizes the sentences of the fathers and of the councils, first practically and then in the theoretical realm of theological statements. The function of reason was thus to collect, to harmonize, and to comment on the given sentences of the fathers. The man who did this most successfully was Peter the Lombard, whose *Four Books of Sentences* was the handbook of all medieval scholasticism. His *Sentences* were commented on by others when they wrote their own systems.

The next function of reason was to interpret the meaning of the given tradition which was expressed in the sentences. This means that the contents of faith had to be interpreted, but faith was presupposed. Out of this situation came the slogan: *credo ut intelligam*, I believe in order to know. This means that the substance of faith was given; it was something in which one participated. In the Middle Ages one did not exert a will-to-believe. The creed was given just as nature is given. Natural science does not create nature; instead, the natural scientist calculates the structures and movements of the given nature. Similarly, reason has the function of interpreting the given tradition; it does not create the tradition. This analogy can help us to understand the Middle Ages much better.

The next step was carried through, less speculatively and very cautiously, by those thinkers who took Aristotle into their theology,

especially Thomas Aquinas. They held that reason is adequate
to interpret authority. At no point is reason against authority; the
living tradition can be interpreted in rational terms. Reason does
not have to be destroyed in order to interpret the meaning of the
living tradition. This is the Thomistic position even today.

The final step was the separation of reason from authority.
Duns Scotus and William of Ockham, the nominalist, asserted
that reason is inadequate to the authority, the living tradition;
reason is not able to express it. This was stated very sharply in
later nominalism. However, if reason is not able to interpret the
tradition, the tradition becomes authority in a quite different
way; it becomes the commanding authority to which we have to
subject ourselves even though we do not understand it. We call
this "positivism". The tradition is given positivistically; there it
is, we simply have to look at it, accept it, and subject ourselves
to it as it is given by the church. Reason can never show the
meaning of the tradition; it can only show different possibilities
which can be derived from the decisions of the church and the
living tradition. Reason can develop probabilities and improba-
bilities, but never realities. It cannot show how things should be.
They are all dependent on the will of God. The will of God is
irrational and given. It is given in nature, so we must be empiricists in order to find out how the natural laws are. We are not in
the center of nature. We are in the orders of the church, in canon
law, so we must subject ourselves to these decisions in a positivistic way; we must take them as positive laws, for we cannot
understand them in rational terms.

In Protestantism both things came to an end, the authority of
the church and to a certain extent reason. Then reason elaborated
itself completely and became creative in the Renaissance. In the
Reformation, tradition was transformed into personal faith. But
the Counter-Reformation tried to keep reason in bondage to
tradition, only this tradition was not so much living as formulated
tradition, tradition which became identical with the authority of
the pope. This is very important for our present situation. All of
us have to deal even today with the problem of living tradition.
Living tradition is often confused with authority, and this is
wrong. Authority can be natural and factual, without involving a
break within ourselves, disrupting our autonomy and subjecting
us to a foreign law or heteronomy. In the early Middle Ages

authority was natural, so to speak, as our relation to nature is natural. By the end of the Middle Ages the situation was changed. Then that concept of authority arose against which we must fight, an authority which demands subjection to one tradition against other traditions. Today dictators even go to the extreme of excluding all other traditions. The so-called "iron curtains" which we build to a certain extent by not admitting books from the East, etc., are attempts to keep the people in one definite tradition and to prevent it from touching other traditions, because every authoritarian system knows that nothing is more dangerous for a given tradition than contact with other traditions. This places the individual at the point of decision with respect to other traditions. The "iron curtain" method was not necessary in the early Middle Ages because there was no other tradition; one lived in this tradition as naturally as we live in nature.

C. Trends in Scholasticism

1. *Dialectics and Tradition*

The first form in which autonomous thinking arose in the Middle Ages was dialectics. This word "dialectics" is difficult to use today because of its innumerable meanings; its original meaning had been lost. The original meaning in Greek is "conversation", talking to each other about a problem, going through "yes and no", one representing the "yes" and the other the "no". We have already mentioned how the jurists, who represented the canon law, had to harmonize for practical reasons the different authorities, councils, and theologians. Out of this need there arose the method of dialectics, of "yes and no". This method was applied to theological problems. However, the dialectical method of "yes and no" is something of which the guardians of tradition are afraid, because once a "no" is permitted, one cannot know where it may lead. This is as true today, when you think of our fundamentalists and traditionalists, as it was in the early Middle Ages.

The early Middle Ages were not able to stand many "no's", in view of the primitive peoples to which they had to speak, in view of the fact that the church tradition was the only one in which people lived at that time, and in view of the fact that everything was in the process of transformation and consolidation. So the pious traditionalists arose against the dialectical theologians. Here I am thinking, for example, of Bernard of Clairvaux as the representative of the pious traditionalists, and of Abelard's dialectics. The question was whether dialectics can produce something new in theology, or was it to be used only for the sake of explaining the given, namely, the tradition and the authorities?

2. *Augustinianism and Aristotelianism*

When dealing with Augustine we pointed out that Aristotle was missing in his development. Now in the high Middle Ages the Augustinians came into conflict, or at least into contrast, with the newly arising Aristotelians. The Augustinians were represented by the Franciscan order; the Aristotelians were represented by the Dominican order. We have Augustinians against Aristotelians, or Franciscans against Dominicans. One of the heads of the Franciscan order was Bonaventura, a cardinal of the church, who opposed Thomas Aquinas, the great Dominican theologian. One of the fundamental problems of the philosophy of religion was developed when Augustine and Aristotle, or when Plato and Aristotle—since Augustine was Neo-Platonic in his thinking—met again and continued their eternal conversation, a conversation which will never cease in the history of human thought because they represent points of view which are always valid and which are always in conflict with each other. We have the more mystical point of view in Plato, Augustine, Bonaventura, and the Franciscans, and the more rational, empirical point of view in the line from Aristotle to Thomas Aquinas. From the point of view of the foundation of religion and theology this is perhaps the most important of the trends in the Middle Ages. Almost all the problems of our present-day philosophy of religion were discussed in this conflict which was especially strong in the thirteenth century.

3. *Thomism and Scotism*

A third contrast or conflict was between Thomism and Scotism. In a sense this is a continuation of the other struggle, since Duns

Scotus was a Franciscan and Thomas a Dominican. Yet, it was a new problem, also decisive for the modern world, involving the conflict between intellect and will as ultimate principles. For the Dominicans, for Thomism, that is, for the Aristotelian rationality which Thomas introduced into the church, the intellect is the predominant power. Man is man *qua* intellect. For the Augustinian line which leads to Duns Scotus will is the predominant power which makes man man, and God God. God is first of all will, and only secondarily intellect. And will is the center of man's personality, and intellect is secondary. The world is originally created by will and is for this reason irrational and to be taken empirically. On a secondary level it is intellectually ordered, but this order is never final and cannot be taken in by us in deductive terms. In the modern world this same conflict goes on, for example, when thinkers like Henri Bergson and Brand Blanshard of Yale present contrasting systems in terms of the will and intellect.

4. *Nominalism and Realism*

The fourth of the conflicting trends is nominalism against the so-called realism. In order to make this conflict understandable we must know what realism is. If you want to understand what medieval realism was, then simply translate it by "idealism". Medieval realism is what we call idealism, if we are not thinking of idealism in a moral sense or in a special epistemological sense, but in terms of the ideas or essences of things which have reality and power of being. Medieval realism is almost the exact opposite of what we call realism today, and realism today is almost identical with what medieval people called nominalism. For medieval man the universals, the essences, the nature of things, the nature of truth, the nature of man, etc., are powers which determine what every individual thing, such as a tree, or every individual man will always become when he or it develops. This could be called mystical realism or idealism. *Universalia realia*—the universals are realities; this is medieval realism. Of course, the universals are not things in time and space. That is a misunderstanding which makes it a little too easy to reject universals by saying: "I have never seen manhood; I have only seen 'Paul' and 'Peter.'" This is something medieval people knew as well. However, they maintained, all "Pauls" and "Peters" always have noses and eyes and feet and language. This is a phenomenon which can be understood only in terms of the universal, the power of being, which we call manhood, which makes it possible for every man to become a man with all these potentialities. These potentialities may be undeveloped or even destroyed, but every individual has them.

Nominalism holds the opposite view: Only Peter and Paul, only this particular tree at the corner of 116th Street and Riverside Drive exists, and not "treehood", not the power of treehood, which makes it become a tree. Here you have an example of the difference in feeling. If as a nominalist you look at a tree, you feel: "This is a real thing; if I run against it, I will hurt my head." But it is also possible in looking at it to be astonished that with all the seeds sown in the soil, this particular structure of a tree develops, shooting up and spreading its branches. Then in this big tree you can see "treehood", and not just a big tree. And in Peter and Paul you can see not only these particular individuals, but also the nature of man, manhood, as a power which makes it possible for all men to have this character. This is an important discussion which was carried on in logical terms, and is still being carried on. There is hardly a day that I do not fight against nominalism on the basis of my comparatively medieval realistic kind of thinking, which conceives of being as power of being. That is a sin against the "holy spirit" of nominalism, and thus also very much against the "unholy spirit" of logical positivism and many other such spirits. And I fight this fight because I believe that although extreme realism is wrong, namely, that realism against which Aristotle was fighting in Plato which regards universals as special things somewhere in heaven, there are nevertheless structures which actualize themselves again and again. So I can say, the power of being always resists non-being. For this reason I believe that we cannot be nominalists alone, although the nominalist attitude, the attitude of humility toward reality, of not desiring to deduce reality, is something which we must maintain.

The immediate importance of nominalism was that it disrupted the universals, which were understood not only in terms of abstract concepts but also of embracing groups, such as family, state, friends, craftsmen, all groups which precede the individual. At the same time, the danger of medieval realism was that the individual was prevented from developing his potentialities.

Therefore, nominalism was an important reaction, so important
that I would say that without it the estimation of the personality
in the modern world—the real basis of democracy—could not
have developed. While I am usually critical of our being nominalists, I do praise its emphasis on the fully developed individual
and his potentialities, which withstands any danger of our
becoming Asiatic. In face of such a danger medieval nominalism
must be understood as positively as medieval realism. Medieval
realism maintains the powers of being which transcend the individual; medieval nominalism preserves or emphasizes the value
of the individual. The fact that the radical realism of the early
Middle Ages was rejected saved Europe from Asiatization, that is,
from collectivization. The fact that at the end of the Middle Ages
all universals were lost resulted in the imposition of the power of
the church on individuals, making God himself into an individual
who, as a tyrant, gives laws to other individuals. This was the
distortion which nominalism brought along with itself, whereas
the affirmation of the personal was its creative contribution. Thus,
when you read about nominalism and realism in text-books of
logic, do not be betrayed into the belief that this is in itself a
basically logical problem. Of course, it must be discussed in
terms of the science of logic as well, but it really has to do with
the attitude toward reality as a whole which expresses itself also
in the logical realm.

5. Pantheism and Church Doctrine

Partly connected with realism in the Middle Ages is pantheism,
the tendency toward the complete extinction of the individual.
This was done in different ways. First, it was expressed in what
is called Averroism. Averroes, the greatest of the Arabian philosophers, said that the universal mind which produces culture
is a reality in which the individual mind participates. But the
individual mind is not something independent. This was in line
with Asiatization, and Averroes was rejected. Secondly, pantheistic elements were expressed in German mysticism of the type of
Meister Eckhart. This was able to dissolve all the concreteness
of medieval piety, and led to the philosophy of the Renaissance.
The church rejected it in the name of the individual authoritarian
God.

D. The Religious Forces

Next we shall consider the religious forces of the Middle Ages. The greatest and most fundamental of these religious forces was the hierarchy. The hierarchy represented the sacramental reality on which the existence of the church, state, and culture as a whole depended. It administered the Mass which was the central sacramental event. Then the hierarchy carried through the work of educating the Germanic-Romanic tribes which entered the church from their barbaric state. In doing so the hierarchy tried to influence not only the individual through the sacrament of penance, but also the social status of reality. The sacrament of penance was the correlate to the sacrament of the Mass; the Mass is objective, penance subjective. The ecclesiastical hierarchy wanted to control the world. Civil powers, or the secular hierarchies with the emperor at the top, arose and came into conflict with the church hierarchy. The emperor aspired to do the same thing from the secular point of view which the church tried to do from the religious, namely, to establish one body of Christian secular life, a life which is always at the same time both secular and religious, instead of having two separate realms as we do.

By assuming secular functions the hierarchy was always in danger of becoming secularized itself. Other religious forces resisted this tendency, one of which was monasticism. Monasticism represents the uncompromising negation of the world, but this negation was not a quietistic one. It was a negation coupled with activity directed to transforming the world—in labor, science, and other forms of culture, church architecture and building, poetry and music. It was a very interesting phenomenon and has little to do with the deteriorated monasticism against which the Reformers and humanists were fighting. On the one hand, it was a radical movement of resignation from the world, leaving the control of the world to the secular clergy, but on the other hand, it did not fall merely into a mystical form of asceticism, or into a ritualistic form as the Eastern church was in danger of doing; it applied itself to the transformation of reality.

The monks produced the great medieval aesthetic culture, and even today some of the monastic orders represent the highest form of culture in the Catholic Church. The Benedictines, in particular, have preserved this tradition until the present time. The monks were also the real bearers of theological science, perhaps even of all science. The Franciscans and especially the Dominicans produced the greatest theologians. Other monks did agricultural work, irrigation of land, drying up swamps, and all sorts of things needed in the newly conquered countries in central and northern Europe where conversions had been made. These monastic groups were, as we might say today, the active, ascetic vanguard of the church. They were free to perform cultural activities and yet were bound to the fundamentals of the church. Later on attempts were made to introduce this monastic spirit into other groups as well. We can mention two groups, the knights and the crusaders. The knights fought against the pagans and conquered eastern Germany. If you want a sweeping historical statement, consider that these chivalric orders which fought for the Christianization, and also Germanization, of eastern Europe a thousand years ago have now been conquered in this twentieth century, with the help of the Christian nations of the West. That is to say, the Slavic groups have retaken what was taken from them by the military monastic orders of the Middle Ages, and Christianity is now suppressed for the sake of the Communist form of a non-Christian secularism. It was a great world-historical event, as great as the battles of the knights in the Middle Ages, when in the twentieth century, especially in the Berlin Conference of 1945, eastern Europe was surrendered and the Germanic population which had lived there for a thousand years was thrown out. If this situation is seen in perspective, you see a little of the importance of these medieval orders.

The crusades, and the spirit of the crusaders, can be seen as the result of the introduction of the monastic spirit into the lower aristocracy. They were to conquer Palestine and the Byzantine Empire in the East. But in the end they were also repelled.

Sectarianism was another religious force; it should not be understood so much from a dogmatic point of view, as is usually done. Of course, the sects sometimes did have strange doctrines and for this reason left the church. But the real reason was psychological and sociological and much less theological. Sectarianism is the criticism of the church for the gap between its claim and its reality. It is the desire of special groups to represent ideals of consecration, sanctification, and holiness. It is an attempt to carry through some of the monastic radicalism in terms which are anti-hierarchical. To a certain extent the sectarian movements were lay movements. As the word *sectare* means, they "cut" themselves off from the body of the church. However, the non-sectarian way of introducing monastic ideals, at least in part, into secular life was through the so-called *tertiarii*, the "third orders". There was a first order of St. Francis (the order for men), a second order for women, the nuns, and later on a third order was created for the laymen. They did not enter the cloister, nor were they celibate. They subjected themselves partly to the discipline of the monastic orders, and as such produced a kind of lay piety which became stronger toward the end of the Middle Ages, and prepared the way for the Reformation.

Then we must mention the great individuals of church history as bearers of medieval piety. They were not great individuals in the sense of the Renaissance. Rather, they were great individuals as representatives of something objective, namely, of the "holy legend". The holy legend starts with the Bible and continues through all the centuries. "Legend" does not simply mean "un-historical"; it is a mixture of history and interpretation, involving stories which are attached usually to great individuals who themselves had no connection with them. Thus, legendary history is a history of representatives of the spirit of the church. This meant that the Catholic Christian of the Middle Ages was aware of a continuity through all history, going back to biblical times, even back to Noah and Adam in the Old Testament period. This continuity in history was represented by great individuals who are interesting, however, not as individuals but as representatives of the tradition and the spirit in which the people lived. This seems to me more important than the superstitious use of the individuals, for example, by praying to those who had become saints. The holy legend was a reality which, like nature, was something within which one lived. It is a reality in which the living tradition expresses itself symbolically. Those who study religious art will see that up to Giotto the great figures of medieval art are not so much individuals as representatives of the divine presence in a special event or form or character.

Another of the religious forces was the popular superstitions of daily life. The forms of daily life can be called superstitions, if by "superstition" we have in mind the identification of a finite reality with the divine. Such superstitions permeate the entire Middle Ages; for example, the relics of the saints, or from the life of Christ. Another superstition was expressed in the ever-repeated miracles or in the attitude toward holy objects, which were used not so much as pointers to the divine but as powers which contain the divine in themselves. The positive side of this was that it consecrated the daily life. Let me show you this by a picture. Take a medieval town, the town of Chartres, for instance. Not only its cathedral is important—which you must look at to understand the Middle Ages—but also the very way in which it stands on the hill in the middle of a small town. It is a tremendous cathedral, overlooking the whole surrounding country. In it you find symbols of the daily life—the nobility, the craftsmen, the guilds, and the different supporters of the church. The whole daily life is within the walls of the cathedral in consecrated form. When people went into it, their daily life was represented in the sphere of the holy; when they left it, they took with them the consecration they had received in the cathedral back into their daily lives. This is the positive side of it. The negative side is that all this is expressed in superstitious forms of poor pictures, sculptures, relics, and all kinds of holy objects.

Something else of great importance in the daily life of the medieval man was the experience of the demonic. This was a reality for these people. The vertical line which leads up to the divine also leads down to the demonic. And the demonic is a power which is present in the cathedral as something already conquered. Exorcism, expelling the demonic, was one of the daily practices in the cathedral. When entering the cathedral one sprinkled oneself with holy water. This had the effect of purifying oneself from the demonic forces which had been brought along from the daily life. Baptism was primarily exorcism of the demonic forces before forgiveness of sins could be received. Demonic figures are seen supporting the weight of the churches. This is perhaps the greatest symbol—the power of the divine conquers the power of the demonic within the daily life. Toward the end of the Middle Ages, when the Renaissance brought in the demonic symbolism and reality of the later ancient world, the demonic prevailed over against the divine in terms of anxiety. The church of this period lived in a constant anxiety about the presence of the demonic within itself and in others. This is the background to the trials of witches and in part also to the persecution of heretics. It is the basis for the demonic persecution of the demonic; there is no better way to describe these witchcraft trials. It is the feeling for the "underground" in life which could erupt any moment in many individuals in terms of neurotic anxiety. At first the churches were able to conquer it, but not at the end of the Middle Ages. So they started the great persecutions of sorcerers, which were even more cruel and bloody than those of the heretics. As in every persecution fear was behind this hostile attitude toward oneself and others, the tremendous anxiety about non-being in terms of demonic symbols.

E. The Medieval Church

It is interesting that in the systems of the medieval theologians there is no special place for the doctrine of the church. This indicates, among other things, that the church was self-evident; it was the foundation of all life and not a matter of a special doctrine. Of course, in the discussions about the hierarchy, the sacraments, and the relation to the civil power, a doctrine of the church was implicitly developed.

Our first consideration is: What was the relation of the church to the kingdom of God in medieval thinking? The answer to this question is the basis on which the other questions about the relation of the church to the secular power, to culture, etc., can be answered. The background to this is what we said about Augustine's interpretation of history. We must review this in order to understand the situation.

In the Augustinian interpretation of history we have a partial identification and partial non-identification of the church with the kingdom of God. They are never completely identified because Augustine knew very well that the church is a mixed body. It is full of people who formally belong to it but who in reality do not belong to it. On the other hand, he identified the church with the kingdom of God from the point of view of the sacramental graces present in the hierarchy. Now, either this identification or this non-identification could become the point of emphasis. This was always the problem of the Middle Ages. The church, of course, tried to identify itself with the kingdom of God in terms of the hierarchical graces. However, it is not correct to think that any medieval representative, whether theologian, pope, or bishop, identified his own goodness or holiness with the kingdom of God, but always his sacramental holiness, his objective sacramental power. The objectivity of this sacramental reality is decisive for understanding medieval thought. On the other hand, the actual church was a mixed body and the representatives of the sacramental graces were distorted. So from this point of view it was possible to attack the church. The discussion in the Middle Ages was carried on in continuous oscillation between these two poles.

Parallel to this there was in Augustine also a partial identification and a partial non-identification of the state with the kingdom of earth, which was also designated as the kingdom of Satan. The partial identification was based on the fact that in Augustine's interpretation of history states are the result of compulsory power. He called them "robber states", states produced by groups of gangsters, who are not considered criminals only because they are powerful enough to take the state into their own hands. This consideration, which reminds one of the Marxist analysis of the state, is contrasted, however, to the idea of natural law that the state is necessary to repress the sinful powers which would lead to chaos if left unchecked.

Here again the emphasis could be either on the identity of the state with the kingdom of Satan, or at least the kingdom of the sinful world, or on the non-identification of the two, stressing the possibility that the state has a divine function to restrain chaos. All of this is understandable only in the kind of period in which Augustine lived, when the Roman Empire, and later the Germanic-Romanic kingdoms, were realms of non-Christian power. Even when Constantine accepted Christianity, the power play was still going on, the substance of the ancient culture still existed, and was not yet replaced by the religious substance of the church. But then the situation changed. With the expansion of Christianity westward the church became the cultural substance of life, the power which determined all the individual relations, all the different expressions of art, knowledge, ethics, social relations, relation to nature, and all other forms of human life. The ancient substance was partly received by Augustine and partly removed, and what was left in it was subjected to the theonomous principles of the church.

In such a situation one could no longer say that the state is the kingdom of Satan because now the substance of the state is the church. So a new situation arose which had consequences not only for the relation of the church to the state, but also for the state itself. How was the Germanic system related to the church? Before the Germanic tribes were Christianized, they had a religious system in which the princes, the leaders of the tribes, represented not only the earthly but also the sacred power. They were automatically representing both realms. This was continued in the Germanic states insofar as the clergy belonged to the feudal order of these tribes. A man like Hinchmar, the great bishop of Rheims in France, represented the feudal protest of a sacred political power—political and sacred at the same time—against the universality of the church. The German kings, who had to give political power to the higher feudal lords, also had to give power to the bishops as higher feudal lords. The church called this simony, from the story of Simon who wanted to buy the divine power. This was connected with the fact that these feudal lords had to give something for what they received. All of this was bound up with the territorial system of the Germanic-Romanic tribes, a system which stood in opposition to the universality of the church.

Opposition against the feudal bishops and the local kings or princes came from three quarters: (1) from the lower clergy; (2) from the popes, especially Gregory VII; (3) from the proletarian masses, which were anti-feudal, especially in northern Italy. The pope used the lower bishops who were nearer to the lower clergy than the pope himself, so in the name of the pope they could resist the feudal clergy in their own territories. This was the situation which finally led to the great fight between Gregory VII and Henry IV. Usually this is called the struggle between church and state, but this is misleading. "State" in our modern sense is a concept which comes from the eighteenth century. Thus, when we speak of the "state" in Greece, in Rome, or in the Middle Ages, we should always put it in quotation marks. What did exist were legal authorities, with military and political power.

The conflict was not due to the state's encroaching upon the rights of the church, as was often the case later. It was a much more fundamental thing. Since the church was the representative of the spiritual substance of everyone's daily life, of every function, craft, business, profession, there was no separation of realms as developed after the Reformation. There was one reality with different sides. Then the question arose as to who should head this one reality. There must be a head, and it is dangerous to have two heads. So both sides, the clergy and the princes or feudal lords, claimed to be the head of this one reality. The "state" represented by the feudal order was conscious of also representing the Christian body as a whole, and the church represented by the pope was conscious of playing the same role. The same position was claimed by both sides, a position which embraced the secular as well as the religious realms. The king aspired and claimed to represent and be the protector of all Christendom. This was especially true when the king became the German emperor and as such the continuation of the Holy Roman Empire. On the other hand, Pope Gregory VII claimed the same thing from the hierarchical side. He made claims which surpassed everything which had been done before. He identified himself with all bishops as the universal bishop. All episcopal grace comes from the pope; in him Peter is present, and in Peter Christ himself is present. There is no bishop who is not dependent on the pope for his episcopal sacramental power. The pope is the universal monarch in the church. But he even went beyond this: the church is the soul of the body, and the body is the secular life. Those who represent the secular life are related to him who represents the spiritual life, as the limbs of the body are related to the inner self which is the soul. As the soul shall govern the limbs of the body, so the pope shall govern the kingdoms and all feudal orders.

This was expressed by the famous doctrine of the "two swords". There are two swords, the earthly and the spiritual. As the bodily existence is subjected to the spiritual existence, so the earthly sword of the king and of the feudal lords is subjected to the spiritual sword of the pope. Therefore, every being on earth has to be subject to the pope at Rome. This was the doctrine of Pope Boniface VIII, in whom the papal aspirations were radically expressed. The emperors fought against this, and compromises were made, but generally speaking the popes prevailed, at least as long as there was this one reality of Christendom about which popes and emperors were fighting.

However, new forces arose in the Middle Ages. First and foremost among them were the national states. The national states claimed independence from both the pope and the emperor. National feeling was behind them. The importance of Joan of Arc was that in her French nationalism first arose and came into direct conflict with the pope. At the end of the Middle Ages the national states had taken over much of the papal power. Again France was leading: Philip the Fair took the papacy to Avignon in France, and the resulting schism between the two popes radically undercut the papal authority. The princes and kings, who gradually became independent and who created the national states, were at the same time religious lords. Thus in England the theory arose that the king represents Christ for the Church of England, as the pope is the vicar of Christ.

Another theory arose which was directed against the pope. The bishops of these developing national states did not want to be simply subjects of the pope; they wanted to regain the position the bishops had at the time, let us say, of the Council of Nicaea. They developed the idea of *conciliarism*; the council of bishops is the ultimate authority of the church. This idea is in contrast to *curialism* (from *curia*, the papal court); the papal court is the monarchic power over church and state. Thus, in alliance with the nationalist reaction against empire and papacy, conciliarism was a radical movement which threatened the pope. In the long run, however, the pope finally had the power to destroy the reform councils in Basle and Constance, where conciliarism had triumphed for a while. The national separations and splits of all kinds, plus the desire of the later Middle Ages to have a unity in spite of everything, made it possible for ecclesiasticism and monarchism to prevail in the Roman Church.

There were also important movements of criticism against the church, the sectarian and lay movements at the end of the Middle Ages. The greatest critic of the church in the theoretical realm was William Ockham, who fought for the German national state against the universal monarchy of the pope. But the most effective was Wyclif of England. Wyclif criticized the existing church in a radical way from the point of view of the *lex evangelica*, the evangelical law, which is in the Bible. He translated the Bible and fought against the hierarchy with the support of the national king. Already at that time the relationship between the king of

England and the pope became very precarious. The pope did not succeed in inducing the king to persecute Wyclif and his followers.

Finally the hierarchy (i.e., as a universal reality) came to an end in the revolutionary movement of the Reformation. The Protestant churches took the form of the territorial church which had long before been prepared under the princes. With the power of the pope and the hierarchy vanishing it happened that the church no longer had a backbone. So the prince received the title of "highest bishop". This means that he replaced the hierarchical, sacramental bishops, and became the highest administrator within the church, as a lay member at that; he was the predominant lay member who could keep the church in order. In this way the Protestant churches became subjected to the earthly powers, and to this day they have this problem. In Lutheranism it was the problem of the church's relation to the princes, their cabinets, and authoritarian governments. In the Calvinist countries, and also in America, it is the socially ruling classes which are decisive for the church and make up its administrative backbone.

F. THE SACRAMENTS

From the point of view of the actual religious life the sacraments were perhaps the most important thing in medieval church history. When we discuss the sacraments in the Middle Ages, if we are Protestants, we must forget everything we have in our immediate experience of the sacraments. In the Middle Ages the sacraments were not things which happened at certain times during the year and which were merely regarded as comparatively solemn acts. The preached word did not need to accompany the sacraments. Thus Troeltsch could call the Catholic Church the greatest sacramental institution in all world history.

Previously we have said that the Middle Ages were dominated by one problem, namely, to have a society which is guided by a present reality of a transcendent divine character. This is different from the period in which the New Testament was written, where the salvation of the individual soul was the problem. It is different from the period of Byzantium (*ca.* 450–950) where mysteries interpret all reality in terms of the divine ground, but not much is changed. It is different from the post-Renaissance period, end-ing in the nineteenth century, in which the world is directed by human reason, by man as the center of reality. It is different also from the early Greek period in which the mind was looking for the eternal Immovable. All of these periods had their particular problem. The problem of the Middle Ages, accordingly, was the problem of the world (society and nature) in which the divine is present in sacramental forms. In the light of this we can ask: What does "sacramental" mean? It means all kinds of things in the history of the church. It means the deeds of Christ, the sufferings of Christ (the stations of the cross); it means the Gospels, which can be called sacraments; it means symbols in the Bible; it means the symbolic character of the church buildings, and all the activities going on in the church, in short, everything in which the holy was present. This was the problem of the Middle Ages— to have the holy present.

The sacraments represent the objectivity of the grace of Christ as present in the objective power of the hierarchy. All graces— "graces" may be translated as substantial powers of the New Being—are present in and through the hierarchy. The sacraments are the continuation of the basic sacramental reality of God's manifestation in Christ. In every sacrament there is present a substance of a transcendent character. Water, bread, wine, oil, a word, the laying on of hands—all these things become sacramental if a transcendent substance is poured into them. This substance is like a fluid which heals. One of the definitions of a sacrament is: "Against the wounds produced by original and actual sin, God has established the sacraments as remedies." Here in medical symbolism what is meant is clearly expressed: the healing power is poured into the substances.

The question often raised in Protestantism is how many sacraments there are. Up to the twelfth century there were many sacramental activities. It was always more or less clear which of them were the most important, namely, baptism and the Lord's Supper. It took more than a thousand years of church history to discover that seven sacraments are the most important. After this discovery the term "sacrament" in a special sense became reserved for just these seven sacraments. This is unfortunate for the understanding of what a sacrament is. We must keep in mind the universal concept of the sacrament: the presence of the holy. Therefore, *sacramentalia* are being performed in the churches all the time; these are activities in which the presence of the divine is experienced in a special way. The fact that there are seven sacraments has many reasons behind it—traditional, practical, church-political, psychological, and many others. There are seven sacraments in the Roman Church; for a long time there were five. In Protestant churches there are two; in some groups, at least, of the Anglican Church there are actually and theoretically three sacraments. But the number does not matter. The question is: What does sacramental thinking mean? This is what Protestants have to learn; they have forgotten it.

In the Roman Church the main sacraments are baptism and the eucharist; but there is also penance as the center of personal piety. There is ordination which is the presupposition for the administration of all the other sacraments. There is marriage as the control of the natural life. Confirmation and extreme unction are supporting sacraments in the life of the individual. Thus, we see that the *raison d'être* for some of the sacraments is "biographical", while other sacraments stem from the establishment of the church.

Now what is a sacrament? A sacrament is a visible, sensuous sign instituted by God as a medicament in which under the cover of a visible thing the power of God is hiddenly working. The basic ideas are: divine institution, visible sign, medicament (the medical symbol is very important), the hidden power of God under the cover of the sensuous reality. A sacrament is valid if it has a material substance, a form, that is, the words by which it is instituted, and the intention of the minister to do what the church intends to do. These three elements are necessary. The sign (we would say, the symbol) contains the matter. Therefore, the sacrament has causality; it causes something in the inner part of the soul, something divine. But it does not have ultimate causality. It is dependent on God as the ultimate causality. The sacraments mediate the grace. "Grace" should always be translated as divine power of being, or power of New Being, which justifies or sanctifies—these two words being identical in Catholicism, while in Protestantism quite distinct from each other. Grace, or the divine power of the new being, is poured by the sacraments into the essence of the soul, into its very innermost center. And there is no other way to receive justifying and sanctifying grace than through the sacraments. The substance which is poured into the center of the soul has effects upon the different functions of the soul, or mind, as we would say. The intellect is driven toward faith by the sacramental grace; the will is driven toward hope; and the whole being is driven toward love.

The decisive statement is that the sacrament is effective in us *ex opere operato*, by its mere performance, not by any virtue. There is only one subjective presupposition, namely, the faith that the sacraments are sacraments, but not faith as a special relationship to God. It is a "minimum" theory; those who do not resist the divine grace can receive it even if they are not worthy, if only they do not deny that the sacrament is the medium of the divine grace. The theory of *ex opere operato* (by its very performance) makes the sacrament an objective event of a quasi-magical character. This was the point at which the Reformers were most radical.

The whole life stood under the effects of the sacraments. Baptism removes original sin; the eucharist removes venial sins; penance removes mortal sins; extreme unction removes what is still left over of one's sins before death; confirmation makes a person a fighter for the church; ordination introduces one into the clergy, and marriage into the natural vocation of man or wife. However, above them all is the sacrament of the Mass. This is the sacrifice of Christ repeated every day in every church in Christendom, in terms of the transubstantiation of bread and wine into body and blood. This sacrifice is the foundation of the presence of the divine and of the sacramental and hierarchical power of the church. This was, therefore, the sacrament of sacraments, so to speak. Officially it was a part of the Lord's Supper, but objectively it was and is the foundation of all sacraments, for here the priest has the power to produce God, *facere deum*; making God out of the bread and wine is the fundamental power of the church in the Middle Ages.

Penance was in a kind of tension with all the others. It was the sacrament of personal piety. There was much discussion about it. What are the conditions of the forgiveness of sins in the sacrament of penance? Some made them very easy, some more heavy. All believed that a person's repentance is necessary—light or heavy—and, on the other hand, that a sacrament is necessary. But no scholastic gave an answer as to how the sacrament and the personal element are related to each other. It was just at this point that the medieval church exploded, that is, by the intensification of the subjective side in the sacrament of penance. This was the experience of Luther and, therefore, he became the reformer of the church.

G. ANSELM OF CANTERBURY

Next we shall take up two men of the twelfth century, Anselm of Canterbury and Abelard of Paris. The basis of Anselm's theological work was the same as for all the scholastics, the assertion that in the Holy Scriptures and their interpretation by the fathers all truth is directly or indirectly enclosed. His phrase *credo ut intelligam* (I believe *in order to* understand, not I understand in order *to believe*) must be understood in the light of how he understood faith and tradition. Faith is not belief as a special act of an individual, but is participation in the living tradition. This living tradition, the spiritual substance in which one lives, is the foundation, and theology is interpretation built on this foundation.

The content of eternal truth, of principles of truth, is grasped by the subjection of our will to the Christian message and the consequent experience arising from this subjection. This experience is given by grace; it is not produced by human activities. Here the term "experience" becomes important. "Experience" must be distinguished from what we mean by it today, if we mean anything at all, since the term is used so widely that it has become most questionable and almost meaningless. In any case, at that time experience did not mean "religious" experience, generally speaking; such a thing did not exist then. Rather, experience meant participation in the objective truth implicit in the Bible and authoritatively explained by the church fathers. Every theologian must participate in this experience. Then this experience can become knowledge, but not necessarily so. Faith is not dependent on knowledge, but knowledge is dependent on faith. Again we can use the analogy we have used before: Natural science presupposes participation in nature, but participation in nature does not necessarily lead to natural science. On this basis reason can act with complete freedom to transform experience into knowledge. Anselm was a great speculative thinker at a time when the word "speculation" did not yet have the meaning of gazing into the clouds; instead, it meant analyzing the basic structures of reality.

Knowledge based on experience leads to a system. Here we come to one of the features of all medieval thinking. The medieval thinkers knew that in order to think consistently, you must think systematically. In the term "systematic theology" which we use in our teaching there is a remnant of this insight that knowledge must have the character of a system in order to be consistent. On the other hand, people are often attacked today when they use the word "system", just because they want to think systematically, and not sporadically and fragmentarily. But the church cannot afford—as an individual thinker can—to have here an insight and there an insight which have nothing to do with each other or even contradict each other. What would be bad in systematic theology is the derivation of consequences from principles which have no foundation in experience. But this is not the meaning of "system". Its meaning is the ordering of experience cognitively in such a way that the contents of experience do not contradict each other and the whole truth is reached. As Hegel rightly said, the truth is the whole.

Thus, reason can elaborate all religious experiences in rational terms. Even the doctrine of the trinity can be dealt with by reason on the basis of experience. In other words, autonomous reason and the doctrine of the church are identical. Again this is to be compared with our relationship to nature when we say that mathematical structure and natural reality belong to each other. Mathematical reason is able to grasp nature, to order and to make understandable natural movements and structures. In the same way theological reason is able to make understandable and to connect with each other the different religious experiences. This is the courageous way in which Anselm attacked the problems of theology. In saying that even the trinity can be understood in rational terms, he is following the Augustinian heritage. We can call it dialectical monotheism, a monotheism in which movement is seen in God himself. God is a living God; therefore, there is a "yes" and a "no" in himself. There is not a dead identity of God with himself, but a living separation and reunion of his life with himself. In other words, the mystery of the trinity is understandable for dialectical thought. This mystery is included in reason itself and is not against reason. How could it be, since, according to classical theology, God has reason in himself as his Son, the Logos? Reason, therefore, is valid so far as God and the world are essentially considered. Autonomy is not destroyed by the mystery. On the other hand, autonomy is not empty and formalistic. It does not empty the mysteries of the divine life, but only points to it in dialectical terms. The content, the substance and the depth of reason, is a mystery which has appeared in revelation.

This means that Anselm was neither autonomous in an empty formalistic sense, nor heteronomous in subjecting his reason to a tradition which he did not understand, which was almost a magical mystery. Anselm's attitude is what I call theonomous. This is a concept I often use in my own writings and discussions. Whenever you are asked, "What do you mean by theonomy?" then you can answer, "Anselm's way of philosophizing, or Augustine's way, or . . ."—now I hesitate to say it—"Hegel's". I mention Hegel in spite of all my criticism of him. This theonomous way means acknowledging the mystery of being, but not believing that this mystery is an authoritarian transcendent element which is imposed upon us and against us, which breaks our reason to pieces. For this would mean that God would be breaking his Logos to pieces, which is the depth of all reason. Reason and mystery belong together, like substance and form.

There is one point, however, at which I deviate from Hegel and go along with Anselm. Actually, it is more than a point, but a total turning of the whole consideration: the Logos becoming flesh! This is not a matter of dialectical reason. This is not only dialectical, not only mystery, but paradoxical. Here we are in the sphere of existence, and existence is rooted in the freedom of God and man, in sin and grace. Here reason can only acknowledge and not understand. The existential sphere, reason itself, is ruled by will and decision, not by rational necessity. Therefore, it can become anti-reason, anti-structure, anti-divine, anti-human. This means that it is not mystery and revelation which place a limitation upon rational necessity. The mystery of being is preserved by good dialectics, and destroyed by bad dialectics. But beyond mystery and dialectics there is something paradoxical. This means that although man has contradicted himself and always does so, there is a possibility of overcoming this situation because a new reality has appeared under the conditions of

existence, conquering it. This is the Christian paradox! It is a
matter of serious concern that we do not create a gap between
the divine mystery and the divine Logos. Again and again the
church has affirmed that they belong together. If one denies that
the structure of reason is adequate to the divine mystery, he is
completely dualistic in his thinking; then God would be split in
himself.

Anselm's theonomous thought is expressed in his famous arguments for the existence of God, or as I like to say, his so-called
arguments for the so-called existence of God, because I want to
show that they are neither "arguments" nor do they prove the
"existence" of God. But they do something much better than
this. There are two arguments, the cosmological and the ontological. The cosmological argument is given in his *Monologion*
and the ontological argument in his *Proslogion*. I want to show
that these arguments are not arguments for the existence of an
unknown or doubtful piece of reality, even if it is called "God".
They are quite different from this.

The cosmological argument says: We have ideas of the good,
of the great, of the beautiful, of the true. These ideas are realized
in all things. We find beauty, goodness, and truth everywhere,
but, of course, in different measures and degrees. But if you want
to say that something has a higher or lower degree of participation in the idea of the good or the true, then the idea itself must
be presupposed. Since it is the criterion by which you measure, it
is not itself a matter of measure and degree. The good itself, or
the unconditionally good—being or beauty—is the idea which is
always presupposed. This means that in everything finite or
relative, there is implied the relation to an unconditioned, an
absolute. Conditionedness and relativity imply and presuppose
something absolute and unconditioned. This means that the
meaning of the conditioned and the unconditioned are insepar-
able. If you analyze reality, especially your own reality, you
always discover in yourself elements which are finite, but in-
separably related to something infinite. This is a matter of conclusion from the conditional to the unconditional, yet it is a
matter of analysis which shows that both elements correspond
to each other. Reality by its very nature is finite, pointing to the
infinite to which the finite belongs and from which it is separated.

That is the first part of the cosmological argument. So far it is an existential analysis of finitude, and to this extent it is good and true, and the necessary condition for all philosophy of religion. Actually, it is *the* philosophy of religion. However, this idea is mixed with a metaphysical realism which identifies universals with the degrees of being. As we discussed before, medieval realism attributes power of being to the universals. In this way a hierarchy of concepts is constructed in which the unconditionally good and great, and being, is not only an ontological quality, but becomes an ontic reality, *a* being besides others. The highest being is that which is most universal. It must be one, otherwise another one could be found; it must be all-embracing. In other words, the meaning or quality of the infinite suddenly becomes a higher infinite being, the highest or unconditionally good and great being. The argument is right as long as it is a description of the way in which man encounters reality, namely, as finite, implying and being excluded from infinity. The argument is doubtful and yields a conclusion which can be attacked if it is supposed to lead to the existence of a highest being.

In the *Proslogion* Anselm himself criticizes this argument because it starts with the conditional and makes it the basis of the unconditional. His criticism is right with respect to the second part of his argument, but not with respect to the first, for in the first part of his argument he does not base the infinite on the finite, but analyzes the infinite within the finite. But Anselm wanted more than this; he wanted a direct argument which does not need the world in order to find God. He wanted to find God in thought itself. Before thought goes outside itself to the world, it should be certain of God. This is what I really mean by theonomous thinking.

This is the argument; it is difficult to follow because it is extremely scholastic and far from our modes of thought. Anselm says: "Even the fool is convinced that there is something in the intellect than which nothing greater can be thought, because as soon as he (the fool) hears this, he understands it; and whatever is understood is in the understanding. And certainly, that than which nothing greater can be thought cannot be only in the intellect. If, namely, it were in the intellect alone, it could be thought to be in reality also, which is more. If, therefore, that than which nothing greater can be thought is in the intellect alone, that than which nothing greater can be thought is something than which something greater can be thought. But this is certainly impossible. Therefore, beyond doubt, something than which nothing greater can be thought exists in intellect as well as in reality. And this art Thou, our Lord." Now, this last sentence is remarkable because I have not read such a sentence in any of our logical treatises in the last few hundred years. After going through the most sophisticated logical argumentation, it ends with "And this art Thou, our Lord." This is what I call theonomy. It is not a thinking which remains autonomous in itself, but a thinking which goes theonomously into the relationship of the mind to its divine ground.

I shall now attempt a point-by-point analysis of the meaning of this argument.

(1) Even the fool—the fool of Psalm 53, who says in his heart, "there is no God"—understands the meaning of the term "God". He understands that the highest, the unconditional, is conceived of in the term "God".

(2) If he understands the meaning of God as something unconditional, then this is an idea which exists in the human mind.

(3) But there is a higher form of being, that is, being not only in the human mind, but being in the real world outside of the human mind.

(4) Since being both within and outside of the human mind is higher than being merely in the intellect, it must be attributed to the unconditional.

Each step in this argument is such that it can be easily refuted, and refutations were given already in Anselm's time. For instance, the refutation is that this argument would be equally valid for every highest thing, say, for a perfect island. It is more perfect for it to exist in reality than only in the mind. Moreover, the term "being in the mind" is ambiguous. It means actually being thought, being intended, being an object of man's intentionality. But "in" is metaphorical and should not be taken literally.

To the first criticism Anselm answered that a perfect island is not a necessary thought, but the highest being, or the unconditioned, is a necessary thought. To the second criticism he could argue that the unconditional must overcome the cleavage between subjectivity and objectivity. It cannot be only in the mind; the power of the meaning of the unconditional overcomes subject and object, embracing them both. If Anselm had answered in this way, the fallacious form of the argument would have been abandoned. Then the argument is not an argument for a highest being, but an analysis of human thought. As such the argument says: There must be a point at which the unconditional necessity of thinking and being are identical, otherwise there could be no certainty at all, not even that degree of certainty which every skeptic always presupposes. This is the Augustinian argument that God is truth, and truth is the presupposition which even the skeptic acknowledges. God is identical, then, with the experience of the unconditional as true and beautiful and good. What the ontological argument really does is to analyze in human thought something unconditional which transcends subjectivity and objectivity. This is necessary, otherwise truth is impossible. Truth presupposes that the subject which knows truth and the object which is known are in some way in one and the same place.

However, it is impossible to conclude from this analysis to a separate existence. This touches on the second part of the argument. At this point we cannot follow medieval realism. The so-called ontological argument is a phenomenological description of the human mind, insofar as the human mind by necessity points to something beyond subjectivity and objectivity, and points to the experience of truth. If you go beyond this, you are open to a devastating criticism, as the whole history of the ontological argument proves. The history of this argument is dependent on the attitude toward form or content. If the *content* of the argument is emphasized, as all great Augustinians and Franciscans until Hegel have done, the ontological argument is acceptable. If the argumental *form* is emphasized, as equally great thinkers from Thomas Aquinas to Kant have done, the argument must collapse. It is very interesting that this is an argument which has continued from Plato to the present. And its most classical formulation is that of Anselm.

How is it possible for the greatest of thinkers to be divided on this argument? One can hardly say that Thomas was more clever than Augustine, and Kant more clever than Hegel, or vice versa; they are all supreme minds, and yet they contradict each other. How can the phenomenon be explained that this argument is passionately accepted and rejected by the greatest thinkers? The reason can only be that each side is looking at something different. Those who accept the argument look at the fact that in the human mind, in spite of its finitude, something unconditional is present. The description of this unconditional element is not an argument. I am among those who affirm the ontological argument in this descriptive sense. On the other hand, people like Thomas, Duns Scotus, and Kant reject the argument because they say the conclusion is not valid. And certainly they are right. I try to find a way out of this world-historical conflict—whose consequences are greater than indicated by the scholastic form of it—by showing that these people are doing different things. Its advocates have the correct insight that the human mind, even before it turns to the world outside, has within itself an experience of the unconditional. Its opponents are right when they say that the second part of the argument is invalid because it cannot lead to *a* highest being who exists. Kant's argument that existence cannot be derived from the concept is absolutely valid against it. So one can say: Anselm's intention has never been defeated, namely, to make the certainty of God independent of any encounter with our world, and to link it entirely to our self-consciousness.

I would say that at this point the two ways of the philosophy of religion part company. The one type looks at culture, nature, and history theonomously, that is, on the basis of an awareness of the unconditional. I believe this is the only *possible* philosophy of religion. The other type looks at all this—nature, history, and the self—in terms of something which is given outside, from which through progressive analysis one might finally come to the existence of a highest being called God. This is the form which I deny; I think it is hopeless and ultimately ruinous for religion. In a religious statement I could say that where God is not the *prius* of everything, he can never be reached. If one does not start with him, one cannot reach him. This is what Anselm himself felt when he realized the incompleteness of the cosmological argument.

Anselm is famous in theology also for the application of his principles to the doctrine of the atonement. In his book, *Cur Deus Homo?* (Why a God-man?), he tries to understand the rational adequacy of the substitutional suffering of Christ in the work of salvation. The steps in the doctrine are as follows:

(1) The honor of God is violated by human sin. It is necessary for the sake of his honor for him to react in a negative way.

(2) There are two possible ways to react, either by way of punishment, which would mean eternal separation from God, or by way of satisfaction, giving satisfaction to God so that he can overlook the sins. This is the way in which God in his mercy has decided to solve the problem.

(3) Man is unable to fulfill this satisfaction because he has to do what he can do anyhow, and he cannot do more. Besides, his guilt is infinite, which makes it impossible by its very nature for man to solve the problem. Only God is able to give satisfaction to himself.

(4) On the other hand, because man is the sinner, it is man, not God, who must give the satisfaction. Therefore, someone who is both God and man must do it, who as God *can* do it and who as man *must* do it. The God-man alone is able to do this.

(5) But the God-man could not make satisfaction through his deeds, since he had to do these anyhow out of full obedience to God. He could do it only through his sufferings, because he did not have to suffer; he was innocent. Thus, voluntary suffering is the work through which Christ makes satisfaction to God.

(6) Although our sin is infinite, this sacrifice—since it is made by God himself—is an infinite one; it makes it possible for God to give Christ what he now deserves because of his sacrifice, namely, the possession of man. Christ himself does not need anything; what he needs and wants to have is man, so God gives him man.

Behind this legalistic, quantitative thinking there is a profound idea, namely, that sin has produced a tension in God himself. This tension was felt. Anselm's theory became so popular because everyone felt that it is not simple for God to forgive sins, just as it is not simple for us to accept ourselves. Only in the act of suffering, of self-negation, is it possible at all. Here lies the power of this doctrine of the atoning work of Christ. The church has never dogmatized Anselm's theory. It has wisely restricted itself from doing so, because there is no absolute theory of atonement. Abelard, as we shall see, and Origen as well as others have had different theories of the atonement. The church has never decided, but it is obvious that it liked Anselm's most, probably because it has the deepest psychological roots. This is the feeling that a price must be paid for our guilt, and that since we cannot pay it, God must do it.

Then the question arose: How can man participate? To this the

juristic mind of Anselm had no answer. At this point Thomas
Aquinas said: It is the mystical union between head and members, between Christ and the church, which lets us participate in
all the steps of Jesus himself.

H. ABELARD OF PARIS

We have discussed Anselm of Canterbury as a typically theonomous thinker, theonomous in the sense that he does not crush
reason by heteronomous authority, and theonomous in the sense
that he does not leave it empty and unproductive, but filled with
the divine substance as it is given through revelation, tradition,
and authority. Anselm represents the more objective pole in
medieval thought, objective in the sense that the tradition is the
given foundation, but not exclusive of an intensive personal kind
of thinking and searching. On the other hand, in Abelard of Paris
we have a representative of the subjective side, if "subjective"
does not mean willful but taking into the personal life, as subjective reality. It is unfortunate that the words "objective" and
"subjective" have become so indefinite and distorted in all respects.
We should not think that if something is objective, it is real and
true, whereas if it is subjective, it is willful. "Objective" here refers
to the reality of the given substance of the Bible, tradition, and
authority. "Subjective" refers to something which is taken into the
personal life, and as such experienced and discussed.

Abelard was a philosopher and theologian in the twelfth century, who lived in the shadow of the Cathedral of Notre Dame in
Paris. Subjectivity, which characterizes his spiritual attitude and
character, is visible in the following points:

(1) Abelard was enthusiastic about dialectical thinking, showing the "yes" and "no" in everything. He was full of contempt for
those who accept the mysteries of the faith without understanding what the words mean through which the mysteries are
expressed. He did not wish to derive the mysteries from reason,
but to make them understandable to reason. Of course, there is
always the danger that the mystery will be emptied, but this
danger is inherent in thinking itself. Thinking unavoidably destroys the immediacy of life, once it is begun. The question is
whether a higher immediacy can be re-established. This is also
true of the theological lectures you hear here. To hear them means

being endangered. This is the reason some of the more fundamentalistic people would be very much afraid if their future theologians would be educated in a place like Union Theological Seminary in New York, which likes—as Abelard did—dialectical thinking. But if this danger is not risked, faith can never become a real power.

(2) Abelard represents the type of jurisprudential thinking which was introduced into Western Christianity by Tertullian. He was, so to speak, the lawyer who defended the right of the tradition by showing that the contradictions in its sources—which no one can deny—can be solved. In doing this he was supporting the church; but, of course, the same dialectics which have the power to defend also have the power to attack. Some of the traditional theologians sensed this danger in dialectics, even before the danger became actual. This is also the reason some more or less orthodox theologians do not like apologetics; the same means by which you defend Christianity can be used to attack it.

(3) Abelard was a person of strong self-reflection. This was almost a new event in a period which was so objective in the sense of being related to the contents and not to oneself. In Abelard there was not merely a commitment to truth or goodness, but at the same time to a reflection about his being committed. We all know about this; we have a feeling of repentance and we reflect on having this feeling. We have an experience of faith and we reflect on this experience. This is characteristically modern, and it first appeared in Abelard. From this perspective we can understand his famous autobiography, *Historia Calamitatum* (History of My Misfortunes). The title is in line with Augustine's *Confessions*, but the important difference is that his self-analysis is not made in the face of God, as with Augustine. The self-analysis is done in relation to himself, in relation to what he has experienced. The title reveals the danger in which we all live as modern men. When Augustine spoke of confessions, he related himself to God as he looked at himself. If we speak of "misfortunes" or "calamities", there always remains a feeling of resentment, and resentment is a sign of subjectivity. This in Abelard was supported by his tremendous ambition, his lack of consideration for others, for instance, his teachers, and his continuous attacks on authorities.

(4) This subjectivity is visible also in the realm of feeling.

Abelard was one of those who discovered this as a special realm. An example of this was his romance with Heloise, an event with all the tragedy and greatness of the romantic form of love, although this was much earlier than its development in the period of romanticism. It represents the discovery of *erōs* against two things which had been predominant, first, paternalistic authority, and secondly, simple sexuality, which has nothing to do with the personal relationship, but which the church had allowed and limited and which was used as an element in the paternalistic family. Instead of this, we have in the romance of Abelard and Heloise a relationship in which the sexual and the spiritual dimensions are united. This was something new and threatening in a period in which the barbaric tribes were just becoming educated and receptive of the Christian gospel. Abelard was, so to speak, ahead of his time.

Abelard's book *Sic et Non* (Yes and No) used a dialectical method which was older than Abelard. It came from the canonistic literature (the sacred law literature) in ecclesiastical jurisprudence. The papal lawyers tried to harmonize the decrees of the various popes and synods. The practical problem was that the pope and his advisers had to make decisions, and they wanted these to be based on the tradition of law. So the law had to be harmonized. However, the dogmatic decisions of the popes and synods were a part of canon law, so they too had to be harmonized through "yes and no". When Abelard wrote his book, he tried to harmonize the doctrines, not to show dogmatic differences in order to arouse doubt and skepticism. On the contrary, he wanted to show that a unity is maintained in the tradition which can be proved by methods of harmonization. This was also accepted by the church authorities because they needed it; in fact, all scholastics accepted the "yes and no" method of Abelard. They asked questions, put opposing views against the answers, discussed the opposing views, and finally came to a decision.

The first step in this method is the attempt to deal historically with the texts of the fathers, the synods, the decrees, and the Bible. The question whether the texts in question are authentic had to be raised. Further, one had to show in what historical situation and under what psychological conditions these texts were written. Any changes in the texts had to be examined. The sphere and the configuration in which these changes occur in the same author had to be investigated and described. If all this has been done, then it might be shown that what seemed to be contradictions are not such at all, but only different forms in which the very same idea is expressed. It happens often in the history of thought that statements contradict each other only when taken as isolated statements out of the *Gestalt*, the structure, to which they belong. While appearing contradictory, they may actually say one and the same thing.

The second step is the elaboration of the literal meaning of a word—the philological task. This may lead to the discovery of different senses of a word, even in the same writer. In my lectures I continuously discover that the semantic problem is predominant, that if we use words like "faith" or "Son of God", they have as many meanings as there are people in the room, each with a different nuance. Now, if we ask ourselves: Is there any danger in this method of semantic analysis, or more widely, to what degree can logical calculus, semantic purification and reduction, be applied to the contents of the Christian message?—then I would say there is no absolute possibility of applying it, because when we deal with the existential things of life, every word has an edge which makes it what it is, which gives it its color and power; if that is removed, you leave a bone—a conceptual bone—without flesh and skin. This is why I am not convinced by the criticisms of logical positivists, in spite of my interest in semantics, because I believe that if they have their way completely, all words in realms like theology, metaphysics, ontology, art theory, or history will lose their full meaning and be reduced to mathematical signs from which the real power and meaning of such words escape.

The application of the authority of the Bible as the ultimate criterion is the next step. This sounds very Protestant, like so much biblicism in the Middle Ages, but it really is not. It was not a new experience of the Bible out of which Abelard spoke, as was the case with Luther. It was rather the application of the Bible as a law, as the ultimate legal judge. This is quite different from the Protestant interpretation of the Bible as the place where the message of justification can be found. The legal relationship to the tradition in Abelard is different from the creative traditionalism of Anselm. Though he was less dialectical than Abelard, Anselm was more creative and even more courageous, and at the same time more sensitive to the substance of the tradition.

Abelard shows subjectivity in all his doctrines, ethical and theological. His doctrine of ethical autonomy is connected with the subjective reason. He was a predecessor of Kant, in spite of the tremendous difference in time and situation. He taught that it is not an act in itself that is good or bad, but the intention makes it so. Kant expressed the same idea—nothing is good except a good will. So for Abelard the act itself is indifferent; only the intention is decisive. "In the intention consists the merit." Therefore, what makes us sinful is not nature itself, not even the desire itself, but the intention, the will. The contents of a moral system are not the important thing, but whether or not the conscience follows them. The contents of the moral system are always questionable when applied to a concrete situation. They can never be taken as absolutes, but the conscience must be the guide. The perfect good, of course, is an exact correspondence between the objective norm and the subjective intention, provided the conscience shows what is actually right. But often this is not the case. When it is not, it is better to follow our conscience, even if it is objectively wrong. He says: "There is no sin except against our conscience." In one sense even Thomas Aquinas accepted this notion. Aquinas said: If a superior in my order, to whom I have sworn obedience, asks me to do something which is against my conscience, I shall not do it, although I am obliged to be obedient to him. The conscience was regarded as ultimate judge, though it may be objectively erroneous. The Protestants and Kant were anticipated by these formulations, but in Abelard's time they could not work, because he neglected the educational element. If the uneducated masses are told that they should follow their conscience, but they have no sufficiently strict objective norms, they will wander and go astray. In this respect, as in so many others, Abelard anticipated ideas which later became actual, for example, in eighteenth-century France.

Abelard denied that in Adam all have sinned. Sin is not sensuality, but an act of the will. There is no sin without an agreement of the will, and since we did not agree with our will when Adam sinned, it is not sin for us. Here we see how subjectivity, exactly as in the eighteenth century, dissolves the doctrine of original sin, because this doctrine shows the tragic side of sin, the objective and not the personal, subjective side.

In christology Abelard emphasized the human activity of

Christ, and denied in a radical way that Christ was a transformed God or Logos or higher divine being. For him the personal activity of Christ is decisive, not his ontological origin in God.

He is best known to Protestants and most often quoted for his idea of salvation. As we have seen, Anselm in his doctrine of atonement makes a deal between God and Christ, out of the situation produced by human sin. He describes atonement in quantitative terms of satisfaction. For Abelard, however, it is the love of God which is visible in the cross of Christ; this produces our love. It is not an objective mechanism between transcendent powers which enables God to forgive, as it is in Anselm, but it is the subjective act of divine love which evokes in us a love for him. Salvation is man's ethical—in the sense of personal—response to the forgiving act of divine love. This is one of the types of the doctrine of atonement. It is a doctrine of atonement in the personal center. The mechanism of atonement through substitutionary suffering is ruled out. Anselm's doctrine lies in the mythological realm in which God and Christ trade with each other; Christ sacrifices and gets something back from God in return. In this respect Abelard is pre-Protestant and pre-autonomous. This is subjectivity in the sense of reason and centered personality. Many of these ideas in Abelard were rejected; he was too early for the educational situation in which the church found itself. For instance, if you tell someone whom you want to educate that the act of confession (i.e., repentance) is valid only if it arises out of love toward God, and not from fear, then you undercut the educational effect of the preaching of the law. Abelard as a theologian did not think in terms of what is good for the people, but in terms of what is ultimately true, and what is good for those who are autonomous. Although some of his doctrines were rejected, he became one of the most influential people in the development toward scholasticism, because of the greatness of his dialectical method.

I. BERNARD OF CLAIRVAUX

Bernard of Clairvaux, a man of the same century as Abelard, fought with him over the possibility of applying dialectics to Christian beliefs. Bernard is the most eminent representative of Christian mysticism. As the foe of Abelard he succeeded in bringing Abelard before a council which rejected him. Yet, it is only half-true to call him an adversary of Abelard, because Bernard was also in favor of the subjective side, subjectivity in terms of mystical experience. He wanted to make the objective Christian doctrines, the decisions of the fathers and the church councils, matters of personal appropriation. The difference was that while Abelard did this in terms of reason, Bernard did it in terms of mystical experience. This experience is based on faith, as with every medieval theologian, and faith is described as an anticipation of the will. This is Augustinian voluntarism which Bernard is expressing. Faith is daring and free, an anticipation of something which can become real personally only through full experience. Certainty is not given in the act of faith; it is a daring anticipation of a state to which one may attain. Faith is created by the divine Spirit, and the experience which follows confirms it.

However, Bernard's mysticism was even more important and influential than these ideas which foreshadow the Franciscan school and much of later medieval thought about faith. In a seminar on Christian mysticism we have dealt with the question, "Can mysticism be baptized?" Can it be Christian? Mysticism is much older than Christianity, and much more universal. What about the relation of Christianity to mysticism? In our seminar we have come to the conclusion that mysticism *can* be baptized if it becomes a concrete Christ-mysticism, very similar to the way it is in Paul—a participation in Christ as Spirit. This is just what Bernard of Clairvaux did. The importance of Bernard is that he is the "baptizing father" in the development of Christian mysticism. Whenever it is said, as some Barthians do, that Christianity and mysticism are two different things, that either one is a Christian or a mystic, that the attempt of almost two thousand years to baptize mysticism is wrong, then one must point to Bernard in whom a mysticism of love is expressed. Only if you have a mysticism of love can you have a Christian mysticism.

Mysticism has two types of content in Bernard. First, there is the picture of Jesus as it is given in the biblical record, through which the divine is transparent. The stress is on participation in his humility, not on an ethical command, although this follows after it. We participate in the reality of God in Jesus. The mystical following of Jesus is participating in him. When we read about how Francis of Assisi and Thomas à Kempis tried to follow Jesus, we should never forget that this was not the way in which a Jew follows Moses; it was not another law, but it was meant as a participation in the meaning of what Jesus is. In this way the mystics of the Middle Ages overcame a legal interpretation of obedience to Christ. We cannot really follow him except we participate in him mystically. This participation is dynamic, not static and legalistic. This concrete, active mysticism of love to Christ is the presupposition of the second type of content in Bernard's mysticism. This is the abstract mysticism; it is called "abstract" because it abstracts from anything concrete. It is a mysticism of the abyss of the divine. This side of the mystical experience is that which Christian mysticism has in common with all other forms of mysticism. There are three steps, according to Bernard:

(1) Consideration (you look at things from outside; they remain objects for your subjectivity).

(2) Contemplation (participating in the "temple", going into the holiness of the holy).

(3) *Excessus* (going outside oneself, an attitude which exceeds the normal existence, one in which man is driven beyond himself without losing himself, it is also described as *raptus*, being grasped).

In the third stage man goes over into the divinity, like a drop of wine which falls into a glass of wine. The substance remains, but the form of the individual drop is dissolved into the all-embracing divine form. One does not lose one's identity, but it becomes a part of the divine reality.

These two forms of mysticism must always be distinguished: concrete mysticism, which is mysticism of love and participating in the Savior-God, and abstract mysticism, or transcending mysticism, which goes beyond everything finite to the ultimate ground of everything that is. When we examine these two forms, we can say that at least for this life Bernard's mysticism stands within the Christian tradition. As for the second type, we can say that this makes love in eternity impossible. But then we must add that Paul said something similar in his statement that God will be all in all. This means that when we come to the ultimate, we cannot think simply in terms of separated individuals, although we must still think in terms of love. And this is no easy task. In any case, the decisive thing is that in Bernard there is something different than in Pseudo-Dionysius, and this is his concrete mysticism, Christ mysticism, love mysticism. It is still mysticism, because mysticism is participation, and participation involves partial identification.

In coming to the end of this discussion on the early Middle Ages, we must briefly consider Hugh of St. Victor, the most influential theologian of the twelfth century. More than Anselm, Abelard, or Bernard, he was a fulfiller of systematic thinking. He wrote a book, *On the Sacraments of the Christian Faith*. The term "sacrament" is used in the broadest sense; all the works of God and everything in which the divine becomes visible are sacraments. He distinguishes two groups of the works of God. He calles them the *opera conditionis*, the works of condition, and the *opera reparationis*, the works of reparation. This offers a deep insight into medieval life. All things are visible embodiments of the invisible ground behind them. Nevertheless, this does not lead to a pantheistic form of theology, because although all the works of God are sacraments, they are concentrated into seven sacraments. If not only bodily realities, but also activities of God are called sacraments, then the idea of sacrament becomes full of dynamism. Thus, we have an interpretation of the world in dynamic sacramental form, centered around the seven sacraments of the church, particularly around the Mass and penance.

J. JOACHIM OF FLORIS

In Joachim of Floris we have an interpretation of history which became extremely influential upon the Middle Ages as well as upon modern thought. Joachim was an abbot of a monastery in Calabria in southern Italy. He wrote a number of books in which he developed a philosophy of history which became an alternative to the Augustinian interpretation of history and formed the background to most of the revolutionary movements in the Middle Ages and in modern times. Augustine's interpretation of history was the basis for most conservative movements during the same time. I want to confront the Joachimist interpretation of history with the Augustinian.

The Augustinian view places the reign of Christ, the thousand-year period, in the present time and identifies it with the control of this period by the hierarchy and its divine graces. The sacramental power of the hierarchy makes it the immediate medium of Christ, so that the thousand-year period, the monarchy of Christ, is the monarchy of the church. Since this is the last period, according to Daniel, there is no future any more; the thousand years are here and we live in them. Criticism can only be directed to the church so far as it is a mixed body, not to its foundation, which is final. In this way Augustine removed the threat of millenarianism—the doctrine of the thousand years—which holds that the millennium is still to come in the future, and in the light of which the church and its hierarchy could be criticized.

Joachim renewed the idea of the thousand years of Christ which still lie in the future. He spoke about the three dispensations which unfold in history and which are characterized by historical figures. The first period runs from Adam to John the Baptist, or to Jesus Christ; it is the age of the Father. This age is overcome by the very fact of the Christ. The second period runs from King Uzziah (Isaiah 6) to the year A.D. 1260. This way of figuring is arrived at by the fact that according to the genealogies of the Old Testament, this age is supposed to embrace forty-two generations. The third dispensation runs from Benedict in the sixth century after Christ, when Western monasticism started; it is called the age of the Spirit. It has twenty-one generations after Christ, which lead up to the year 1260.

This construction seems to be very artificial. The ages overlap; the second overlaps with the first age from King Uzziah to the birth of Christ, or to John the Baptist. The second is overlapped by the third from Benedict to 1260. What does this overlapping mean? It represents a profound insight into historical developments. Historical periods never start sharply but always unfold with some overlapping. There is no such thing as "the end of the Gothic period" and "the beginning of the Renaissance", no "end of the Renaissance" and "beginning of the Baroque", no "end of the Baroque" and "beginning of the Rococo", etc. Every new period is conceived and born in the womb of the previous one. No one was more aware of this than Karl Marx when he constructed his interpretation of history, describing how each new period was prepared in the womb of the preceding one—for instance, the socialist in the womb of the bourgeois period, and the latter in the womb of the late feudal period. It is like birth;

there is a certain period in which mother and child are together in the same body. According to this idea of overlapping, the germs of the new period are prior to what he called *fructificatio* (fructification), mature realization. A period is never mature when its first beginnings become visible. In this trinitarian scheme applied to history, the succeeding period is always present for a certain amount of time in the preceding one. In this way Christ is one moment in the three periods of history, and history goes beyond him. This is the same problem we have in the Fourth Gospel, whether or not the Spirit goes beyond the Christ. The Fourth Gospel decides in a double way: on the one hand, it decides partly for the Spirit going beyond the Christ when it says that many things cannot be said now, but the Spirit will come and help you; and, on the other hand, the Spirit does not take of its own but from Christ, who is present in the second period, the period of the Son.

These ideas about the meaning of historical development should be taken seriously. They should not be rejected just because of these names in the Old Testament, which are certainly arbitrary. Every historian knows about the arbitrariness of every periodization of history. Historians will tell you that the period which we call the "Renaissance" was shared in by only a few people—artists, scholars, and politicians in Italy, and later by some people in England, Holland, and Germany. The masses of people still lived under the conditions which had prevailed for the past century.

What are the characteristics of these stages? Being a profound observer Joachim knew that the first stage was to be determined sociologically. This is a period in which marriage is the decisive sociological form, work and servitude (slavery, feudalism, etc.) are economically decisive, and which religiously can be identified as the period of law. In the second period the clergy and the organized church are decisive. The sacramental reality makes the law unnecessary; because of grace it is a time for faith instead of good works. It is not an age of autonomy, but one in which the clergy represent for everyone the presence of the divine. The third period is monasticism, when the monastic ideal will grasp all mankind and the birth of new generations will cease. This is, therefore, by necessity the last period. The graces given by the Holy Spirit in this period are higher than the sacramental graces of the second period, and still higher than the law of the first period. Whereas the second period was prepared already in Judaism, which had some sacramental graces, the third period was prepared in church history, with the foundation in monasticism. The inner part of this period is freedom, that is, autonomy, not being subject any more to state or church authorities. The appropriate attitude is contemplation instead of work, and love instead of law.

So we have here a sociological understanding of the different periods of history, but sociology is not the "cause" of everything, as it is in Marxism but it is a necessary condition. At the same time it is an interpretation of religion which shows the difference between works (under the law), grace accepted by faith, and autonomous freedom in contemplation and love. The scheme is trinitarian; the dynamic element which is always implied in trinitarian theology has become horizontal, transferred to the movement of history. It is the historization of the trinitarian idea: Father, Son, and Spirit have different functions in history. Of course, all three are always present—God cannot be divided—but they are present with a different emphasis. This means that something is still ahead. The perfect society, the monastic society, will still come, and when measured by it not only the Old Testament society but also the New Testament society, the church, must be criticized.

Another idea is that truth is not absolute, but is valid for its time—*bonum et necessarium in suo tempore*—the good and necessary according to its time. This is a dynamic concept of truth, the idea that truth changes in history according to the situation. The early church had to apply this principle always to the Old Testament. The truth of the Old Testament is different from that of the New Testament, and yet it also is the divinely inspired Word of God. To account for this theologians spoke about dispensations or covenants. The idea of the *kairos* was used, which means that as the time is different, so the truth is different. This idea was placed against the absolutism of the Catholic Church, which identified its own being with the last period of history, that is, with the ultimate truth. For Joachim there is a higher truth than that of the church, namely, the truth of the Spirit. From this it follows that the church is relative. It is *inter utrumque*, between both the period of the Father and the period of the Spirit. Its shortcomings are due not only to distortions, but also to its relative validity. In this scheme the church is relativized. Only the third period is absolute; it is not authoritarian any more, but autonomous. Every individual has the divine Spirit within himself. This means that the ideal for Christianity lies in the future and not in the past. He called it *intellectus spiritualis* and not *literalis*, that is, a spiritually formed intellect and not an intellect dependent on literalistic laws.

From this it follows that in the future the hierarchy as well as the sacraments will come to an end. They will not be needed because everything will be directly related to God spiritually, and no authoritarian intervention will be necessary. Joachim spoke of a *papa angelica*, an angelic pope, which is more a principle than a man. It is a pope who represents the presence of the Spirit without authority. The hierarchy will be transformed into monasticism, and so will the laity. When this happens the last period will have been reached. In this third stage there will be perfection, contemplation, liberty, and Spirit. This will happen in history. For Augustine the final end is only transcended; nothing new will happen in history any more. For Joachim the new is in history.

Joachim also spoke of the "eternal gospel", which is not a book. The gospel is the presence of the divine Spirit in every individual, according to the prophecy of Joel, which is often used in this context. It is a *simplex intuitus veritatis*, a simple intuition of truth which all can have without intermediate authority. Freedom means the authority of the divine Spirit in the individual. This is theonomy, not rationalistic autonomy, theonomy which is filled with the presence of the divine Spirit. History produces freedom in the course of its progress. The idea is progressivistic; the goal is ahead.

These were revolutionary ideas which understandably Thomas Aquinas fought against in the name of the church. The church has its classical period in the past, not in the future. The classical period of the church is the apostolic age. The church is based on history; history has brought the church about, but the church is itself not in history. It is beyond it because it is at the end of history. Joachim's ideas are important because they had a dynamic, revolutionary, explosive power. The extreme Franciscans used his prophecies and applied them to their own order, and on

that basis they revolted against the church. Many sectarian movements, including the sects of the Reformation on which much of
American life is dependent, were directly or indirectly dependent
on Joachim of Floris. The philosophers of the Enlightenment who
taught that there will be a third period of history in which everyone will be taught directly by the inner light—the light of reason
—were dependent on Joachim's ideas. The socialist movement
rests on the same idea when in its classless society everybody will
be directly responsible to the ultimate principles. It is not the
case, of course, that all these people knew Joachim and his ideas
directly, but there was a tradition of revolutionary thinking in
Western Europe, some of the fundamental ideas of which first
appeared in Joachim. Much of American utopianism must be
understood in the light of this movement in the West. So far as
I know none of this revolutionary thinking can be found in the
Eastern religions, because by definition they are non-historical
religions. In Joachim a new insight into the dialectics of history
appeared. His influence was mediated by the radical Franciscan
monks.

K. The Thirteenth Century

The thirteenth century is the high point of the Middle Ages. The
whole destiny of the Western world was decided at this time in a
very definite way. All the scholastics were dependent on Peter
Lombard, whom we have not yet discussed, although he belongs
to the twelfth century. He was not as original as the others, but
he represents the systematic, didactic type of the Middle Ages.
He organized the statements of the fathers in a book entitled
The Four Books of Sentences, which became the text-book of the
Middle Ages, if there ever was a text-book. Every great scholastic
started by writing a commentary on Lombard's *Sentences.*

The thirteenth century can be described theologically in three
steps, represented by three names: Bonaventura, Thomas
Aquinas, and Duns Scotus. There are others between them whom
we will mention occasionally. Duns Scotus was the greatest of
them all as a scholar, and he was also the starting point of new
developments on which the whole modern period is dependent.
Thomas Aquinas is the classical theologian of the Roman Church,
and was established as such again in modern times by the pope.

Bonaventura represents the spirit of Augustine and St Francis, in his being, in his mysticism, and in his theology.

What are the presuppositions of the thirteenth century which made it the high point of the Middle Ages? First, I want to mention the crusades, not because of their political and military significance but because they brought about the encounter of Christianity with two highly developed cultures, the original Jewish and the Islamic cultures. One could perhaps even say that a third culture was encountered at that time, namely, the classical culture of ancient Greece, which was mediated into the medieval world by the Arabian theologians. The fact of an encounter with another, if it is serious enough, always involves a kind of self-reflection. Only if you encounter someone else are you able to reflect on yourselves. As long as you go ahead without resistance, you are not forced to look back upon yourselves. When you encounter resistance, you reflect. This is what Christianity had to do. It began to reflect on itself in a much more radical way. The second presupposition was the appearance of the complete Aristotle in his genuine writings, and with him the appearance of a scientific philosophical system which was methodologically superior to the Augustinian tradition. Thirdly, there was the rise of several new types of monastic orders, the preaching and mendicant orders, which both intensified and popularized the religious substance. They produced world-wide organizations through all countries and contended with each other theologically. Since they were not nationally provincial, they could compete on a world-wide scale and produce theological systems of the highest significance in conflict with each other. Since the thirteenth century these two orders became the bearers of the theological process. They both used Aristotle, but they used him differently. They used the new knowledge of Judaism and Islam, but they used it differently.

This leads us to a description of the two types of orders, the Franciscan and the Dominican, named after two personalities, Francis of Assisi and Dominic. Francis continued the monasticism of Augustine and Bernard. Like them he emphasized personal experience, but he introduced the idea of the active life in contrast to the contemplative life. From the beginning this was always nearer to the Western mind than to the East. Francis also produced a new relationship to nature; not only human hierarchical orders, but also sun and stars and animals and plants belong to the power of the divine life. The best thing to do to understand him is to look at the pictures of Giotto, who painted almost nothing else than the story of St. Francis, who had become the new holy legend. Thus, Francis became the father of the Renaissance; by his feeling of fraternity with all beings, he opened up nature for religion. He opened up nature with respect to its ground of being, which is the same as it is in man.

Francis introduced also the idea that the lay people must be brought into the circle of the holy. In the sacramental system the clergy and the monks were the real representatives, while the laymen were only passive. To bring the laity into the circle he created the so-called "third order", the *tertiaries*. The first is the male order, the monks; the second is the corresponding female order, the nuns; the third is the laymen who remain married and subject themselves to some of the principles of the monastic orders. All of this was placed by Francis under the authority of the pope. Giotto's famous picture, in which Innocent III, the greatest pope, and Francis, the greatest saint of the Roman Church, met each other, depicts a classical moment in world history. Nevertheless, this represented a threat to the hierarchical system. The danger became actual in the revolution of the Franciscan radicals who tried to unite Francis and Joachim, and who became the prototypes of many later anti-ecclesiastical and anti-religious movements. The lay principle was also dangerous because it could spell the end of the absolute authority of the hierarchy. Dangerous also was the new relationship to nature and the vision of the divine ground in it which in the long run would undermine Catholic supernaturalism. Generally speaking, Francis belonged to the Augustinian-Anselmian-Bernardian tradition of the mystical union of Christianity with the elements of culture and nature.

In contrast to Francis, Dominic was not such an original personality. He assumed the task of preaching to the people and of defending the faith. This was something new—defending either by mediation or by conversion or by persecution, that is, either in terms of apologetics or in terms of missions or in terms of church power. In all three ways the Dominicans became the order of the Inquisition and of the Counter-Reformation until, at a later time, the Jesuits took over. The Dominican order produced the classical system of mediation, of apologetic theology, that of Thomas Aquinas, and the greatest preachers, among whom was Meister Eckhart. More than any other school, they brought Aristotle into the West. Their instrument was the intellect, even in their mysticism, whereas the Franciscan-Augustinian tradition laid stress more on the will. Finally, the voluntarism of the Franciscans broke down the intellectualism of the Dominicans, thus opening the way for Duns Scotus, Ockham, and the nominalists.

This was the spiritual background for the tremendous development of the thirteenth century. Without constant reference to these movements, the theology of this period cannot be understood. When we think of Thomas Aquinas, we must understand him as a mediating theologian. He understood, better than anyone else, the mediating function of theology. In German theology the term *Vermittlungstheologie* has been used of the nineteenth century in a derogatory sense. I have come to its defense by saying that all theology is mediation, the mediation of the message of the gospel with the categories of the understanding as they exist in any given period of history.

The dynamics of the high Middle Ages are determined by the conflict between Augustine and Aristotle, or between the Franciscans who were Augustinians and the Dominicans who were Aristotelian. This contrast, however, should not be taken too exclusively. For all medieval theologians were Augustinian in substance. And since the thirteenth century they were all Aristotelian with respect to their philosophical categories. Yet, these schools did have different emphases which have been reflected ever since in the philosophy of religion.

Let us make clear what Aristotle meant for the Middle Ages the moment he was discovered at the beginning of the thirteenth century, with the help of the Arabian philosophers.

(1) Aristotle's logic had always been known, but it was used as a tool and had no direct influence on the content of theology. When the whole work of Aristotle was rediscovered, it was found to be a complete system in which all realms of life were discussed—observations about nature, politics, and ethics. It represented an independent secular world-view, including a system of values and meanings. The question was: How could a world which had been educated in the Augustinian ecclesiastical tradition deal with this secular system of ideas and meanings? It

was similar to the question theology has raised in recent centuries: How can the scientific revolution since the seventeenth century be mediated with the Christian tradition?

(2) Aristotle offered basic metaphysical categories, such as form and matter, actuality and potentiality. He came with a new doctrine of matter, of the relation of God to the world, and on this basis an ontological analysis of reality.

(3) Perhaps the most important thing he gave was a new approach to knowledge. The soul has to receive impressions from the external world. Experience is always the beginning in Aristotle, whereas in the Augustinian tradition immediate intuition was the point of departure. The Augustinians stood, so to speak, in the divine center, and judged the world from there. The Aristotelians looked at the world, and concluded to the divine center.

The whole movement of Augustinianism in relation to Aristotelianism must be viewed in the light of this question of knowledge. The question is: Is our knowledge a participation in the divine knowledge of the world and himself, or must we on the contrary recognize God by approaching the world from the outside? Is God the last or the first in our knowledge? The Augustinians answered that the knowledge of God precedes all other knowledge; it comes first and we must start with it. We have the principles of truth within ourselves. God is the presupposition even of the question of God, as he is the presupposition of every quest for truth. "He is", says Bonaventura, "most truly present to the soul and immediately knowable." The principles of truth are the divine or eternal light within us. We start with them; we begin with our knowledge of God, and from this we go to the world, using the principles of the divine light within us. This divine light or these principles are the universal categories, especially the *transcendentalia*, those things which transcend everything concrete and given, such as being, the true, the good, the one. These are ultimate concepts of which we have immediate knowledge, and this knowledge is the divine light in our soul. Only on the basis of this immediate knowledge of the ultimate principles of reality can we find truth in the empirical world. These principles are present in every act of knowing. Whenever we say what something is, whenever we make a logical judgment about something, the ideas of the true, of the good, of being itself, are present. Bonaventura can say: "Being itself is what first appears in the intellect", and being itself is the basic statement about God. This means that every act of cognition is made in the power of the divine light. The Franciscans said that this divine light and these principles within us are uncreated, and we participate in them. Somehow this means that there is no such thing as secular knowledge. All knowledge is in some way rooted in the knowledge of the divine within us. There is a point of identity in our soul, and this point precedes every special act of knowledge. Or, we could say that every act of knowledge—about animals, plants, bodies, astronomy, mathematics—is implicitly religious. A mathematical proposition as well as a medical discovery is implicitly religious because it is possible only in the power of these ultimate principles which are the uncreated divine light in the human soul. This is the famous doctrine of the inner light, which was also used by the sectarian movements and by all the mystics during the Middle Ages and the Reformation period, and which in the last analysis underlies even the rationalism of the Enlightenment. The rationalists were all philosophers of the inner light, even though this light later on became cut off from its divine ground.

This attitude we call theonomous. The Franciscans tried to maintain a theonomous outlook in spite of the fact that they had to use such Aristotelian concepts as form and matter, potentiality and actuality. So from Augustine to Bonaventura we have a philosophy that is implicitly religious, or theonomous, in which God is not a conclusion from other premises, but prior to all conclusions, making them possible. This is the philosophy which in my article, "The Two Types of Philosophy of Religion" (in *Theology of Culture*), I call the ontological type; it can also be called the mystical type, the type of immediacy. I also like to call it the theonomous type in which the divine precedes the secular.

The opposite type is the Thomist philosophy of religion. Thomas Aquinas cuts off the immediate presence of God in the act of knowing. Of course, he acknowledges that God is the first in himself, but he is not the first for us. Our knowledge cannot start with God, although everything starts with him; but our knowledge must reach him by starting with his effects—the finite world. In starting with the effects of God we can conclude to their cause. In other words, man is separated from being itself, from truth itself, and from the good itself. Of course, Thomas could not deny that these principles are in the structure of man's intellect, but he calls them created light, not uncreated light. They are not the divine presence in us; instead, they are the works of God in us; they are finite. Thus, in the act of knowledge, we do not have God, but with these principles we can attain to God. It is not that we start with the divine principles in us and then discover the finite world, as the Franciscans; but we start with the finite world and then perhaps we can discover God in our acts of cognition.

In opposing this Thomist theory the Franciscans said that this method which must start—in a good Aristotelian way—with sense experience is good for *scientia* (for "science" in the broadest sense of the word) but it destroys *sapientia,* wisdom. *Sapientia* means the knowledge of the ultimate principles, the knowledge of God. One of Bonaventura's followers made the prophetic statement that the moment you pursue the Aristotelian-Thomist method and start with the external world, you will lose the principles. You will gain the external world—he agreed with that because he knew that empirical knowledge can be acquired in no other way—but you will lose the wisdom which is able to grasp intuitively the ultimate principles within yourself. Thomas answered that the knowledge of God, like all knowledge, must begin with sense experience and reach God on this basis in terms of rational conclusions.

The divergence between these two approaches to the knowledge of God is the great problem of the philosophy of religion, and, as I will now show, it is the ultimate cause of the secularization of the Western world—I am using "cause" in the cognitive realm, for there are other causes too. The Aristotelian method is placed against the Augustinian, and gradually this method of starting with the external world prevailed. Thomas knew that the conclusions reached in this way, though they are logically correct, do not produce a real conviction about God. Therefore, they must be completed by authority. In other words, the church guarantees the truth which can never be fully reached merely by an empirical approach to God. The situation is clear: In Bonaventura we have a theonomous knowledge in all realms of life; we have no knowledge whatsoever without beginning with God. In Thomas we have autonomous knowledge, reached by the scientific method, as far as it goes. But Thomas knew that it does not go far enough, so it must be completed by authority. This is the meaning of the heated struggle between the Augustinians and the Aristotelians in the thirteenth century. There was a gap in the Thomist approach, but at that time the gap was not yet visible. By his genius, his power to take in almost everything, his power to mediate, his personal, even mystical, piety, Thomas was able to cover the gap, but the gap was there and had consequences reaching far beyond what Thomas himself realized. This came out in Duns Scotus.

Duns Scotus was not a mediating but a radical thinker. He was one of those who tear up what seems to be united. He fought against the mediations of Thomas Aquinas. On the other hand, he did not follow his own Franciscan predecessors. He followed Thomas by accepting Aristotle, but he realized the consequences which Thomas was able to cover. For Duns Scotus there is an infinite gap between the finite and the infinite. Therefore, the finite cannot reach God cognitively at all, either in terms of immediacy—as the older Franciscans wanted—nor in terms of demonstrations, as Thomas and the Dominicans wanted. He criticized—and insofar as you are nominalists, you will like this criticism—even the *transcendentalia*, the ultimate principles. He says: Being itself (*esse ipsum*) is only a word; it points to an analogy between the infinite and the finite, but only an analogy. The word "being" does not cover God as well as the world. The gap is such that you cannot cover both of them with one word, not even in terms of the *verum, bonum, unum* (the true, good, and one), and that means in terms of being itself. Therefore, there is only one way that is open to receive God, the way of authority, the way of revelation received by the authority of the church.

The result is that in Duns Scotus we have two positivisms: the religious or ecclesiastical positivism, which means that we must simply accept what is given to us by the church since we cannot reach God cognitively, and the positivism of the empirical method, which means we must discover what is positively given in nature by the methods of induction and abstraction. Now the gap of which I spoke has become visible. In Thomas it was closed; in Duns Scotus it was opened up and has never been closed again. It is still our problem, as it was the problem of the thirteenth century.

The gap opened up by Duns Scotus became very large a century later in Ockham, the real father of nominalism. In his view God cannot be approached at all through autonomous knowledge; he is out of reach. Everything could be the opposite of what it is. Therefore, God can be reached only by subjecting ourselves to the biblical and ecclesiastical authorities. And we can subject ourselves to them only if we have the *habitus*, the habit, of grace. Only if grace is working in us can we receive the authority of the church. Cultural knowledge, the knowledge of science, is completely free and autonomous, and religious knowledge is completely heteronomous. The original theonomy of the Augustinian-Franciscan tradition has been broken into complete scientific autonomy on the one side, and complete ecclesiastical heteronomy on the other side. This is the situation which prevailed at the end of the Middle Ages. Since the Middle Ages were based on a system of mediation, they came to an end when these mediations broke down.

If we compare these positions on the traditional question of reason and revelation, we can say: In Bonaventura reason itself is revelatory insofar as in its own depths the principles of truth are given. This does not, of course, refer to the historical revelation in Christ, but to our knowledge of God. In Thomas reason is able to express revelation. In Duns Scotus reason is unable to express revelation. In Ockham revelation stands alongside of reason, even in opposition to it. At the end of the Middle Ages the religious and secular realms are separated, but not in the way in which they are today, for the Middle Ages still wanted to maintain its traditional unity. Therefore, the church developed its radical heteronomous claim to rule over all realms, and thus to control them from the outside. Then the desperate fight between autonomous secularism and religious heteronomy developed. The late Middle Ages should not be confused with the earlier Middle Ages. As long as the tradition retained its force, the Middle Ages were not heteronomous; they were theonomous. But by the end of the Middle Ages, an independent secular realm became established. This led to the question whether the church could control this independent realm. The Renaissance and the Reformation were the means by which the church was deprived of this power.

The theory of double truth appeared at this time. Some people seriously believed—they were not merely being diplomatic, to hide themselves—that in reality a statement on the same matter can be both theologically true and philosophically false, and vice versa. Thus, they could accept the whole heteronomous system of the church and, at the same time, continue to develop their autonomous thought. If a philosophical proposition conflicted with the theological tradition, they could take refuge in the "double truth" theory. For many this was a way of evasion, but it was also a belief that these realms are so separated that you can say in one realm the opposite of what you say in the other.

We have been dealing with the epistemological problem, but behind it there is the problem of God. The medieval idea of God has three levels.

(1) The first and fundamental level is the idea of God as *primum esse*, the first being, or *prima causa*, the first cause. The word "cause" here is not meant in the sense of "cause and effect" in the realm of finitude. And the word *prima* does not mean first in a temporal way, but in the sense of the "ground" of all causes. So the term "cause" is here used more symbolically than literally. God is the creative ground in everything, *creatrix universalium substantia*, the creative substance of everything that is. This is the first statement about God. God is the ground of being, as I like to express it, or being-itself, or the first cause; all these terms point to the same meaning.

(2) This substance cannot be understood in terms of the inorganic realm—as fire or water, as the ancient physicists did—nor in the biological realm as a life process. It must be understood as intellect. The first quality of God as the ground of being is intellect. Intellect does not mean intelligence; it means the point in which God is for himself subject and object at the same time; it means God knowing himself and knowing the world as that which he is not. The ground of being, or in other words, the creative substance, is the bearer of meaning. The consequence is that the world is meaningful; it can be understood in words which have meaning. The *logos*, the word, can grasp it. To understand reality, we must presuppose that it is understandable. Reality is understandable because its divine ground has the character of intellect. Knowledge is possible only because the divine intellect is the ground of everything.

(3) The third point is that God is will. This comes from the Christian Augustinian tradition, whereas the emphasis on intellect comes from the Greek Aristotelian tradition. If the concept of will is applied to God and the world, it refers to the dynamic ground of everything, not to the psychological function which we observe in ourselves. Will is the productive power of the ground of being. This will has the nature of love—in good Augustinian tradition. The creative substance of the world has meaning and love; it is intellect and will, symbolically speaking. Just as we said that God knows himself, so now we must say that God wills or loves himself as the absolute good, indeed, as the ultimate aim of everything. He loves the creatures in giving them in a graded way the good of which he is the ultimate ground. Therefore, all the creatures long for him; he is the object of their love, the love toward that in which every being sees its ultimate good.

That is the medieval idea of God. This God is not called a person. The word "person" was never applied to God in the Middle Ages. The reason for this is that the three members of the trinity were called *personae* ("faces" or "countenances"): the Father is *persona*, the Son is *persona*, and the Spirit is *persona*. *Persona* here means a special characteristic of the divine ground, expressing itself in an independent hypostasis. Thus, we can say that it was the nineteenth century which made God into *a* person, with the result that the greatness of the classical idea of God was destroyed by this way of speaking. Of course, this personal structure, including being, intellect, and will, is analogous to our experience of our own being, so if we call ourselves "persons", we must also speak of God as "person". But this is quite different from calling God *a* person. First of all, he is being itself; he is the ground of being in everything. The personal side is expressed in intellect and will, and their unity. But to speak of God as *a* person would have been heretical for the Middle Ages; it would have been to them a Unitarian heresy, because it would have conflicted with the statement that God has three *personae*, three expressions of his being.

On the question of the relationship between intellect and will in God the same controversy took place as on the epistemological problem. For the Thomist tradition, intellect is characteristic of God and man. Thomas argues that man can be distinguished from an animal only because he has intellect. An animal would be human if it could intellectually place purposes before the will. But the animal only wills without purposes, in the sense in which we ascribe that ability to man. Thus, for Thomas it is the intellect which makes man human, and which is the primary characteristic of God. Intellect is the power of insight into the universally true and good. Duns Scotus opposed this doctrine. For him God and man are will. Will is universally creative. There is no reason for the divine will other than the divine will itself. There is nothing which determines the will. The good is good because God so wills it. There is no intellectual necessity for the world to be as it is, that salvation should happen as it does. Everything is possible for God except that he cease to be God. Duns Scotus spoke of God's *potentia absoluta*, the absolute power of God. God uses his absolute power only in order to create a given world in which there are definite orders. On this level he spoke of God's *potestas ordinata*, the ordered power of God. He distinguishes these two things. The world as we know it, as well as the plan of salvation as we know it by revelation, is not *necessarily* as it happens to be; it is as it is by the ordered power of God. Implied in this distinction is something threatening. The world is not as it is from eternity; there is no real necessity that it be as it is. The absolute power of God stands threateningly behind the ordered power, and may change everything. Duns Scotus did not believe that this would happen, but it could happen.

What does such an idea mean? It means that we have to accept the given, that we cannot deduce it, that we have to be humble toward reality. We cannot deduce the world or the process of salvation in terms of necessity. Compare this to Anselm's doctrine of atonement, in which he tried to deduce in terms of necessity the way of salvation between God and Christ and man. Duns Scotus would say there is no such necessity; instead, this is a positive order of God. In this idea of the absolute power of God we have the root of all positivism, in science as well as in politics, in religion as well as in psychology. The moment that God became defined as will—determined by his will and not by his intellect—the world became incalculable, uncertain, unsafe. So we are compelled to subject ourselves to what is positively given. All the dangers of positivism are rooted in this concept of Duns Scotus. So I consider him the turning point in the history of Western thought.

L. THE DOCTRINES OF THOMAS AQUINAS

We shall discuss a few of the most important doctrines of Thomas Aquinas. The first is his doctrine of nature and grace. His famous statement reads: "Grace does not remove nature, but fulfills it." This important principle means that grace is not the negation but the fulfillment of nature. The radical Augustinians, or more exactly, the Manichaean distorters of Augustine, would not accept this statement. They would say that grace removes nature. For Thomas Aquinas, with whom I am in agreement on this point, nature and grace are not two contradictory concepts. Grace contradicts only estranged nature, but not nature as such. But now Thomas says that nature is fulfilled in supernature, and supernature is grace. This is the structure of reality which has existed from creation. God gave to Adam in paradise not only his natural abilities, but beyond these a *donum superadditum*, a gift added to his natural gifts. This is the gift of grace by virtue of which Adam could persist in a state of union with God.

This a point at which Protestantism deviated completely from Thomas Aquinas. Protestantism said that the perfect nature does not need any additional grace; if we are perfect in our created status, there is no need for any grace to come from above. Therefore, Protestantism removed the idea of a *donum superadditum*. This sounds like a mythological story about whether Adam did or did not get this grace, but that is not the interesting point. These mythological stories express a profound vision about the structure of reality. In Thomism the structure of reality has two levels. For Protestantism creation is complete in itself; the created forms of reality are sufficient. God does not need to add anything to them. This is the same basic feeling toward life that we find in the Renaissance, which sees creation as good in itself, with man and his created potentialities in the center, without a supernatural gift added to him. Thomas has two degrees, nature and supernature. Protestantism says that only because nature is distorted by man's fall, by his estrangement from God, is there a need for another power, the power of grace, whose center is forgiveness. Forgiveness is the *restitutio ad integrum*, the restitution of nature to its full potentialities. This idea is ultimately monistic. The created world is perfect in itself; God does not need to give additional graces to his fulfilled creation. Yet, God must come down into existence to overcome the conflicts in it, and this is what grace does. So in Protestantism grace is the acceptance of that which is unacceptable. In Catholicism grace is a substance, which stands in analogy to the natural substances.

The Thomist principle is valid also for the relationship of revelation and reason. Revelation does not destroy reason but fulfills it. Here again I agree with Thomas. I believe that revelation is reason in ecstasy, that in revelation the depth of reason breaks into the form of reason, driving it beyond itself without destroying it. But I would not accept the Thomist form of the doctrine in which reason exists in one realm and revelation in another realm in which reason is completed. Thus we have two forms here. The Catholic world-view is essentially dualistic—nature and supernature. Catholicism defends supernaturalism with all its power. Protestantism, on the other hand, is united with the Renaissance in the monistic tendency—monistic in the sense of having one divine world and having salvation and regeneration (one and the same thing) as the answer of God to the disruption of this world. But this answer is not the negation of the created structure of this world.

In some sense the Protestant dualism is deeper, but it is not a dualism of substances. It is a dualism of the kingdom of God and the demonic powers which stand against it. It is not an identification of the created with the fallen world. The fallen world is the distortion of the created world. Therefore, the new being is not another creation, but the re-establishment of the original unity. One of the consequences of this is that in Protestantism the secular world is immediate to God. In Catholicism the secular world needs the mediation through the supernatural substance, which is present in the hierarchy and their sacramental activities. Here again you have a fundamental difference. Protestantism is emphatically for secularity. This is clearly expressed in Luther's words about the value of the housemaid's work in contrast to the monk's. If it is done in fear of God, the maid's work is more valuable than the asceticism of the monks, even if that is done in the fear of God. Here the emphasis is on the secular act as such, which is the revelation of God if done in the right way. One does not have to become a monk, but if in trying it one claims to be in a supernatural realm, this contradicts the paradox of justification, that as a *sinner* you are justified.

From his epistemology it follows that Thomas would reject the ontological argument for the existence of God. The ontological argument holds that in the center of the human mind there is an immediate awareness of something unconditional. There is an *a priori* presence of the divine in the human mind expressed in the immediate awareness of the unconditional character of the true and the good and of being itself. This precedes every other knowledge, so that the knowledge of God is the first knowledge, the only absolute, sure, and certain knowledge, the knowledge not about *a* being, but about the unconditional element in the depths of the soul. This is the nerve of the ontological argument. However, as I said in connection with Anselm, the ontological argument was also elaborated in terms of a rational argument which concluded from this basis to the existence of a highest being. Insofar as this was done, the argument is not valid, as all its critics—Thomas, Scotus, Kant—have clearly shown. As an analysis of the tension in man between the finite and the infinite, it is valid; it is a matter of immediate certainty.

Thomas Aquinas belongs to those who reject the ontological argument because he saw that as an argument it is invalid. The same is true of Duns Scotus. But now in order to fill the empty space created by the collapse of the ontological argument and of the immediate awareness of the divine in man, Thomas had to find a way from the world to God. The world, although not the first in itself, is the first which is given to us. This is just the opposite of what the Augustinian Franciscans said: the first which is given to us is the principle of truth in us, and only in its light can we exercise the function of doubt. So Thomas had to show another way, the way of the cosmological argument. According to this way, God must be found from outside. We must look at our world and find that by logical necessity it leads to the conclusion of a highest being. Thomas had five arguments for it, which appear again and again in the history of philosophy.

(1) The argument from motion. Motion demands a cause. This cause itself is moved. So we have to go back to an unmoved mover, which we call "God". This is an argument from movement in terms of causality. To find a cause for the movement in the world, we must find something which itself is not moved.

(2) There is always a cause for every effect, but every cause itself is an effect of a prior cause. So we go back from cause to cause, but to avoid an infinite regression, we must speak of a first cause. This cause is not first in a temporal sense, according to Thomas, but it is first in dignity; it is the cause of all causes.

(3) Everything in the world is contingent. It is not necessary that something is as it is. It might have been otherwise. But if everything is contingent, if everything that is can disappear into the abyss of nothing, because it has no necessary existence, this must lead us back to something which has ultimate necessity, from which we can derive all the contingent elements.

(4) There are purposes in nature and man. But if we act in terms of purpose, what is the purpose? When we reach that, we must again ask what that is for. So we need a final purpose, an ultimate end behind all the means. The preliminary purposes become means when they are fulfilled. This leads to the idea of a final purpose, of an ultimate meaning, as we would perhaps say today.

(5) The fifth argument is dependent on Plato. It says that there are degrees of perfection in everything that is. Some things are better or more beautiful or more true than others. But if there are degrees of perfection, there must be something absolutely perfect by which we can distinguish between the more or less of perfection. Whenever we make value judgments, we presuppose an ultimate value. Whenever we observe degrees, we presuppose something which is beyond degree.

In all these arguments there is the category of causality. They conclude from characteristics of this world to something which makes this world possible. I believe that these arguments are valid as analysis. Each of them is true as long as it is not an argument but an analysis. In the doctrine of the arguments for the existence of God we have probably the most adequate analysis of the finitude of reality that has appeared in the writings from the past. They include the existential analysis of man's finitude, and as such they have truth. Insofar as they go beyond this and establish a highest being which as a being is infinite, they draw conclusions which are not justified.

In Thomas Aquinas we have the concept of predestination which combines several motives. Predestination was an Augustinian idea taken over by Thomas on the basis of his principle of intellect, which understands the necessities, and can by necessity derive consequences from what has preceded. On the other hand, Duns Scotus emphasized the will so much that the divine as well as the human will become ultimate realities, ontological ultimates, not determined by anything other than themselves. So Duns Scotus and the Franciscans introduced the element of freedom—the Pelagian element. These Franciscan Augustinians introduced a crypto-Pelagianism into medieval theology, whereas Thomas Aquinas, on the basis of his intellectualism, thought in deterministic terms. This shows that Thomas was religiously much more powerful than the Protestant criticism of Scholastic theology admits. It seems that Luther did not know Thomas Aquinas at all. He knew the late nominalistic theologians, who can rightly be said to have been distortions of scholasticism. So Luther fought against them. But he could have found both his and Calvin's predestinarian thinking in Thomas Aquinas.

The ethical teachings of Thomas Aquinas correspond to his system of grades, as do all the realms of his thought. In his ethics there is a rational substructure and a theological superstructure. They are related to each other exactly as nature and grace are related. The substructure contains the four main pagan virtues, taken from Plato: courage, temperance, wisdom, and the all-embracing justice. These produce natural happiness. Happiness does not mean having a good time or having fun, but the fulfillment of one's own essential nature. In Greek the word for happiness is *eudaimonia*, and there is a philosophical school called eudaemonism. Christianity has often attacked it on the grounds that happiness is not the purpose of human existence, but the glory of God is. I think this is a completely mistaken interpretation of *eudaimonia*. This is exactly what Christian theology calls blessedness, except that this is blessedness on the basis of the natural virtues, and Thomas knew this. Therefore, Thomas was not anti-eudaemonistic. *Eudaimonia* is derived from two Greek words, *eu* and *daimōn*, meaning "well" and "demon"—a divine power which guides us well. (Cf. Socrates' *daimōn*.) The result of this guiding is *eudaimonia*, being led in the right way toward self-fulfillment.

According to Thomas Aquinas, the four natural virtues of philosophy can give natural blessedness, *eudaimonia* in the Greek sense. Virtue was not a term with the bad connotations it has today, for example, abstinence from sexual relations. It meant what the Latin term indicates: *vir*, meaning "man", hence, manliness, power of being. In all these different virtues power of being expresses itself, the right power of being, the power of being which is united with justice. What Thomas did was to combine Christian ethics with the ancient ethics of self-fulfillment, with its natural virtues: the courage to be, the temperance which expresses the limits of finitude, the wisdom which expresses the knowledge of these limits, and finally the all-embracing justice which gives to each virtue the right balance in relation to the others.

On this natural basis the Christian virtues of faith, love, and hope are seen. They are supernatural, because they are given not by nature but by grace. So Thomas' ethical system has these two stories, the natural ethic and the spiritual ethic. This is something more than a theoretical speculation; it was an expression of the sociological situation. The acceptance of the virtues of Plato and Aristotle meant that a city culture had developed. The pagan and the Christian virtues had been combined in the period in which the orders of the knights developed, and they had a great influence on the high Middle Ages. They united pagan courage with Christian love, pagan wisdom with Christian hope, pagan moderation with Christian faith. Humanistic and classical ideals were taken in and developed within the universally Christian culture.

The ethical purpose of man is the fulfillment of what is essential for him. For Thomas what is essential for man is his intellect, which means his ability to live in meanings and in structures of reason. Not the will but the intellect makes him human. Man has the will in common with animals; the intellect, the rational structure of his mind, is peculiar to man.

Thomas combined ethics with aesthetics. He was the first one in the Middle Ages to create a theological aesthetics. "The beautiful is that kind of the good in which the soul rests without possession." You can enjoy a picture without possessing it. By their sheer form you can enjoy the woods or ocean or houses or men depicted in pictures without having to possess them. In art, also in music, there is disinterested enjoyment of the soul. Beautiful is that which is pleasurable in itself. This is a motif which leads in the direction of humanism, but it is not an autonomous humanism, but one which is always but the first step toward something which transcends human possibilities.

In similar fashion he dealt with the problem of church and
state. There are the values represented by the state, and the
higher, supernatural values embodied in the church. The church
has authority over the states, the different national governments,
because it represents something higher. If necessary the church
can ask the people to be disobedient. The Thomistic ethics which
we have been discussing have been fully as influential in the
Western world as his dogmatic statements. They can be found in
the second part of the second section of his *Summa Theologica.*

M. William of Ockham

William of Ockham is the father of nominalism. The conflict between nominalism and realism was the destiny of the Middle
Ages and is still today the destiny of our own time. Today it
continues, at least in part, as a conflict between idealism and
realism, whereby realism today is what nominalism was in the
Middle Ages, and idealism is what medieval realism was. Ockham
criticized the mystical realism of the Middle Ages for regarding
the universals as real things, as having an independent existence.
If the universals exist apart from things, they simply reduplicate
the things. If they exist in the mind only, they are not real things.
Therefore, realism is nonsense. Realism is meaningless because
it cannot say what kind of reality the universals have. What is
the reality of "treehood"? Ockham says it is only in the mind,
and so has no reality at all; it is something which is meant, but
it is not a reality. The realists of that time said the universal "treehood" which directs every tree in a special way is a power of
being in itself. It is not a thing—no realist ever said that—but
it is a power of being. The nominalists said that there are only
individual things and nothing else. It is against the principle of
economy in thinking to augment the principles (cf. Ockham's
razor). If you can explain something like the universals in the
simplest way, for instance, by saying that they are meant by the
mind, then you should not establish a heaven of ideas as Plato
did.

This criticism was rooted in the development toward individualism which became increasingly powerful in late medieval
life. It was a change from the Greek and medieval moods. The
Greek feeling toward the world starts with the negation of all

individual things; the medieval subordinates the individual to the collective. So this was not simply a logical game which the nominalists won for the time being. Rather, it represented a change of attitude toward reality in the whole of society. You will find nominalism and realism discussed in books on the history of logic, and rightly so, but that does not give the full impact of what this controversy meant. This was a debate between two attitudes toward life. Today these attitudes are expressed in terms of collectivism and individualism. However, the collectivism of the Middle Ages was only partly totalitarian; it was basically mystical. This mystical collectivism—basically the church as the mystical body of Christ—is different from our present-day collectivism. Yet, it was collectivism. The realists fought for it, while the nominalists dissolved it. And as soon as nominalism became successful, this was the actual dissolution of the Middle Ages.

Now, if only individual things exist, what are the universals, according to Ockham? The universals are identical with the act of knowing. They rise in our minds, and we must use them, otherwise we could not speak. They are natural. He called them the *universalia naturalia*. Beyond them are the words which are the symbols for these natural universals which arise in our minds. They are the conventional universals. Words can be changed; they exist by convention. The word is universal because it can be said of different things. Thus, these people were also called "terminists" because they said the universals are merely "terms". They were also called "conceptualists" because they said the universals are mere "concepts", and have no real power of being in themselves. The significance of a universal concept is that it indicates the similarity of different things, but that is all it can do. All of this boils down to the point that only individual things have reality. Not man as man, but Paul and Peter and John have reality as individuals. Not treehood, but this particular tree on the corner has reality, and all other particular trees. We call them trees because we discover some similarity between them.

This nominalistic approach was applied also to God. God is called by Ockham *ens singularissimum*, the most single being. This means that God himself has become an individual. As such he is separate from all other individuals. He looks at them and they look at him. God is no longer in the center of everything, as he was in the Augustinian way of thinking. He has been removed

from the center to a special place at a distance from other things.
The individual things have become independent. The substantial
presence of God in all of them has no more meaning, because
such a notion presupposes some kind of mystical realism. Hence,
God has to know things, so to speak, empirically, from the outside. Just as man approaches the world empirically, because he
is no longer thought to be in the center, so also God knows everything empirically from the outside, not immediately by being the
center in which all reality is united. This is a pluralistic philosophy in which there are many individuals, of which God is one,
although the most important one. In this way the unity of all
things in God has come to an end. The consequence of their
individual separation is that they cannot participate in each
other immediately in virtue of their common participation in a
universal. Community, such as we have in the Augustinian type
of thinking, is replaced by social relations, by society. As a consequence of this nominalism we live today in a society in which
we relate to each other in terms of co-operation and competition,
but neither of these has the meaning of participation. Community is a matter of participation; society is a matter of common
interests, of being separated from each other and working with
or against each other.

We do not know each other except by the signs, the words,
which enable us to communicate and to have common activities.
This was an anticipation of our life in a technological society
which developed first in those countries in which nominalism was
predominant, as in England and America. Attitudes concerning
the relations between man and man, and between man and
things, are nominalistic in America and in the traditions of
American philosophy, as is largely the case in England and in
some West European countries. The substantial unity which was
preserved by realistic thinking has disappeared. This means that
we have knowledge of each other not through participation but
only by sense perceptions—seeing, hearing, touching. We deal
with our sense perceptions and the reflections of them in our
minds. This, of course, produces positivism; we have to look at
what is positively given to us.

Many things follow from all this. A rational metaphysics becomes impossible. For example, it is impossible to construct a
rational psychology which proves the immortality of the soul, its

pre- or post-existence, its omnipresence in the whole body, etc. If such things are affirmed, they are matters of faith, not of philosophical analysis. Similarly all aspects of rational theology become impossible. God does not appear to our sense perceptions. He remains unapproachable since we have no direct or immediate relationship to him, as we do in Augustinian thought. We cannot have direct knowledge of God. We can have only indirect reflections, but they never lead to certainty, only to probability of a lower or higher degree. This probability can never be elevated to certainty; instead it is very doubtful. It is quite possible that there is not one cause of the world, but many causes. The most perfect being—the definition of God—is not necessarily an infinite being. A doctrine like the trinity which is based on mystical realism—the three *personae* participate in the one divinity—is obviously improbable. These things are all matters of irrational belief. Science must go its way and faith must guarantee all that is scientifically irrational and absurd.

If this is the case, it is easy to see that authority becomes the most important thing. Faith is subjection to authority. For Ockham the authority he has in mind is more the authority of the Bible than that of the church. Ockham dissolved the realistic unity not only in thought but also in practice. He sided with the German king against the pope. He produced autonomous economics as well as autonomous national politics. In all realms of life he was for the establishment of independent spheres. This means that he contributed radically to the dissolution of medieval unity.

N. German Mysticism

Meister Eckhart was the most important representative of German mysticism. What did these mystics try to do? They tried to interpret the Thomistic system for practical purposes. They were not speculative monks sitting alongside of the world, but they wanted people to have the possibility of experiencing what was expressed in the scholastic systems. Thus, the mysticism of Meister Eckhart unites the most abstract scholastic concepts—especially that of being—with a burning soul, with the warmth of religious feeling and the love-power of religious acting. He says: "Nothing is so near to the beings, so intimate to them, as being-itself. But God is being-itself." The identity of God and

being is affirmed. "*Esse est deus*"—being-itself is God. This is
not a static concept of being. When I have used the concept of
being, I have often been attacked for making God static. This is
not even true of Meister Eckhart's mysticism. Being is a continuous flux and return; he calls it *Fluss und Wiederfluss*, a stream
and a counter-stream. It always moves away from and back to
itself. Being is life and has dynamic character.

In order to make this clear he distinguishes between the divinity
and God. The divinity is the gound of being in which everything
moves and counter-moves. God is *essentia*, the principle of the
good and the true. From this he can even develop the idea of the
trinity. The first principle is the being which is neither born nor
giving birth; the second is the process of self-objectivation, the
Logos, the Son; the third is the self-generation, the Spirit, which
creates all individual things. For the divinity he uses the terms of
negative theology. He calls it the simple ground, the quiet desert.
It is the nature of the divinity not to have any nature. It is beyond
every special nature. The trinity is based on God's going out and
returning back to himself. He re-cognizes himself, he re-sees himself, and this constitutes the Logos. The world is in God in an
archetypical sense. "Archetype" is a word which has been
revived today by Jung; it is the Latin translation of the Platonic
"idea". The essences, the archetypes of everything, are in the
depths of the divine. They are the divine *verbum*, the divine
Word. Therefore, the generation of the Son and the eternal
creation of the world in God himself are one and the same thing.
Creaturely being is receiving being. The creature does not give
being to itself; God does. But the creature receives being from
God. This is a divine form of being. The creature, including man,
has reality only in union with the eternal reality. The creature has
nothing in separation from God. The point in which the creature
returns to God is the soul. Through the soul what is separated
from God returns to him. The depths of the soul in which this
happens Eckhart called the "spark", or the innermost center of
the soul, the heart of the soul, or the castle of the soul. It is the
point which transcends the difference of functions in the soul; it
is the uncreated light in man. In this way the Son is born in every
soul. This universal event is more important than the particular
birth of Jesus.

However, all this is in the realm of possibility. Now it must be brought into the realm of actuality. God must be born in the soul. Therefore, the soul must separate itself from its finitude. Something must happen, which he calls *entwerden*, the opposite of becoming, going away from oneself, losing oneself. The process of salvation is that man gets rid of himself and of all things.

Sin and evil show the presence of God, as everything does. They push us into a situation of awareness of what we really are. This is an idea which Luther took over from Meister Eckhart. God is the *nunc aeternum*, the eternal now, who comes to the individual in his concrete situation. He does not ask that the individual first develop some goodness before he will come to him. God comes to the individual in his estrangement. To receive the divine substance, serenity or patience, not moving, is needed. Work is not the means of coming to God; it is the result of our having come to him. Eckhart fought against making the religious relationship a matter of purposing. All this is a strange mixture between quietism—being quiet in one's soul—and a tremendous activism. The inner feeling must become work, and vice versa. This also removes the difference between the sacred and the secular worlds. They are both expressions of the ground of being in us.

This mysticism was very influential in the church for a long time, and is still influential in many people. This Dominican mysticism is a counter-balance to the nominalistic isolation of individuals from each other. One could say that in the religious realm the impulses of German mysticism prevailed. In the secular realm the nominalistic attitude prevailed. Both nominalism and German mysticism were to some degree preparations for the Reformation.

O. THE PRE-REFORMERS

The period prior to the Reformation is quite different from the high Middle Ages. During this period the lay principle becomes important and biblicism begins to prevail over church tradition. Perhaps the most important expression of this situation is the Englishman, John Wyclif. He had a large number of ideas which the Reformers used, and he certainly prepared the soil in England for the Reformation. What the pre-Reformers all lacked was the one fundamental principle of the Reformation—Luther's breakthrough to the experience of being accepted in spite of being unacceptable, which in Pauline terms is called justification by grace through faith. This principle does not appear before Luther. Almost everything else in the Reformation can be found in the so-called pre-Reformers. Thus, when we speak of the pre-Reformers, we have in mind mainly those critical ideas applied against the Roman church which were later also used by the Reformation. If it is argued that they should not be called pre-Reformers, what is meant is that they lacked the main principle of the Reformation, the real breakthrough to a new relationship to God.

Wyclif was dependent on Augustine, but also on Thomas Bradwardine in England who represented an Augustinian reaction against the Pelagian ideas connected with nominalism. Thomas Bradwardine was an important link between Augustine and the English Reformation. The title of his book is characteristic, *De Causa Dei contra Pelagium*, which means the cause of God against Pelagius, not the Pelagius who was Augustine's enemy, but the Pelagianism which he found in nominalistic theology and in the practice of the church. Against this he followed Augustine and Thomas Aquinas with respect to the doctrine of predestination. He says: "Everything that happens, happens by necessity. God necessitates whatever act is done. Every act or creature which is morally evil is an evil only accidentally." This means that God is the essential cause of everything, but evil cannot be derived from him. From this it follows, as for Augustine, that the church is the congregation of the predestined. The true church is not the hierarchical institution of salvation. This true church is in opposition to the mixed body in the church, to the hierarchical institution which, as it now exists, is nothing else than a distortion of the true church. The basic law of the church is not the law of the pope, but the law of the Bible; this is the law of God or of Christ. These ideas were not meant to be anti-Catholic. Neither Bradwardine nor Wyclif thought of leaving the Roman Church. There was only one church, and even Luther needed much time before he separated himself.

There were dangers for the Roman Church in the Augustinian principles. After Augustine a semi-Pelagianism removed the dangers of Augustinianism from the Roman Church. Now these dangers appear again in the name of Augustine, as represented by Thomas Bradwardine and John Wyclif. The idea of pre-destination means that many people are not predestined, many of the hierarchs, for example. This provides a basis for looking for symptoms in the hierarchy which show that they are not pre-destined. These symptoms are discovered by applying the law of Christ, such as the Sermon on the Mount, or the sending of the disciples—all ideas and laws which are dangerous in an organized hierarchical church.

From his criticism of the hierarchy Wyclif revised the doctrines of the church and its relationship to the state. This also has a long tradition. Since the twelfth century there had been in England a movement represented by one who was called the Anonymous of York, a man who wrote on behalf of the king, making the king the Christ for the British nation. There was an anti-Roman tendency which favored having a British territorial church, similar to the Byzantine situation. The king is the Christ for the nation, depicted in hymns and in pictures as the Christ, just as Constantine in Byzantium was the Christ for the whole Eastern church. These analogies are preparations for the revolt of the crown of England against the pope.

Wyclif differentiated between two forms of human domination or government, the natural or evangelical domination, which is the law of love, and the civil domination, which is a product of sin and a means of force for the sake of the bodily and spiritual goods. On the one hand, we have the natural law, which in the classical tradition is always the law of love, and all that it includes. This is the law which should rule. On the other hand, there is un-fortunately a need for civil government, which is necessary because of sin. Force and compulsion are inescapable means to maintain the goods of the nation, bodily and spiritually. The first law, the law of love, is sufficient for the government of the church. Since the church is the body of the predestined, force is not needed here. Its content is the rule which Jesus gave, the rule of serving. The law of Christ is the law of love, which expresses itself in service. From this it follows that the church must be poor; it must not be economically and politically in control. It must be the church which is poor, the church as it was anti-cipated by the radical Franciscans and originally by Joachim of Floris.

The church, however, is not entirely holy. For ministers to be wealthy is an abuse which should be removed, by the power of the king, if necessary. If the church responds with excommunication, the king should not fear this, for it is impossible to excommunicate a man unless he has first excommunicated himself. The real excommunication of a Christian is severing himself from communion with Christ. This means that the hierarchy has lost its chief power; it can no longer decide about the salvation of the individual. It can be criticized when it acts against the law of Christ, which is the law of poverty, the law of spiritual rule. From this it follows, further, that there is no dogmatic necessity to have a pope. This was also in the line of Joachim of Floris, who spoke of a *papa angelica*, an angelic pope, which is really a spiritual principle. Wyclif says that if we are ruled by a spiritual principle, it is all right to have a pope, but not necessary. These ideas are in line with the sectarian protest against the rich and powerful church, yet they remain on the whole within the framework of official doctrine. They are not the same as the Reformation protest, because they are based on the principle of law—not the law of the church but the law of Christ—and not on the gospel.

Since the basis of Wyclif's attack was the law of Christ as given in the Bible, he developed the authority of Scripture against that of the tradition and against the symbolic interpretation of the Bible. He even reaches the point, also on biblical grounds, that the *predicatio verbi*, the preaching of the Word, is more important than all the ecclesiastical sacraments. The transition in the Middle Ages from realism to nominalism is accompanied by a transition from the predominance of the eye to the ear. In the early centuries of the Christian Church the visual function was predominant in religious art and in the sacraments. Since Duns Scotus, and even more since Ockham, the hearing of the Word becomes most important, and not the seeing of the sacramental embodiment of the reality. Even before the Reformation the emphasis on the word develops; it came to the foreground in nominalism. Why? Because realism sees the essences of things. "Idea" comes from *idein*, "seeing". *Eidos*, "idea", means picture, the essence of a thing which we can see in every individual thing. Of course, this is an intuitive spiritual seeing, but it is still seeing, and it is expressed in the great art. The great art shows the essence of things, visible to the eye. In nominalism we

have individuals. How can they communicate? By words. Therefore, if God has become the most individual being, the *ens
singularissimum* in Ockham's language, then we receive a communication from him not through a kind of intuition of his divine
essence, as expressed in all his creations, but by his word which
he speaks to us. Thus, the word became decisive in contrast to
the visual function. The importance of the word as over against
the sacraments appears already in Wyclif. This is not yet Reformation theology, because here the word is the word of the law;
it is not yet the word of forgiveness. This is the difference between the Reformation and the pre-Reformation.

If there is to be a pope, he must be the spiritual leader of the
true church, the church of the predestined, otherwise he is not
really the vicar of Christ, the spiritual power from which all
spiritual power is derived. But the pope is a man who falls into
error. He is not able to give indulgences; only God can do that.
This is the first statement against the system of indulgences—
before Luther's Ninety-five Theses. If the pope is not living in
humility, charity, and poverty, he is not the true pope. When the
pope accepts the dominion over the world, as he has done, then
he is a permanent heretic. The pope did just that by means of
the "Donation of Constantine", which was the great foundation
of the political power of the pope, making him the prince of
Rome and sovereign over the Western half of the empire, in spite
of the fact that this document was historically a falsification. It is
heretical for the pope whose power is spiritual to become a prince.
If he does this, he is the Antichrist. This is a term which comes
from the Bible and was used during the Reformation. It has been
used in church history especially by sectarians in their criticism of
the church. They said that if the pope claims to represent Christ,
but is actually a ruler of this world opposed to Christ, then he is
the Antichrist.

I once spoke with Visser 't Hooft, general secretary of the
World Council of Churches, about the Hitler period in Holland.
He said: We Dutch people, and many other Christians, at first
had the feeling that Hitler might be the Antichrist because of all
the anti-divine things he did. But then we realized that he is not
good enough to be the Antichrist. The Antichrist must maintain
at least some of the religious glory of the real Christ, so that it
would be possible to confuse them and to adore him. But Hitler

had none of this. Then we knew, he said, that the end of time had not yet come, and Hitler is not the Antichrist.

This was not a question about a dogma concerning the Antichrist. In these ideas Visser 't Hooft was standing in the real tradition of the sectarian movements. Today if we call someone the Antichrist, it is understood simply as name-calling. But when Luther called the pope the Antichrist, he was not name-calling, but speaking dogmatically; that is, in the very place where Christ is supposed to be represented, everything is done which stands against Christ.

The church's involvement in big business is further evidence of its Antichrist character. The Vatican had become the banking house of the world, especially in Luther's time, but before also. The bishops were bankers in a lesser way, but all this, Wyclif insisted, must be abolished. Even the monks had lost their ideal of poverty and accommodated themselves to the general desire of the church to be wealthy.

These criticisms brought Wyclif to even more radical conclusions. He attacked transubstantiation by saying that the body of Christ is, spatially speaking, in heaven. He is actually, or *virtualiter* (i.e., with his power) in the bread, but not spatially. This contradicts the idea of transubstantiation completely. When the church rejected him, although he knew he was right on biblical grounds, he came to realize that the official church can err with respect to articles of faith. This was also Luther's great experience, that the church rejected a true criticism of its errors. On the basis of the Bible as the real law of Christ, he was able to criticize any decision of the church which was unbelievable. He criticized the number of sacraments and particular sacraments, such as marriage. He criticized the idea in Catholicism that the sacraments have the *character indelebilis* (indelible character), according to which a special character which cannot be lost adheres to those who are baptized, confirmed, or ordained. He even criticized the celibacy of the priests. He criticized the idea of the treasury of the saints, and the superstitious elements in the popular religion. Monasticism should be abolished because it introduces division in the one church. There should not be a division in the status of Christians. There should be a *communis religio*, a common religion, to which everyone belongs. What the Catholic Church calls monastic counsels, such as love of the enemies, should be fulfilled by all Christians. In terms of the negative side, one could say that Wyclif anticipated nearly all the positions of the Reformers. He was supported by the king, because the English crown had for a long time opposed the interference of Rome in the affairs of the nation, not only religiously but also politically. Wyclif was attacked very much, but always protected. After his death his movement slowly ebbed away, but the seeds were in the soil and became fertile when the real Reformation broke through.

This shows that the Roman Church could not be reformed on the basis of a sectarian criticism, radical as it was in Wyclif. A reform could occur only by the power of a new principle, the power of a new relationship to God. And this is what the sixteenth-century Reformers did.

CHAPTER IV

Roman Catholicism from Trent to the Present

BEFORE taking up the Reformation we are going to discuss the Counter-Reformation from the Council of Trent to the present time. During the Reformation period there were many councils which attempted to overcome the split in the church. The demand for a general council never stopped. When the Council of Trent was convened, instead of being a universal council, it was a council of the Counter-Reformation. At Trent sessions of this council were held during several decades, with many interruptions. The Protestant Reformers were excluded from it.

A. THE MEANING OF COUNTER-REFORMATION

The Counter-Reformation was not simply a reaction, but was real reformation. It was reformation insofar as the Roman Church after the Council of Trent was not what it was before. It was a church determined by its self-affirmation against the great attack of the Reformation. When something is attacked, and then re-affirms itself, it is not the same. One of the characteristic results is that it becomes narrowed down. The medieval church should not be seen in the light of post-Tridentine Catholicism. The medieval church was open in every direction, and included tremendous contrasts, for example, Franciscans and Dominicans (Augustinians and Aristotelians), realists and nominalists, biblicists and mystics, etc. In the Counter-Reformation many possibilities which the Roman Church had previously contained were shut off. The Roman Church tended to become "counter"—the "counter" of Reformation—just as the Protestant church, with its prophetic principle, became the principle of protest against Rome.

This is the unwholesome split of Christianity. The Reformation, instead of becoming the reformation of the whole church, became the dogma of the protesting group, the Protestants. The non-Protestants reformed themselves, but in terms of "counter", in terms of opposition to something, not of immediate creativity. This is always the historical situation: if a group has to resist, it narrows down. Take simply the attack of Communism on the Western world, and you see how the freedoms for which America stands are tremendously narrowed down in defense of these freedoms. The Reformation itself was very wide open. But when all kinds of attacks were directed against the Reformation, the result was a very narrow Protestant Orthodoxy—here we call it "fundamentalism"—which represented a narrowing down of the Reformation in resistance against the attacks.

B. The Doctrine of Authorities

This leads us to a presentation of the doctrine of the authorities which the Council of Trent defined.

(1) The traditional Holy Scriptures and the Apocrypha of the Old Testament are both Scriptures and of equal authority. Luther had removed the Apocrypha of the Old Testament from canonic validity. He would have liked to remove many more books from the biblical canon, e.g., the Book of Esther, and others. Why is it important that he removed the Apocrypha? Because they are characterized by legalism, a legalism in terms of proverbs, to a great extent. This legalistic spirit had been in the Roman Church for a long time, and now was preserved in terms of the authority of the apocryphal books. So we have two Bibles, the Roman and the Protestant, and they are not identical.

(2) Scripture and tradition are equal in authority; the phrase was "with equal piety and reverence accepted". This was the form in which the Council of Trent negated the Scripture principle. What the tradition is, was not defined. Actually the tradition became identical with the decisions of the Vatican from day to day. But the tradition was not defined; the fact it was left open made it possible for the pope to use it in whatever way he pleased. Of course, he was not free to use it absolutely willfully, because there was an actual tradition deposited in the councils and former decisions, but the present decision is always decisive.

And the present decision about what the tradition is lies in the hands of the pope.

(3) There is only one translation which has ultimate authority, the Vulgate of St. Jerome. This was a decision against Erasmus, who had edited a text of the New Testament in terms of higher criticism. Erasmus' text was used by the Reformers. The pope excluded this kind of higher criticism for dogmatic purposes by making the Vulgate the only sacred translation.

(4) When the principle of biblicism prevails, the question always arises: Who interprets the Bible? Trent's unambiguous answer was: the Holy Mother Church gives the interpretation of Scripture. In Protestantism it was the theological faculties. The difference is that the pope is one man, and his decision is final; there were many theological faculties in Protestantism, and since they disagreed with each other so much, their authority in the long run was ineffective.

This doctrine of authorities in the church was a restatement of what the Reformers attacked. It makes the position of the pope unimpeachable; he cannot be attacked or criticized. He is beyond any possibility of being undercut by a competing authority, even the Bible's, because he alone has the ultimate decision in the interpretation of the sacred text.

C. The Doctrine of Sin

The Council of Trent offers an interpretation of man different from that of the Reformers. For Trent sin is a transformation of man into something worse—*in deterius commutatum*—commuted into something worse, or deteriorization. This was said against the Reformers who held that man has completely lost his freedom by his fall. This freedom that is completely lost is the freedom to contribute to one's relationship to God, not the psychological sense of freedom, which no one denied in these discussions. However, for the theology of Trent man's freedom is not lost or extinguished, but only weakened. The sins before baptism are forgiven in the act of baptism, but after baptism concupiscence remains. However, this concupiscence should not be called sin, according to the Roman Church. For the Augsburg Confession sin is a lack of faith; the Roman Church says that although concupiscence comes from sin and inclines to sin, it is not sin itself.

This means that man is not completely corrupted; even his natural drives are not sin. This had one important consequence in that Catholicism—except perhaps in America where from the beginning it has been influenced by the general climate—is not puritan. Catholicism can be radically ascetic, but it is not puritan in the ordinary life. When we Protestants from the northern and eastern sections of Germany went to Bavaria, we had the feeling that we were then in a gay country in comparison to the religious and moral climate in the Protestant areas. This difference had a basis in doctrine. For the Reformers concupiscence is sin in itself; for the Roman Church it is not. Therefore, it can admit many more liberties in the daily life, more gaiety, and more expressions of the vital forces in man, than Protestantism can.

On the other hand, the doctrine of sin in the Reformers was based on the fact that sin is unbelief. Against this the Roman Catholic Church says: No, sin is neither unbelief nor separation from God. Sin is understood as acts against the law of God. This means that the religious understanding of sin was covered over by the Council of Trent. This is another fundamental difference. From this point on, sin was understood in the Roman Church in terms of particular acts which can be forgiven. When Catholics confess their sins to a priest, they receive absolution and are liberated from them. This again contributes to a much fuller affirmation of the vital elements of life in predominantly Catholic countries. By contrast, in Protestantism sin is separation from God; "sins" are only secondary. Therefore, something fundamental must happen. A complete conversion, transformation of being, and reunion with God are necessary. This lays a much greater burden on every Protestant than any Catholic has to bear. On the other hand, the Catholic position is in principle legalistic and divides sin into "sins". When Protestants do this, as they sometimes do, they follow the Catholic and not the Reformation line of thought.

D. THE DOCTRINE OF JUSTIFICATION

The central inssue between the Reformers and the Roman Catholic Church was the doctrine of justification by faith alone (*sola fide*), the formula which the Reformers used for polemical purposes. In the Council of Trent the Roman Church repeated the Thomistic tradition on the doctrine of justification, but with a diplomatic tendency. The Catholic Church knew that this was, as the Reformers called it, the *articulus stantis aut cadentis ecclesiae,* the article by which the church stands or falls. Since this was the main point of the Reformation opposition, the Roman Church felt it had to be as conciliatory as possible. It avoided some of the distortions of this doctrine in nominalism which the Reformers had attacked. Nevertheless, it remained clear in the main statement that the *remissio peccatorum,* the forgiveness of sins, is not *sola gratia,* by grace alone. Other elements are added. It speaks of a preparation for the divine act of justification whereby a *gratia praeveniens,* a prevenient grace, is effective in man which can be rejected or accepted, whichever way a man decides. Thus, man must cooperate with God in his prevenient grace. After grace is received by man, it is given to him in the degree of his cooperation. The more man cooperates with God in his prevenient grace the more is the grace of justification given to him.

Justification as a gift contains two things: faith on the one hand, and hope and love on the other. Faith alone is not sufficient. According to the Council's decision, it is even possible that justification may be lost by a Christian through a mortal sin, but that faith still remains. Now the Reformers would say: If you are in faith, you can never lose your justification. But the Roman Church understood faith in terms of its ancient tradition, which defined faith as an intellectual and a moral act. Of course, if faith is an intellectual and a moral act, it can be lost, and nevertheless justification can be there. However, faith for the Reformers is the act of accepting justification, and this cannot be lost if there shall be justification.

Nothing has been more misunderstood in Protestant theology than the term *sola fide,* by faith alone. This has been understood not only by the Romans but also by Protestants themselves as an intellectual act of a man. This act of "faith" forces God to give his forgiveness. But *sola fide* means that in the moment that our sins are forgiven, we can do nothing else than receive this forgiveness. Anything else would destroy the activity of God, his exclusive grace. This central position of the Reformers that grace can only be *received* by faith alone was first misunderstood and then rejected. This means that from this moment on the split in the church became final. No reconciliation was possible between these

two forms of religion—the Reformation doctrine which holds that
our act of turning to God and receiving his grace is unambiguously
a receptive act, one in which God gives something to us and we
do not do anything, and the Catholic doctrine which teaches that
we must act and prepare for grace, that we must cooperate with
God, and that faith is an intellectual acknowledgment, which
may or may not be there. All the anathemas of the Council of
Trent on this point are based on this misunderstanding of *sola
fide*.

E. THE SACRAMENTS

While the fathers of Trent tried to approximate the Protestant
position on justification to some degree, they made no such effort
at all on the sacraments. Here caution was unnecessary because
every caution would have undercut the very essence of the
Roman Church. So the Council of Trent states: "All true justice
starts, and if it has started, is augmented, and if it has been lost, is
restituted, by the sacraments." This is the function of the sacraments; it is the religious function altogether.

Not much was said about the way in which the sacraments are
effective nor about the personal side in the reception of the sacraments. The formulation was made that the sacraments are effective
ex opere operato non ponentibus obicem, i.e., by their very operation for those who do not resist. If you do not place an impediment
(*obicem*) within yourselves in the way of the effectiveness of the
sacraments, then no matter what your subjective state, they
are effective by their mere performance (*ex opere operato*). This
was another crucial point for the Reformers, that there cannot be a
relationship to God except in the actual person-to-person encounter with him in the realm of faith. This is much more than
non-resistance; it is an active turning toward God. Without this
the sacraments are not effective for Protestants as they are for
Catholics.

With respect to the number of the sacraments, which had been
reduced by Luther and Calvin to two sacraments, there are seven,
all of them instituted by Christ. This is *de fide*, a matter to
be accepted on faith for the Catholic. This means no historical
doubt is allowed whether they were really instituted by Christ
or not. When you read the words *de fide* in connection with

a dogmatic formulation in a Catholic book, this means that this is a dogma of the Roman Church which you cannot doubt or deny, except at the risk of being cut off from the Roman Church.

There is no salvation without the sacraments. The sacraments are saving powers, not merely strengthening powers, as in Protestantism. They have a hidden force of their own, mediated to all those who do not resist the grace. Baptism, confirmation, and ordination have an indelible character—another statement against the Reformers' position. One is baptized for life; this had the practical consequence in the Middle Ages that all the baptized fell under the law of heresy. Those who belonged to other religions, such as Jews and Muslims, fell under another law which limits alien religions, but were not persecuted for heresy, as Christians were. The indelible character of a sacrament was a life-and-death matter in the practice of the Roman Church. The same is true of the indelible character of ordination. This meant that the excommunicated priest could perform valid marriages in prison. The sacramental power in him overcomes his state of excommunication as an individual. This stands against the Protestant doctrine of the universal priesthood. In Catholic doctrine not every Christian has the power to preach and to administer the sacraments, but only those who are ordained; being ordained means having received sacramental power. The sacramental power is even embodied in the ritual form of the sacraments. If there is a given ritual formula, no priest, no bishop, can change it or omit something from it without sinning. The sacramental power is communicated from its origin in the actuality of the church to the forms which are used; no arbitrariness is possible.

Infant baptism is valid; the water of baptism washes away the contamination of original sin. To have faith during one's later life in the power of baptism as the divine act which initiates all Christian being, as Luther demanded, is not sufficient for the forgiveness of sins. This means that baptism loses, religiously speaking, its actual power for the later life. It is not a point to which one religiously returns; its meaning lies in the fact of the *character indelebilis*.

The doctrine of transubstantiation was preserved, and wherever it is preserved you always find a clear test of it, namely, the demand to adore the Host. For Protestants the bread is not the body of Christ except in the act of performance. For Catholics the bread and the wine are the body and blood of Christ after they have been consecrated. So when you enter an empty Catholic church—as you do when you travel in European countries, because they are the objects of greatest interest—you come into a sacred atmosphere. You are not coming into a house which is used on Sundays, and sometimes during the week, but a house in which God himself is present twenty-four hours a day, in the holiest of holies, on the altar, in the shrine. This determines the whole mood which prevails in such a church. God is always there in a definite way on the altar. I believe that the reason the attempts of some Protestant churches to remain open for prayer and meditation during the day have a very limited effect on people is that nothing is happening in them. If, however, you go into a Roman Church, something has happened, the effects of which are still there—the presence of God himself, of the body of Christ, on the altar.

On this basis the Roman Church also preserved the Mass against the criticism of the Reformers, not only the Mass for the living, but the Mass—the sacrifice of the body of Christ—for those who have died and are in purgatory. In these respects the Council of Trent made practically no reform at all, nor did it provide a better theological foundation. It simply confirmed and consecrated the tradition.

The attitude toward the sacrament of penance was a little different. This was another point against which Protestantism directed an attack. The sacrament of penance was, generally speaking, maintained as a sacrament, and even the weakest aspect of this sacrament, the doctrine of attrition, which Luther ironically called the repentance evoked by the gallows, the kind of repentance induced by fear, was retained as a necessary preparation. Contrition, the real repentance, *metanoia* in the New Testament, is not sufficient. It is fulfilled only in connection with the sacrament and with the word of absolution. This word does not simply declare that God has forgiven, but itself gives the forgiveness. It is not that the priest gives the forgiveness, but through the priest, and only through the priest, does God grant forgiveness. Moreover, Christians need more than the word of absolution from the priest. They also need satisfactions, because the punishment is not removed with the guilt. Therefore, some punishments must be imposed on the people even after they have taken part in the sacrament. The satisfactions are such things as praying the "Our Father" a hundred times, or giving money, or making a pilgrimage, etc. This was the point with which the Reformers disagreed the most.

Marriage is retained as a sacrament, although in contradiction to this, virginity is evaluated more highly than marriage. This is still the situation in the Roman Church. Now what was still somewhat in flux before the Reformation became fixed. It was fixed against the Reformation. This shows how the Roman Church lost its dynamic creativity. You can sense this when you read the systematic theologies written by Catholic theologians; they deal with very secondary problems, because all the fundamental problems are solved.

The basic doctrine behind all of them is the sacrament of ordination. Here is the point in which all the others are united. The priest does what constitutes the Roman Church as such; he exercises the sacramental power. Preaching is often secondary and even omitted. Sacrifice and priesthood are by divine ordination— sacrifice in the sense of offering up the body of Christ in the Mass. Both are implied in every ecclesiastical law. Both are presupposed; this church of the sacramental sacrifice is the hierarchical church, and the hierarchical church is the church of the sacramental sacrifice. This is Catholicism in the Roman sense.

F. PAPAL INFALLIBILITY

These decisions confirmed the split in Christianity. Rome actually had accepted only external remedies against abuses. But many problems were left. The first was the problem of the pope in relation to councils. This leads us to the development from Trent to the Vatican Council in 1870. At Trent two opinions were fighting against each other. The first was that the pope is the universal bishop, the vicar of Christ. This means that every episcopal power is derived from the power of the pope; every bishop participates in the pope and the pope participates in him, because he is the vicar of Christ. The other opinion was that the pope is the first among equals, representing the unity and the order of the church. This is the point of view of conciliarism; the councils finally have the power to make the ultimate decisions. The former is the point of view of curialism; the Curia, the court of the pope, is the central power of decision. This question was not decided at Trent. It took a few more centuries.

One of the presuppositions for the decision that was to be made at the Vatican Council was that the historical development more and more destroyed those groups which were most dangerous for the pope in the Roman Church; these groups were the national churches. For example, the movement for an independent French church—called Gallicanism—was a real threat to Rome. There were similar movements in Germany, Austria, and other places, where the national churches under the leadership of their bishops resisted many papal aspirations. The civil rulers formed alliances with the national bishops against the pope. But this was undermined by the historical development. One of the reasons was that the rulers, such as the leaders of the French revolution (Napoleon), or the German princes, used the pope against the local ecclesiastical powers. Diplomacy always plays the one side off against the other. The national princes used their own bishops against the encroachments by the pope, and they used the pope against the power of their own bishops. The result of these oscillations was that finally the pope prevailed. In 1870 the Vatican Council made the statement on the infallibility of the pope. This decision has many presuppositions. First, it was necessary to give a definite meaning to the term "tradition". One distinguished now between ecclesiastical and apostolic tradition. The apostolic tradition is composed of the ancient traditions which came into the church through ways which are not given in the Bible. The ecclesiastical tradition is the tradition about which the pope has to decide in the course of the church's history. The ecclesiastical tradition, which was the only living tradition, was identical with the papal decisions. This is the positive statement.

And now its negative side: The Jesuits more and more undercut all other authorities. In contrast to Thomas Aquinas, they undercut conscience and made themselves leaders of the consciences of the princes, and of the other people too. Most of the decisive political personalities surrounded themselves with Jesuits to advise them, as leaders of their conscience. Now if you guide the conscience of a prince, you can apply this guidance to all political decisions, because in all political decisions there are moral elements. This is what the Jesuits did. They turned the consciences of the Catholic princes toward all the cruelties of the Counter-Reformation. Thus, the conscience could no longer serve as an authority.

The authority of the bishops was undercut by the Jesuits. Episcopal power in the councils was undercut by the interpretation given by the Jesuits. The councils themselves and their decisions have to be confirmed by the pope. This meant the complete victory of the pope over the councils. The pope was accepted by the majority of the bishops at Trent as the one who has to confirm the Council of Trent. The result is that no council which is not confirmed by the pope can have validity any more. The pope is removed beyond criticism.

Even the church fathers were undercut by the Jesuits. The Jesuits were especially anti-Augustinian. There is only one father of the church, namely, the living pope. All earlier church fathers are full of heretical statements, of errors, even of falsifications. As you see from this, the Jesuits were very modern people. They knew about the historical problems and used them to undermine the authority of the church fathers. Protestant historiography did the same thing, to make possible the prophetic authority of the Reformers. So both sides used criticism, the Jesuits to give absolute power to the pope, and the Protestants to liberalize the authority of the Bible.

The constitution of 1870, *Pastor Aeternus*, declared the pope to be the universal power of jurisdiction over every other power in the church. There is no legal body which is not subject to the pope. Secondly, he is declared universal bishop. This means practically that through the local bishop he has power over every Catholic, and if this does not work he can exercise direct episcopal power and bring the subjects of a bishop into revolt against him. Thirdly, the pope is infallible when he speaks *ex cathedra*. This is the most conspicuous decision of the Vatican Council, one which brought about the separation of some Catholics, who called themselves the "Old Catholics", from the Roman Church. They remained a small group in Western Germany, and never succeeded in taking over the Roman Church.

The first *ex cathedra* decision since 1870 was made in our generation, in 1950, about the bodily assumption of the Virgin Mary. Before he made this decision the pope asked most of the bishops. The majority was on his side; a minority was opposed to it. The tradition on this point is more than a thousand years old. We have pictures from many periods in church history of Mary being elevated into heaven and crowned by Christ, or received by God. Now the question was: Is this a pious opinion in the church which is to be tolerated, or is it a matter *de fide*? As long as it is a pious opinion, any Catholic can disagree with it, without losing the salvation of his soul. The moment that it is declared *de fide*, as it was done in 1950 by the pope, every Catholic is bound to accept it as truth, and nothing can relieve him of this necessity. Many Catholics were deeply shaken by this, but they subjected themselves to it.

Infallibility of the pope does not mean that there exists a man whose every word is infallible. For eighty years, from 1870 to 1950, no pope had said anything which is infallible in the strictest sense. But then in 1950 he did, which reminded us that this dogma about the infallibility of the pope is taken absolutely seriously, without restriction. From a Protestant or humanist point of view there can be no approach to this doctrine and its implications.

This was finally confirmed in the fourth point of *Pastor Aeternus*: The pope is irreformable by an action of the church. You must compare this with the impeachment proceedings which are possible against any president of the United States; they are rare, but they have happened and can happen again. This sort of thing happened against the popes in the Middle Ages; some were removed and others were put in their place. All this came to an end in 1870, because there is no power which can remove a pope. The pope is in this sense absolute and irremovable. No impeachment is possible. In this way every dogma formulated by the pope is implicitly valid. This means, for instance, that the doctrine of the Immaculate Conception of Mary the Virgin in the birth of Christ, which had been formulated before 1870, now became *de fide*. Prior to this time the Dominicans, who were against the Franciscans on this matter, could say that it is not a valid dogma. It became a valid dogma because of the implication that the pope has accepted it *ex cathedra*.

G. Jansenism

There was a strong movement in the Roman Church back to the original Augustinianism of the church. This movement is called

Jansenism, named after Cornelius Jansen. The Jesuit, Molina, wrote against the Thomistic Dominicans who taught the doctrine of predestination. The Jesuits opposed this doctrine and fought for human freedom. Now Jansen and the Jansenists, the most important of whom was Blaise Pascal, arose and fought against the Jesuits. But the Jesuits prevailed and the popes followed them. The Jesuit was the modern man in the Roman Church. He was disciplined, very similiar to the totalitarian form of subjection we see today. He was completely devoted to the power of the church, and at the same time nourished on much intellectual education and modern ideas, deciding for freedom and reason.

The Jansenist movement attempted to return to a genuine Augustinian tradition, but was opposed and finally destroyed by the Jesuits. In the process, however, the Jesuits lost a lot of their standing in the public eye, and in the eighteenth century were thrown out of many Catholic countries. One interesting point in the discussion was that if the sentences of Cornelius Jansen are condemned, then this condemnation covers not only the matter of content, but also the question of fact (*question de fait*), whether he really said what he was accused of saying. This seems very foolish, but the important point behind it is that when the pope inquires into someone's text, and then condemns it, he is right not only in rejecting its ideas, but also in his statement that these ideas are really in the text. This means that the pope is the interpreter of every text. If the pope says that this is what the text means, no philological defense in the face of that is possible. Here we see the natural extension of the totalitarian and authoritarian principle even to historical facts. The pope decides what is a historical fact, not only what is true in theological terms.

Jansenism produced other writings. There was a man, Quesnel, who tried to introduce Augustinian principles again and to defend them against the Jesuits. But again the pope took the side of the Jesuits and Augustine was removed from Counter-Reformation Catholicism to a large extent. In the bull *Unigenitus* the pope drove out the best in the Roman tradition. He drove out Augustine's doctrine of grace, of faith, and of love. For instance, it is anathema if someone says with Augustine: "In vain, Lord, thou commandest if thou dost not give what thou orderest." For Augustinianism the commandments of God can be fulfilled only if God gives what he commands. Now, after the Jansenist controversy, somebody who says this in the Roman Church is condemned, and implicitly this means that Augustine is condemned.

When you meet modern progressive Catholics—there are more of them in Europe than in America, where Catholicism, with a few exceptions, has lost its spiritual power—you will find that they always fall back upon Augustine and are always on the verge of being thrown out, of being excommunicated or forbidden to express themselves. In my recent trips to Germany I had discussions several times with Catholic groups and became astonished at how near we were to each other. But these people feel that if they agree with me on Augustinian principles, they are in danger. And they are! This means that the condemnation of Augustinianism in the Jansenist struggle is like a sword which hangs over every form of spiritualized Catholicism.

H. PROBABILISM

The last problem I want to discuss is probabilism. Opinion given by authorities in the Roman Church on ethical questions are probable. The Jesuits said: If an opinion is probable, one is allowed to follow it even though the opposite opinion should be more probable. This means that on ethical matters one has no autonomy; that is something the church would radically deny. One must always follow the guidance of the Roman priest, especially of the confessor. But the confessor himself has many possibilities. Since he must talk to a person, not in the power of his spirit, but on the basis of authorities, and since these authorities always contradict each other, or are at least different, he can advise a person to do something which is probably right, even though other courses of ethical action are more probable. If he can find an acknowledged authority of the church who has said something about a problem, one can follow it, even if it is not safe, even if other things seem to be better. The result of this doctrine was a tremendous ethical relativism, laxity, and chaos. This, of course, was most advantageous in the eighteenth century when the church was following the new morals of an emerging bourgeois society. This was so abused that finally a reaction arose in the Roman Church.

Alfonso Maria di Liguori reacted against it, but did not really overcome it, because he also said that it is not I who can decide, but my confessor. And how can the confessor decide? Finally the principle of the probable triumphed. Another development connected with this was that now every sin becomes a venial sin. Here again Jesuitism and the bourgeoisie—the greatest enemies—joined together to remove the radical seriousness of sin which the Jansenists and the early Protestants maintained.

I. Recent Developments

Much more can be said about present-day Catholicism. I have already said a few things about more recent decisions of the pope. Let me refer to one decision which is not so well known as the decision about the bodily assumption of the Holy Virgin. This was the papal encyclical *Humani generis* in which the pope said things which went beyond what was said in the Vatican Council about the infallibility of the pope. In the *Vaticanum* the infallibility referred only to statements made *ex cathedra*, when the pope speaks officially on matters of dogma or ethics. But in the *Humani generis* of 1950 he made statements about philosophies, directing a sharp attack against existentialism. This means that if the pope has decided that a philosophy is unsound, no faithful Catholic can work in line with it any more. This goes far beyond anything which the pope has said before. Thomas Aquinas is then placed in the role of *the* Catholic philosopher. This meant that some of the French existentialists—de Lubac and others—had to give up their teaching positions because philosophically they were existentialists, although they answered the existentialist questions in religious terms.

I recall asking Reinhold Niebuhr in March, 1950: "What do you think? Will the pope make this declaration about the assumption of the Holy Virgin *ex cathedra*?" Then he answered: "I don't think so; he is too clever for that; it would be a slap in the face of the whole modern world and it would be dangerous for the Roman Church to do that today." Only a few months later it was done! This means that even such a keen observer as Reinhold Niebuhr could not imagine that the pope would dare to do such a thing today. But he did it. This means that an authoritarian system has to become more and more narrow in order to fix itself.

It has to do what other totalitarian systems do; they exclude step by step one danger after the other. They try to prevent their subjects from meeting other traditions. The Roman Church had done this right along by means of the "Index of Prohibited Books". These books are forbidden not for the scholars, but for the populace. People are not allowed to read any of the books which appear on the Index, and students have to obtain special permission to read them. But there is another connotation to this papal decision. It meant that the liberal world had become so weak that the pope had no need to fear it. This was our error—Niebuhr's and mine—that we thought the pope would respect the Protestants and the humanists—perhaps even the Communists—all over the world, and not put himself in the position of having almost everybody speak of the superstitious attitude of the Roman Church in making such a dogma. But the pope was not afraid, and probably he was right, because the very weak Protestant resistance against this and similar things cannot hurt the Catholic Church any more. And the humanist opposition is almost nonexistent because it is in a process of self-disintegration. The greatness of the existentialists is that they describe this disintegration, but they themselves are in the midst of it.

Totalitarianism and authoritarianism must be distinguished. Rome is not totalitarian; only a state can be that. But Rome is authoritarian, and it exercises many functions which totalitarian states have exercised. The question which the existence of Catholicism puts before us is whether, with the end of the liberal era, liberalism altogether will come to an end. This leads me to the question, which is very near to my heart, whether with the end of the Protestant era, the Protestant principle will also come to an end. With this we are led to the problem of the Reformation.

We shall have to deal with the Reformation in a brief survey, after having agreed with Professor Handy that in view of the fact that you come from Protestant traditions and are nourished on Protestant ideas, you do not need this as much as you need a knowledge of the ancient and medieval church. But I am not so sure that you do not need it! For the kind of Protestantism which has developed in America is not so much an expression of the Reformation, but has more to do with the so-called Evangelical Radicals. There are the Lutheran and Calvinist groups, and they are strong, but they have adapted themselves to an astonishing degree to the climate of American Protestantism. This climate has been made not by them but by the sectarian movements. Thus, when I came to America twenty years ago, the theology of the Reformation was almost unknown in Union Theological Seminary Reformation was almost unknown in Union Theological Seminary [New York], because of the different traditions, and the reduction of the Protestant tradition nearer to the non-Reformation traditions.

CHAPTER V

The Theology of the Protestant Reformers

A. Martin Luther

THE turning point of the Reformation and of church history in general is the experience of an Augustinian monk in his monastic cell—Martin Luther. Martin Luther did not merely teach different doctrines; others had done that also, such as Wyclif. But none of the others who protested against the Roman system were able to break through it. The only man who really made a breakthrough, and whose breakthrough has transformed the surface of the earth, was Martin Luther. This is his greatness. His greatness should not be measured by comparing him with Lutheranism; that is something quite different. Lutheranism is something which historically has been associated with Protestant Orthodoxy, political movements, Prussian conservatism, and what not. But Luther is different. He is one of the few great prophets of the Christian Church, and his greatness is overwhelming, even if it was limited by some of his personal traits and his later development. He is responsible for the fact that a purified Christianity, a Christianity of the Reformation, was able to establish itself on equal terms with the Roman tradition. From this point of view we must look at him. Therefore, when I speak of Luther, I am not speaking of the theologian who produced Lutheranism—many others contributed to this, and Melanchthon more than Luther—but of the man in whom the Roman system was broken through.

1. *The Breakthrough*

This was a break through three different distortions of Christianity which made the Roman Catholic religion what it was. The breakthrough was the creation of another religion. What does "religion" mean here? "Religion" means nothing else than another personal relationship between man and God—man to God and God to man. This is why a reunion of the churches was not possible, in spite of tremendous attempts to do this during the sixteenth century and later. You can compromise about different doctrines; you cannot compromise about different religions! Either you have the Protestant relation to God or you have the Catholic, but you cannot have both; you cannot make a compromise.

The Catholic system is a system of objective, quantitative, and relative relations between God and man for the sake of providing eternal happiness for man. This is the basic structure: objective, not personal; quantitative, not qualitative; relative and conditioned, not absolute. This leads to another proposition: The Roman system is a system of divine-human management, represented and actualized by ecclesiastical management.

Now first the purpose: The purpose is to give eternal blessedness to man and to save him from eternal punishment. The alternatives are eternal suffering in hell or eternal pleasure in heaven. The way to accomplish the purpose is through the sacraments, in which a magical giving of grace is the one side, and moral freedom which produces merits is the other side—magical grace completed by active law, active law completed by magical grace. The quantitative character comes through also in terms of ethical commands. There are two kinds, commandments and counsels—commandments for all Christians, and counsels, the full yoke of Christ, only for the monks and partly for the priests. For instance, love toward the enemy is a counsel of perfection, but not a commandment for everybody. Asceticism is a counsel of perfection, but not a commandment for everybody. The divine punishments also have a quantitative character. There is eternal punishment for mortal sins, purgatory for light sins, and heaven for people in purgatory, and sometimes for saints already on earth.

Under these conditions no one ever knew whether he could be certain of his salvation, because one could never do enough; one could never receive enough grace of a magical kind, nor could one do enough in terms of merits and asceticism. The result of this was a great deal of anxiety at the end of the Middle Ages. In my book, *The Courage to Be*, I described the anxiety of guilt as one of the three great types of anxiety, and I related this anxiety of guilt historically and socially to the end of the Middle Ages. This anxiety is always present, of course, but it was predominant then and was almost like a contagious disease. People could not do enough to get a merciful God and to get rid of their bad conscience. A tremendous amount of this anxiety was expressed in the art of that period, and also expressed in the demand for more and more pilgrimages, in the collection and adoration of relics, in praying many "Our Fathers", in giving of money, in buying indulgences, self-torturing asceticism, and everything possible to get over one's guilt. It is interesting to look at this period but almost impossible for us to understand it. Luther was in the cloister with this same anxiety of guilt and condemnation. Out of this anxiety he went into the cloister and out of it he experienced that no amount of asceticism is able to give a person a real certainty of salvation in a system of relativities, quantities, and things. He was always in fear of the threatening God, of the punishing and destroying God. And he asked: How can I get a merciful God? Out of this question and the anxiety behind it, the Reformation began.

What did Luther say against the Roman quantitative, objective, and relative point of view? The relation to God is personal. It is an I-thou relationship, mediated not by anybody or anything, but only by accepting the message of acceptance, which is the content of the Bible. This is not an objective status in which one is; it is a personal relationship which Luther called "faith", not faith in something which one can believe, but acceptance of the fact that one is accepted. It is qualitative, not quantitative. Either a person is separated from God or he is not. There are no quantitative degrees of separation or non-separation. In a person-to-person relationship one can say there are conflicts and tensions, but as long as it is a relationship of confidence and love, it is a qualitative thing. It is not a matter of quantity. Likewise, it is unconditional and not conditioned, as it is in the Roman system. One is not a little bit nearer to God if one does more for the church, or against one's body, but one is near to God completely and absolutely if one is united with him at all. And if not united, one is separated. The one state is unconditionally positive, the other unconditionally negative. The Reformation restated the unconditional categories of the Bible.

It follows from this that both the magical and the legalistic

elements in the piety disappear. The forgiveness of sins, or acceptance, is not just an act of the past done in baptism, but it is continually necessary. Repentance is an element in every relationship
to God, and in every moment. The magical and the legal elements
disappear, for grace is a personal communion of God with the
sinner. There is no possibility of any merit; there is only the need
to accept. There can be no hidden magical power in our souls
which makes us acceptable, but we are acceptable in the moment
in which we accept acceptance. Therefore, the sacramental activities as such are rejected. There are sacraments, but they now mean
something quite different. And the ascetic practices are rejected
forever, because none of them can give certainty. At this point a
misunderstanding often prevails. One asks: Now is that not ego-
centric—I think Jacques Maritain told me this once—if Protestants
think about their own individual certainty? However, Luther did
not have in mind an abstract certainty; he meant reunion with
God, and this implies certainty. Everything centers around this
being accepted. This is certain: If you have God, you have him.
If you look at yourself, your experiences, your asceticism, and your
morals, you can become certain only if you are extremely self-
complacent and blind toward yourself. These are absolute categories. The divine demand is absolute. It is not a relative demand
which brings a more-or-less kind of blessedness. The absolute
demand is: Joyfully accept the will of God. And there is only one
punishment, not different degrees of ecclesiastical satisfaction and
degrees of punishments in purgatory, and finally hell. The one and
only punishment is the despair of being separated from God.
Consequently, there is only one grace, reunion with God. That is
all! Luther reduced the Christian religion to this simplicity. Adolph
von Harnack, the great historian of dogma, called Luther a genius
of reduction.

Luther believed that his was a restatement of the New Testament, especially of Paul. But although his message contains the
truth of Paul, it is by no means the whole of what Paul said. The
situation determined what he took from Paul, that is, the doctrine
of justification by faith which was Paul's defense against legalism.
But Luther did not take in Paul's doctrine of the Spirit. Of course,
he did not deny it; there is even a lot of it in Luther, but that is
not decisive. The decisive thing is that a doctrine of the Spirit, of
being "in Christ", of the new being, is the weak spot in Luther's

doctrine of justification by faith. In Paul the situation is different. Paul has three main centers in his thought, which make it a triangle, not a circle. The one is his eschatological consciousness, the certainty that in Christ eschatology is fulfilled and a new reality has started. The second is his doctrine of the Spirit, which means for him that the kingdom of God has appeared, that the new being in Christ is given to us here and now. The third point in Paul is his critical defense against legalism, justification by faith. Luther accepted all three, of course. But the eschatological point was not really understood.

Luther's breakthrough was externally occasioned by the sacrament of penance. There are two main sacraments in the Roman Church, the Mass, which is a part of the Lord's Supper, and the sacrament of penance, which is the subjective sacrament, dealing with the individual and having an immense educational function. This sacrament may be called the sacrament of subjectivity in contrast to the Mass as the pre-eminent sacrament of objectivity. The religious life in the Middle Ages moved between these two. Although Luther attacked the Mass, this was not the real point of criticism; the real issue had to do with the abuses connected with the sacrament of penance. The abuses stemmed from the fact that the sacrament of penance had different parts, contrition, confession, absolution, and satisfaction. The first and last points were the most dangerous ones.

Contrition—the real repentance, the change of mind—was replaced by attrition, the fear of eternal punishment, which Luther called the repentance inspired by the imminent prospect of the gallows. So it had no religious value for him. The other dangerous point was satisfaction, which did not mean that you could earn your forgiveness of sins by works of satisfaction, but that you have to do them because the sin is still in you after it has been forgiven. The decisive thing is the humble subjection to the satisfactions demanded by the priest. The priest imposed on the *communicandus* all kinds of activities, sometimes so difficult that the people wanted to get rid of them. The church yielded to this desire in terms of indulgences, which are also sacrifices. One must sacrifice some money to buy the indulgences, and these indulgences remove the obligations to perform the works of satisfaction. The popular idea was that these satisfactions are effective in overcoming one's guilt consciousness. One can say that here a sort of marketing of eternal life was going on. A person could buy the indulgences and in this way get rid of the punishments, not only on earth but also in purgatory. The abuses brought Luther to think about the whole meaning of the sacrament of penance. This led him to conclusions absolutely opposed to the attitude of the Roman Church. Luther's criticisms were directed not only to the abuses but to the source of them in the doctrine itself. Thus Luther placed his famous Ninety-five Theses on the door of the Wittenberg church. The first of these is a classic formulation of Reformation Christianity: "Our Lord and Master, Jesus Christ, saying 'Repent ye,' wished that the whole life of the believers be penitence." This means that the sacramental act is only the form in which a much more universal attitude is expressed. What is important is the relationship to God. It is not a new doctrine but a new relationship to God which the Reformers brought about. The relationship is not an objective management between God and man, but a personal relationship of penitence first, and then faith.

Perhaps the most striking and paradoxical expression is given by Luther in the following words: "Penitence is something between injustice and justice. Therefore, whenever we are repenting, we are sinners, but nevertheless for this reason we are also righteous, and in the process of justification, partly sinners, partly righteous—that is nothing but repenting." This means that there is always something like repentance in the relationship to God. Luther did not at this time attack the sacrament of penance as such. He even thought that the indulgences could be tolerated. But he attacked the center out of which all abuses came, and this was the decisive event of the Reformation.

After Luther's attack had been made, the consequences were clear. The indulgence money can only help with respect to those works which are imposed by the pope, i.e., the canonical punishments. The dead in purgatory cannot be released by the pope; he can only pray for them; he has no power over the dead. The forgiveness of sins is an act of God alone, and the pope—or any priest—can only declare that God has already done it. There is no treasury of the church out of which the indulgences can come, except the one treasury of the work of Christ. No saint can do superfluous works because it is man's duty to do everything he can anyhow. The power of the keys, that is, the power of the forgiveness of sins, is given by God to every disciple who is with him. The only works of satisfaction are works of love; all other works are an arbitrary invention by the church. There is no time or space for them, because in our real life we must always be aware of the works of love demanded of us every moment. Confession, which is made by the priest in the sacrament of penance, is directed to God. One does not need to go to the priest for this. Every time we pray "Our Father", we confess our sins; this is what matters, not the sacramental confession. About satisfaction Luther said: This is a dangerous concept, because we cannot satisfy God at all. If there is satisfaction, it is done by Christ to God, not by us. Purgatory is a fiction and an imagination of man without biblical foundation. The other element in the sacrament of penance is absolution. Luther was psychologically alert enough to know that a solemn absolution may have psychological effects, but he denied its necessity. The message of the gospel, which is the message of forgiveness, is the absolution in every moment. This you can receive as the answer of God to your prayer for forgiveness. You do not need to go to church for this.

All of this means that the sacrament of penance is completely dissolved. Penitence is transformed into a personal relationship to God and to the neighbor, against a system of means to obtain the release of objective punishments in hell, purgatory, and on earth. All of these concepts were in reality at least undercut by Luther, if not abolished. Everything is placed on the basis of a person-to-person relationship between God and man. You can have this relationship even in hell. This means that hell is simply a state and not a place. The Reformation understanding of man's relationship to God abolishes the medieval view.

The pope did not accept the absolute categories in Luther's view of man's relationship to God. Thus the conflict between Luther and the church arose. Let us make clear, however, that this was not the beginning of the schism. Luther hoped to *reform* the church, including the pope and the priests. But the pope and the priests did not want to be reformed in any way. The last great bull defining the power of the pope said: "Therefore, we declare, pronounce and define that it is universally necessary for salvation that every human creature be subject to the Roman high priest." This is the bull which defines most sharply the unlimited and absolute power of the pope.

2. Luther's Criticism of the Church

Luther criticized the church when it did not follow his criticism of the sacrament of penance. The only ultimate criterion for Christianity is the message of the gospel. For this reason there is no infallibility of the pope. The pope may fall into error, and not only he but also the councils may err. Neither the curialistic theory that the pope is an absolute monarch nor the conciliaristic theory that the great councils of the church are absolutely infallible is acceptable. The pope and councils are both human, and can fall into error. The pope can be tolerated as the chief administrator of the church on the basis of human law, the law of expediency. However, the pope claims to rule by divine right, and makes of himself an absolute figure in the church. This could not be tolerated for Luther, because no human being can ever be the vicar of the divine power. The divine right of the pope is a demonic claim, actually the claim of the Antichrist. When he said this, the break with Rome was clear. There is only one head of the church, Christ himself, and the pope as he is now is the creation of the divine wrath to punish Christianity for its sins. This was meant theologically, not as name-calling. He was theologically serious when he called the pope the Antichrist. He was not criticizing a particular man for his shortcomings. Many people were criticizing the behavior of the pope at that time. Luther criticized the position of the pope, and his claim to be the representative of Christ by divine right. In this way the pope destroys the souls, because he wants to have a power which belongs to God alone.

Luther as a monk had experienced the importance of monasticism in the Roman Church. A double standard of morality grew out of the monastic attitude; there were the higher counsels for those who are nearer to God, and then the rules which apply to everybody. The higher counsels for the monks, such as fasting, discipline, humility, celibacy, etc., made the monks ontologically higher than ordinary men. This double standard was called forth by the historical situation in which the church grew rapidly. The result was that the masses of people could not take upon themselves, as it was said, the whole yoke of Christ, because it was too heavy for them. So a special group did it, following the counsels of a higher morality and piety. These were the *religiosi*, those who made religion their vocation.

Luther attacked the double-standard morality. The divine demand, he said, is absolute and unconditional. It refers to everyone. This absolute demand destroys the whole system of religion. There is no status of perfection, such as the Catholics ascribed to the monks. Everyone has to be perfect, and no one is able to be perfect. Man does not have the power to produce the graces to do the right thing, and the special endeavor of the monks will not do it. What is decisive is the intention, the good will, not the magic habit (*habitus*) of which the Catholic Church spoke. And this intention, this good will, is right even if its content is wrong. The valuation of a personality is dependent on the inner intention of a person toward the good. Luther took this seriously. For him it was not enough to will to do the good, or the will of God; you must will what God wills joyfully, with your voluntary participation. If you fulfill the whole law, but do not do it joyfully, it is worth nothing. The obedience of the servant is not the fulfillment of Christian ethics. Only he who loves, and loves God and man joyfully, is able to fulfill the law. And this is expected of everyone.

This means that Luther turned religion and ethics around. We cannot fulfill the will of God without being united with him. It is impossible without the forgiveness of sins. Even the best people have within them elements of despair, aggressiveness, indifference, and self-contradiction. Only on the basis of divine forgiveness can the full yoke of Christ be imposed on everybody. This is completely different from a moralistic interpretation of Christianity. The moral act is that which follows—it might or might not follow, although essentially it should do so—and the *prius* of it is the participation in the divine grace, in God's forgiveness and in his power of being. This makes all the difference in the world. It is most unfortunate that Protestantism is always tempted to revert to the opposite, to make the religious dimension dependent on morality. Wherever this is done, we are outside the realm of true Protestantism. If someone says: "Oh, God must love me, because I love him and do almost everything he demands"—namely, what the suburban neighbor demands!—then the religious and the ethical relationship is completely reversed. The center of the Reformation, the meaning of the famous phrase, *sola fide*, is rather put this way: "I know that I do not do anything good, that everything seemingly good is ambiguous, that the only thing which is good within me is God's declaration that I am good, and that if I but accept this divine declaration, then there may be a transformed reality from which ethical acts may follow." The religious side comes before the ethical.

The phrase *sola fide* is the most misunderstood and distorted phrase of the Reformation. People have taught that it means that if you do the good work of believing, especially believing in something unbelievable, this will make you good before God. The phrase should not be "by faith alone" but "by grace alone, received through faith alone". Faith here means nothing more than the acceptance of grace. This was Luther's concern, because he had experienced that if it is put the other way around, you are always lost, and if you take it seriously, you fall into absolute despair, because if you know yourself, you know that you are not good. You know this as well as Paul did, and this means that ethics are the consequence and not the cause of goodness.

What did Luther have to say about the sacramental element in the Roman Church, which gave it its tremendous power? The Roman Church is essentially a sacramental church. This means that God is essentially seen as present, not as one who is distant and who only demands. A sacramental world-view is one in which the divine is seen as present in a thing, in an act, or in anything which is visible and real. Therefore, a church of the sacrament is a church of the present God. On the other hand, the Roman Church was one in which the sacraments were administered in a magic way by the hierarchy, and only by the hierarchy, so that all who do not participate in them are lost, and those who do participate, even if they are unworthy, receive the sacrament. To this Luther said that no sacrament is effective by itself without full participation of the personal center, that is, without listening to the Word connected with the sacrament, and the faith which accepts it. The sacrament *qua sacrament* cannot help at all. The magical side of sacramental thinking is thus destroyed.

From this it followed that transubstantiation was destroyed, because this doctrine makes the bread and the wine a piece of divine reality inside the shrine and put on the altar. But such a thing does not occur. The presence of God is not a presence in the sense of an objective presence, at a special place, in a special form; it is a presence for the faithful alone. There are two criteria for this: if it is only for the faithful, then it is only an action. Then if you enter a church and the sacrament is spread, you do not need to do anything, because it is pure bread. It becomes more than this only in action, that is, when it is given to those who have faith. For the theory of transubstantiation, it is there all the time. When you enter an empty Roman church, you must bow down before the shrine because God himself is present there, even though no one else is present besides you and this sacrament. Luther abolished this concept of presence. He denounced the *character indelebilis* as a human fiction. There is no such thing as a "character" which cannot be destroyed. If you are called into the ministry, you must minister exactly as everyone else does in his profession. If you leave the ministry, and become a businessman or professor or shoemaker, you are no longer a minister and you retain no sacramental power at all. Any pious Christian, on the other hand, can have the power of the priest in relation to others. But this does not require ordination.

In this way the sacramental foundation of the whole hierarchical system was removed. But most important was Luther's attack on the Mass. The Mass is a sacrifice *we* bring to God, but in reality we have nothing to bring to God, and therefore the Mass is a blasphemy, a sacrilege. It is a blasphemy because here man gives something to God, instead of expecting the gift of God himself in Christ. And nothing more than this is needed.

3. *His Conflict with Erasmus*

The representative of humanism at this time was Erasmus of Rotterdam. At the beginning Luther and Erasmus were friendly toward each other, but then their attacks on each other created a break between Protestantism and humanism which has not been healed up to the present time, in spite of the fact that Zwingli tried to do it as early as the twenties of the sixteenth century. Erasmus was a humanist, but a Christian humanist; he was not antireligious at all. He believed himself to be a better Christian than any pope of his time. But as a humanist he had characteristics which distinguished him from the prophet. Luther could not stand Erasmus' nonexistential detachment, his lack of passion toward the religious content, his detached scholarly attitude toward the contents of the

Christian faith. He felt that in Erasmus there was a lack of concern for matters of ultimate concern.

Secondly, Erasmus was a scholarly skeptic, as every scholar has to be in regard to the traditions and the meaning of the words he has to interpret. Luther could not stand this skeptical attitude. For him absolute statements on matters of ultimate concern are needed. Thirdly, Luther was a radical, in political as well as in other respects. Erasmus seemed to be a man willing to adapt to the political situation—not for his own sake but in order to have peace on earth. Fourthly, Erasmus had a strongly educational point of view. What was decisive for him was the development of the individual in educational terms. All humanism, then and now, has had this educational drive and passion. Fifthly, Erasmus' criticism was of a rational kind, lacking in revolutionary aggressiveness.

The whole discussion between Luther and Erasmus finally focused on the doctrine of the freedom of the will. Erasmus was for human freedom; Luther against it. But this needs to be qualified. Neither Erasmus nor Luther had any doubts about man's psychological freedom. They did not think of man as a stone or an animal. They knew that man is essentially free, that he is man only because he is free. But on this basis they drew opposite conclusions. For Erasmus this freedom is valid also in coming to God. You can help God and cooperate with him for your salvation. For Luther this is impossible. It takes the honor away from God and from Christ and makes man something he is not. So Luther speaks of the "enslaved will". It is the free will which is enslaved. It is ridiculous to say that a stone has no free will. Only he who has a free will can be said to have an enslaved will, that is, enslaved by the demonic forces of reality. For Luther the only point of certainty can be justification by faith, and no contribution of ours to salvation can give us consolation. Luther said that in Erasmus the meaning of Christ is denied and finally the honor of God is denied.

Here we see a fundamental difference between two attitudes. The attitude of the humanist is detached analysis, and if it comes to synthesis, it is that of the moralist, not that of the prophet who sees everything in the light of God alone.

4. *His Conflict with the Evangelical Radicals*

Luther's conflict with the evangelical radicals is especially important for American Protestants because the prevailing type of Christianity in America was not produced by the Reformation directly, but by the indirect effect of the Reformation through the movement of evangelical radicalism.

The evangelical radicals were all dependent on Luther. Tendencies of this kind existed long before in the Middle Ages, but Luther liberated them from the suppression to which they were condemned. Almost all of Luther's emphases were accepted by the evangelical radicals, but they went beyond him. They had the feeling that Luther stood half-way. First of all, they attacked Luther's principle of Scripture. God has not spoken only in the past, and has now become silent. He always speaks; he speaks in the hearts or depths of any man who is prepared by his own cross to hear. The Spirit is in the depths of the heart, although not of ourselves but of God. Thomas Müntzer, who was the most creative of the evangelical radicals, said that it is always possible for the Spirit to speak through individuals. But in order to receive the Spirit, a man must share the cross. Luther, he said, preaches a sweet Christ, the Christ of forgiveness. We must also preach the bitter Christ, the Christ who calls us to take his cross upon ourselves. The cross is, we could say, the boundary situation. It is internal and external. In an astonishing way Müntzer expressed this in modern existentialist categories. If a man realizes his human finiteness, it produces in him a disgust about the whole world. Then he really becomes poor in spirit. The anxiety of creaturely existence grasps him, and he finds that courage is impossible. Then it happens that God appears to him and he is transformed. When this has happened to him, he can receive special revelations. He can have personal visions, not only about theology as a whole, but about matters of daily life.

On the basis of these ideas these radicals felt that they were the real fulfillment of the Reformation, and that Luther remained half-Catholic. They felt that they were the elect. Whereas the Roman Church offered no certainty to any individual with respect to justification, and whereas Luther had the certainty of justification but not of election, and whereas Calvin had the certainty not only of justification but also to a great extent of election, Müntzer and his followers had the certainty of being elected within a group of the elect; they were the sectarian group.

From the point of view of the inner Spirit, all the sacraments fall down. The immediacy of the procession of the Spirit makes even what was left of the office of the minister unnecessary in the sectarian groups. Instead of that they have another impetus, which could express itself in two ways. One movement would transform society by suffering, and if society could not be changed, they could abstain from arms and oaths and public office and whatever involves people in the political order. Another group of radicals would overcome the evil society by political measures, and even by the sword.

The evangelical radicals are also referred to as enthusiasts. Their emphasis is on the presence of the divine Spirit, not on the biblical writings as such. The Spirit may be present in an individual in every moment, even giving counsels for activities in daily life. Luther had a different feeling. His was basically the feeling of the wrath of God, of God who is the judge. This was his central experience. Therefore, when he speaks of the presence of the Spirit, he does so in terms of repentance, or personal wrestling, which makes it impossible to have the Spirit as a possession. This seems to me the difference between the Reformers and all perfectionist and pietistic attitudes. Luther and the other Reformers placed the main emphasis on the distance of God from man. Hence, the Neo-Reformation theology of today in people like Barth stresses continually that God is in heaven and man is on earth. This feeling of distance—or of repentance, as Kierkegaard said—is the normal relationship of man to God.

The second point in which the theology of the Reformation differs from the theology of the radical evangelical movements has to do with the meaning of the cross. For the Reformers the cross is the objective event of salvation and not the personal experience of creatureliness. Therefore, the participation in the cross in terms of human weakness or moral endeavor to take one's weakness upon oneself is not the real problem with which the Reformation deals. Of course, this is presupposed. We have these same nuances among us today, wherein some of us, following the theology of the Reformation, emphasize more the objectivity of salvation through the cross of Christ, and others more the taking of the cross upon oneself. These two aspects are not contradictions in any way, but as with most problems of human existence, it is more a matter of emphasis than of exclusiveness. It is clear that those of us who are influenced by the Reformation tradition emphasize more the objectivity of the cross of Christ, as the self-sacrifice of God in man, while others coming from the evangelical tradition, so strong in America, emphasize more taking one's own cross upon oneself, the cross of misery.

Thirdly, in Luther the revelation is always connected with the objectivity of the historical revelation in the Scriptures, and not in the innermost center of the human soul. Luther felt that it was pride for the sectarians to believe that it is possible to have immediate revelation in the actual human situation apart from the historical revelation embodied in the Bible.

Fourthly, Luther and the whole Reformation, including Zwingli, emphasized infant baptism as the symbol of the prevenient grace of God, which means that it is not dependent on the subjective reaction. Luther and Calvin believed that baptism is a divine miracle. The decisive thing is that God initiates the action, and that much can happen before the human response. The time difference between the event of baptism and the indefinite moment of maturity does not mean anything in the sight of God. Baptism is the divine offer of forgiveness, and a person must always return to this. Adult baptism, on the other hand, lays stress on the subjective participation, the ability of the mature man to decide.

Luther and the other Reformers were also concerned about the way in which the sects isolated themselves, claiming that they were the true church and that their members were the elect. Such a thing was unthinkable for the Reformers, and I think they were right on this. It is well known that the sects of the Reformation were psychologically lacking in love towards those who did not belong to their sect. Some of you probably have had similar experiences with sectarian or quasi-sectarian groups today. What is most lacking in them is not theological insight, not even insight into their own negatives, but love, that love which identifies with the negative situation in which we all are.

A final difference had to do with eschatology. The eschatology of the Reformers caused them to negate the revolutionary criticism of the state that we find in the sectarian movements. The Reformation eschatology of the coming kingdom of God moved along a

vertical line, and had nothing to do with the horizontal line, which
was, so to speak, given to the devil anyway. Luther often spoke
of the beloved last day for which he longed in order to be liberated, not so much from the "wrath of the theologians" as with
Melanchthon, but from the power play which was no nicer then
than it is now. This difference in mood is visible in a comparison
of the state of things in Europe and America. Under the influence
of the evangelical radical movements the tendency in America is
to transform reality. In Europe, especially after two World Wars,
there is an eschatological feeling—the desire for and vision of the
end in a realistic sense—and a resignation of Christians in the face
of power plays.

5. *Luther's Doctrines*

(a) The Biblical Principle

Whenever you see a monument of Luther, he is represented
with the Bible in hand. This is somewhat misleading, and the
Catholic Church is right in saying that there was biblicism
throughout the Middle Ages. We have stressed before that the
biblicistic attitude was especially strong in the late Middle Ages.
We saw that in Ockham, the nominalist, a radical criticism of the
church was made on the basis of the Bible. Nevertheless, the
biblical principle means something else in Luther. In nominalistic
theology the Bible was the law of the church which could be
turned against the actual church; but it was still law. In the Renaissance the Bible is the source-book of the true religion, to be edited
by good philologists such as Erasmus. These were the two prevailing attitudes: the legal attitude in nominalism, the doctrinal
attitude in humanism. Neither of these was able to break through
the fundamentals of the Catholic system. Only a new principle of
biblical interpretation could break through the nominalistic and
humanistic doctrines.

Luther had many of the nominalistic and humanistic elements
within himself. He valued very highly Erasmus' edition of the
New Testament, and he often fell back on a nominalistic legalism
in his doctrine of inspiration whereby every word of the Bible
has been inspired by the dictation of God. This happened in his
defense of the doctrines of the Lord's Supper, when a literal
interpretation of a biblical passage seemed to support his point

of view. But beyond all this Luther had an interpretation of Scripture in unity with his new understanding of man's relationship to God. This can be made clear if we understand what he meant by the "Word of God". This term is used more often than any other in the Lutheran tradition and in the Neo-Reformation theology of Barth and others. Yet it is more misleading than we can perhaps realize. In Luther himself it has at least six different meanings.

Luther said—but he knew better—that the Bible is the Word of God. However, when he really wanted to express what he meant, he said that *in* the Bible there is the Word of God, the message of the Christ, his work of atonement, the forgiveness of sins, and the offer of salvation. He makes it very clear that it is the message of the gospel which is in the Bible, and thus the Bible contains the Word of God. He also said that the message existed before the Bible, namely, in the preaching of the apostles. As Calvin also later said, Luther stated that the writing which resulted in the books of the Bible was an emergency situation; it was necessary and it was an emergency. Therefore, only the religious content is important; the message is an object of experience. "If I know what I believe, I know the content of the Scripture, since the Scripture does not contain anything except Christ." The criterion of apostolic truth is the Scripture, and the standard of what things are true in the Scripture is whether they deal with Christ and his work—*ob sie Christum treiben*, whether they deal with, concentrate on, or drive toward Christ. Only those books of the Bible which deal with Christ and his work contain powerfully and spiritually the Word of God.

From this point of view Luther was able to make some distinctions among the books of the Bible. The books which deal with Christ most centrally are the Fourth Gospel, the Epistles of Paul, and I Peter. Luther could say very courageous things. For instance, he said that Judas and Pilate would be apostolic if they gave the message of Christ, and Paul and John would not be if they did not give the message of Christ. He even said that anyone today who had the Spirit as powerfully as the prophets and apostles could create new Decalogues and another Testament. We must drink from their fountain only because we do not have the fullness of the Spirit. This is, of course, extremely anti-nominalistic and anti-humanistic. It emphasizes the spiritual character of the Bible. The

Bible is a creation of the divine Spirit in those who have written it, but it is not a dictation. On this basis Luther was able to proceed with a half-religious, half-historical criticism of the biblical books. It does not mean anything whether the five books of Moses were written by Moses or not. He knew very well that the texts of the prophets are in great disorder. He also knew that the concrete prophecies of the prophets often proved to be in error. The Book of Esther and the Revelation of John do not really belong to the Scriptures. The Fourth Gospel excels the Synoptics in value and power, and the Epistle of James has no evangelical character at all.

Although Lutheran Orthodoxy was unable to preserve this great prophetic aspect of Luther, one thing was accomplished by Luther's freedom; it was possible for Protestantism to do something which no other religion in the whole world has been able to do, and that is to accept the historical treatment of the biblical literature. This is often referred to by such misleading terms as higher criticism or biblical criticism. It is simply the historical method applied to the holy books of a religion. This is something which is impossible in Catholicism, or at least possible in a very limited way only. It is impossible in Islam. Professor Jeffery once told the faculty that every Islamic scholar who would try to do what he did with the text of the Koran would be in danger. Research into the original text of the Koran would imply historical criticism of the present text, and this is impossible in a legalistic religion. Thus, if we are legalists with respect to the Bible, in terms of the dictation theory, we fall back to the stage of religion which we find in Islam, and we share none of the Protestant freedom that we find in Luther.

Luther was able to interpret the ordinary text of the Bible in his sermons and writings without taking refuge in a special pneumatic, spiritual, or allegorical interpretation alongside of the philological interpretation. The ideal of a theological seminary is to interpret the Bible in such a way that the exact philological method, including higher criticism, is combined with an existential application of the biblical texts to the questions we have to ask, and which are supposed to be answered in systematic theology. The division of the faculty into "experts" is a very unwholesome state of affairs, where the New Testament man tells me that I cannot discuss a certain problem because I am not an expert, or I say that I cannot discuss a matter because I am not an expert in Old or New Testament. Insofar as we all do this, we are sinning against the original meaning of Luther's attempt to remove the allegorical method of interpretation and to return to a philological approach which is at the same time spiritual. These are very real problems today, and students can do a great deal about them by refusing to let their professors be merely "experts" and no longer theologians. They should ask the biblical man about the existential meaning of what he finds, and the systematic theologian about the biblical foundation of his statements, in the actual biblical texts as they are philologically understood.

(b) Sin and Faith

I want to emphasize Luther's doctrines of sin and faith very much because they are points in which the Reformation is far superior to what we find today in popular Christianity. For Luther sin is unbelief. "Unbelief is the real sin." "Nothing justifies except faith, and nothing makes sinful except unbelief." "Unbelief is the sin altogether." "The main justice is faith, and so the main evil is unbelief." "Therefore the word 'sin' includes what we are living and doing besides the faith in God." These statements presuppose a concept of faith which has nothing whatsoever to do with the acceptance of doctrines. With respect to the concept of sin, they mean that differences of quantity (heavy and light sins) and of relativity (sins which can be forgiven in this or that way) do not matter at all. Everything which separates us from God has equal weight; there is no "more or less" about it.

For Luther, life as a whole, its nature and substance, is corrupted. Here we must comment on the term "total depravity" which we often hear. This does not mean that there is nothing good in man; no Reformer or Neo-Reformation theologian ever said that. It means that there are no special parts of man which are exempt from existential distortion. The concept of total depravity would be translated by a modern psychologist in the sense that man is distorted, or in conflict with himself, in the center of his personal life. Everything in man is included in this distortion, and this is what Luther meant. If "total depravity" is taken in the absurd way, it would be impossible for a man to say that he is totally depraved. A totally depraved man would not say that he is totally depraved. Even saying that we are sinful presupposes something beyond sin. What we can say is that there is no section in man which is not touched by self-contradiction; this includes the intellect and all other things. The evil are evil because they do not fulfill the one command to love God. It is the lack of love toward God which is the basis of sin. Or, it is the lack of faith. Luther said both things. But faith always precedes love because it is an act in which we receive God, and love is the act in which we are united with God. Everybody is in this situation of sin, and nobody knew more than Luther about the structural power of evil in individuals and in groups. He did not call it compulsion, as we do today in terms of modern psychology. But he knew that this is what it was, a demonic power, the power of Satan, which is greater than individual decisions. These structures of the demonic are realities; Luther knew that sin cannot be understood merely in terms of particular acts of freedom. Sin must be understood in terms of a structure, a demonic structure which has compulsory power over everyone, and which can be counterbalanced only by a structure of grace. We are all involved in the conflict between these two structures. Sometimes we are ridden, as Luther described it, by the divine compulsion, sometimes by the demonic. However, the divine structure of grace is not possession or compulsion, because it is at the same time liberating; it liberates what we essentially are.

Luther's strong emphasis on the demonic powers comes out in his doctrine of the devil, whom he understood as an organ of the divine wrath or as the divine wrath itself. There are statements in Luther which are not clear as to whether he is speaking of the wrath of God or of the devil. Actually, they are the same for him. As we see God, so he is for us. If we see him in the demonic mask, then he is that to us, and he destroys us. If we see him in the infant Jesus, where in his lowliness he makes his love visible to us, then he has this love to us. Luther was a depth psychologist in the profoundest way, without knowing the methodological research we know today. Luther saw these things in non-moralistic depths, which were lost not only in Calvinist Christianity but to a great extent in Lutheranism as well.

Faith for Luther is receiving God when he gives himself to us. He distinguished this type of faith from historical faith (*fides historica*), which acknowledges historical facts. Faith is the acceptance of the gift of God, the presence of the grace of God which

grasps us. The emphasis is on the receptive character of faith—
nihil facere sed tantum recipere, doing nothing but only receiving.
These ideas are all concentrated in the acceptance of being
accepted, in the forgiveness of sins, which brings about a quiet
conscience and a spiritual vitality toward God and man. "Faith
is a living and restless thing. The right living faith can by no means
be lazy." The element of knowledge in faith is an existential
element, and everything else follows from it. "Faith makes the
person; the person makes the works, not works the person." This
is confirmed by everything we know today in depth psychology.
It is the ultimate meaning of life which makes a person. A split
personality is not one which does not do good works. There are
many people who do many good works, but who lack the ultimate
center. This ultimate center is what Luther calls faith. And this
makes a person. This faith is not an acceptance of doctrines, not
even Christian doctrines, but the acceptance of the power itself
out of which we come and to which we go, whatever the doctrines
may be through which we accept it. In my book, *The Courage to
Be*, I have called this "absolute faith", a faith which can lose every
concrete content and still exist as an absolute affirmation of life
as life and of being as being. Thus, the only negative thing is what
Luther calls unbelief, a state of not being united with the power
of being itself, with the divine reality over against the forces of
separation and compulsion.

(c) The Idea of God

Luther's idea of God is one of the most powerful in the whole
history of human and Christian thought. This is not a God who
is a being beside others; it is a God whom we can have only
through contrast. What is hidden before God is visible before
the world, and what is hidden before the world is visible before
God. "Which are the virtues (i.e., powers of being) of God?
Infirmity, passion, cross, persecution: these are the weapons of
God." "The power of man is emptied by the cross, but in the
weakness of the cross the divine power is present." About the state
of man Luther says: "Being man means non-being, becoming,
being. It means being in privation, in possibility, in action. It
means always being in sin, in justification, in justice. It means
always being a sinner, a penitent, a just one." This is a paradoxical
way of speaking, but it makes clear what Luther means with

respect to God. God can be seen only through the law of contrast. Luther denies everything which can make God finite, or a being beside others. "Nothing is so small, God is even smaller. Nothing is so large, God is even larger. He is an unspeakable being, above and outside everything we can name and think. Who knows what that is, which is called 'God'? It is beyond body, beyond spirit, beyond everything we can say, hear, and think." He makes the great statement that God is nearer to all creatures than they are to themselves. "God has found the way that his own divine essence can be completely in all creatures, and in everyone especially, deeper, more internally, more present, than the creature is to itself and at the same time nowhere and cannot be comprehended by anyone, so that he embraces all things and is within them. God is at the same time in every piece of sand totally, and nevertheless in all, above all, and out of all creatures." In these formulae the old conflict between the theistic and pantheistic tendencies in the doctrine of God is solved; they show the greatness of God, the inescapability of his presence, and at the same time, his absolute transcendence. And I would say very dogmatically that any doctrine of God which leaves out one of these elements does not really speak of God but of something less than God.

The same thing is expressed in Luther's doctrine of omnipotence. "I call the omnipotence of God not that power by which he does not do many things he could do, but the actual power by which he potently does everything in everything." That is to say, God does not sit beside the world, looking at it from the outside, but he is acting in everything in every moment. This is what omnipotence means. The absurd idea of a God who calculates whether he should do what he could do is removed by this idea of God as creative power.

Luther speaks of creatures as the "masks" of God; God is hidden behind them. "All creatures are God's masks and veils in order to make them work and help him to create many things." Thus, all natural orders and institutions are filled with divine presence, and so is the historical process. In this way he deals with all our problems of the interpretation of history. The great men in history, the Hannibals, Alexanders, Napoleons—and today he would add, the Hitlers—or, the Goths, the Vandals, the Turks—and today he would add, the Nazis and the Communists—are driven by God to attack and to destroy, and in this way God is speaking to us through them. They are God's Word to us, even to the church. The heroic persons in particular break through the ordinary rules of life. They are armed by God. God calls and forces them, and gives them their hour, and I would say, their *kairos*. Outside of this *kairos* they cannot do anything; nobody can apart from the right hour. And in the right hour no one can resist those who then act. However, in spite of the fact that God acts in everything in history, history is nonetheless the struggle between God and Satan and their different realms. The reason Luther could make these two statements is that God works creatively even in the demonic forces. They could not have being if they were not dependent on God as the ground of being, as the creative power of being in them, in every moment. He makes it possible that Satan is the seducer; at the same time he makes it possible that Satan is conquered.

(d) The Doctrine of Christ

What is interesting in Luther's christology is first of all his method, which is quite different from that of the ancient church. I would call it a real method of correlation; it correlates what Christ is for us with what we say about him. It is an approach from the point of view of the effects Christ has upon us. Melanchthon expressed the same idea in his *Loci*. He says that the object of christology is to deal with the benefits of Christ, not with his person and natures apart from his benefits. In describing this method of correlation Luther says: "As somebody is in himself, so is God to him, as object. If a man is righteous himself, God is righteous. If a man is pure, God is pure for him. If he is evil, God is evil for him. Therefore, he will appear to the damned as the evil in eternity, but to the righteous as the righteous, according to what he is in himself." This is a correlative way of speaking about God. For Luther, calling Christ God means having experienced divine effects which come from Christ, especially the forgiveness of sins. If you speak about God apart from his effects, this is a wrong objectifying method. You must speak of him in terms of the effects he can have. The One whose effects are divine must himself be divine—this is the criterion.

What we say about God always has the character of participation—suffering with him, being glorified with him; crucified with him, being resurrected with him. "Preaching the Crucified means preaching our guilt and the crucifixion of our evils." "So we go with him: first servant, therefore now King; first suffering, therefore now in glory; first judged, therefore now Judge. . . . So you must act: first humiliation, in order to get exaltation." "Together condemned and blessed, living and dead, in pain and in joy." This is said of Christ and of us. The law of contradiction, the law of God always acting paradoxically, is fulfilled in Christ. He is the key to God's acting by contradicting the human system of valuation. This paradox is also valid in the church. In its visible form the church is miserable and humble, but in this humility, as in the humility of Christ, there is the glory of the church. Therefore, the glory of the church is especially visible in periods of persecution, suffering, and humility.

Christ is God for us, our God, God as he is in relationship to us. Luther also says that he is the Word of God. From this point of view Protestantism should think through its christology in existential terms, maintaining the immediate correlation of human faith and what is said about Christ. All the formulae concerning his divine and human natures, or his being the Son of God and Son of Man, make sense only if they are existentially understood.

Luther emphasizes very much the presence of God in Christ. In the incarnation the divine Word or Logos has become flesh. Luther's doctrine of the Word has different stages. First, there is the internal Word, which he also calls the heart of God, or the eternal Son. Only this internal Word, which is God's inner self-manifestation, is perfect. As the heart of man is hidden, so the heart of God is hidden. The internal Word of God, his inner self-manifestation, is hidden to man. But Luther says: "We hope that in the future we shall look to this Word, when God has opened his heart . . . by introducing us into his heart." The second meaning of the Word in Luther is Christ as the visible Word. In Christ the heart of God has become flesh, that is, historical reality. In this way we can have the hidden Word of the divine knowledge of himself, although only for faith, and never as an object among other objects. Thirdly, the Word of God is the spoken Word, by prophets, by Jesus, and the apostles. Thus, it becomes the biblical Word in which the internal Word is spoken forth. However, the revealing being of the eternal Word in Christ is more than all the spoken words of the Bible. They witness to him, but they are the Word of God only in an indirect way. Luther was never so bibliolatrous as so many Christians still are today. Word for Luther was the self-manifestation of God, and this was by no means limited to the words of the Bible. The Word of God is in, with, and under the words of the Bible, but not identical with them. The fourth meaning of the Word of God is the word of preaching, but this is only number four. If somebody speaks of the "church of the Word", whereby he is thinking of the predominance of preaching in the services, he is certainly not being a follower of Luther in this respect.

The special character of Luther's doctrine of the incarnation is the continual emphasis on the smallness of God in the incarnation. Man cannot stand the naked Absolute—God; he is driven to despair if he deals with the Absolute directly. For this reason God has given the Christ, in whom he has made himself small. "In the other works, God is recognized according to the greatness of his power, wisdom, and justice, and his works appear too terrible. But here (in Christ) appears his sweetness, mercy and charity." Without knowing Christ we are not able to stand God's majesty and are driven to insanity and hatred. This is the reason for Luther's great interest in Christmas; he wrote some of the most beautiful Christmas hymns and poems. He liked Christmas because he emphasized the small God in Christ, and Christ is the smallest in the cradle. This paradox was for Luther the real meaning of Christmas, that the One who is in the cradle is at the same time the Almighty God. The smallest and most helpless of all beings has within himself the center of divinity. This is Luther's way of thinking of the paradoxical nature of God's self-revelation. Because God acts paradoxically the weakest is the strongest.

(e) Church and State

Anyone who knows the Reformation must ask whether it is possible for a church to live on the basis of the principles of the Reformation. Does not the church have to be a community, organized and authoritarian, with fixed rules and traditions? Is not a church necessarily Catholic, and does not the Protestant principle contradict the possibility of having a church, namely, the principle that God alone is everything and man's acceptance of God is only secondary?

Now, there is no doubt that Luther's doctrine of the church is his weakest point. The problem of the church was the most unsolved problem which the Reformation left to future generations. The reason is that the Catholic system was not replaced and could not be replaced definitively by a Protestant system of equal power, because of the anti-authoritarian and anti-hierarchical form of Protestant thinking. Luther, together with Zwingli and Calvin, chose the ecclesiastical type of church in contrast to the sectarian type of the evangelical radicals. This is a distinction which comes from Ernst Troeltsch, and a very good one. The ecclesiastical type of church is the mother from which we come. It is always there and we belong to it from birth; we did not choose it. When we awaken out of the dimness of the early stages of life, we can perhaps reaffirm that we belong to it in confirmation, but we already belong to it objectively. This is quite different from the churches of the radical enthusiasts, where the individual who decides that he wants to be a member of the church is the creative power of the church. The church is made by a covenant through the decision of individuals to form a church, an assembly of God. Everything here is dependent on the independent individual, who is not born from the mother church, but who creates active church communities. These differences are most noticeable if you contrast the ecclesiastical type of church on the European continent with the sectarian type in America, which is even expressed in the main denominations here.

Luther's distinction between the visible and the invisible church is one of the most difficult things to understand. The main point we must insist on in understanding what Luther means is that they are the same church, not two churches. The invisible church is the spiritual quality of the visible church. And the visible church is the empirical and always distorted actualization of the spiritual church. This was perhaps the most important point of the Reformers against the sects. The sects wanted to identify the church according to its visible and its invisible sides. The visible church must be purified and purged—as all totalitarian groups call it today—of anyone who is not spiritually a member of the church. This presupposes that we can know who is spiritually a member of the church, that we can judge by looking into the heart. But this is something only God can do. The Reformers could not accept this because they knew there is nobody who does not belong to the "infirmary" which is the church. This infirmary is the visible church and is for everyone; nobody can get out of it definitely. Therefore, everybody belongs to the church essentially, even if he is spiritually far away from it.

What is this church? The church in its true essence is an object of faith. As Luther said, it is "hidden in spirit". When you see the actual working of the church, its ministers, the building, the congregation, the administration, the devotions etc., then you know that in this visible church, with all its shortcomings, the invisible church is hidden. It is an object of faith and it demands much faith to believe that in the life of ordinary congregations today, which are by no means of high standing in any respect, the spiritual church is present. This you can believe only if you believe that it is not the people who make the church, but it is the foundation—not the people but the sacramental reality—the Word, which is the Christ. Otherwise we would despair about the church. For Luther and the Reformers the church in its true nature is a spiritual matter. The words "spiritual" and "invisible" usually mean the same thing in Luther. The basis of faith in the church is exclusively the foundation of the church, who is Christ, the sacrament of the Word.

Every Christian is a priest, and thus has potentially the office of preaching the Word and administering the sacraments. They all belong to the spiritual element. For the sake of order, however, some specially fit personalities shall be called by the congregation to fill the offices of the church. The ministry is a matter of order. It is a vocation like all other vocations; it does not involve any state of perfection, superior graces, or anything like that. The layman is as much a priest as any priest. The official priest is the "mouthpiece" of the others, because they cannot express themselves, and he can. Thus, only one thing makes the minister, and that is the call of the congregation. Ordination has no sacramental meaning at all. "Ordaining is not consecrating", he says. "We give in the power of the Word what we have, the authority of preaching the Word and giving the sacraments; that is ordaining." But this does not produce a higher grade in the relationship to God.

In the Lutheran countries the church government very soon became identical with the state government, and in the Calvinist countries with the civil government (trustees). The reason for this is that the hierarchy was removed by Luther. There is no

pope, no bishops, no priests any more in the technical sense. Who
then shall govern the church? First of all the ministers, but they
are not adequate since they have no power. The power comes
from the princes, or from free associations within society, as we
have very often in Calvinism. The princes were called by Luther
the highest bishops of their realms. They are not to interfere with
the inner religious affairs of the church; but they have to run
the administration—the *ius circa sacrum*, the law around the
sacred. The ministers and every Christian are to take care of the
sacred matters.

Such a solution was brought about by an emergency situation.
There were no bishops or ecclesiastical authorities any more, and
the church needed administration and government. So emergency
bishops were created, and there was nobody else who could be
this except the electors and princes. Out of this emergency situation there began to emerge the state church in Germany. The
church became more or less—and I think rather "more" than
"less"—a department of the state administration, and the princes
became the arbiters of the church. This was not intended, but it
shows that a church needs a political backbone. In Catholicism
it was the pope and the hierarchy; in Protestantism it had to
be the outstanding members of the community who take over,
either the princes or social groups, as in more democratic countries.

Luther's doctrine of the state is not easy to deal with because
many people believe that Luther's interpretation of the state is the
real cause of Nazism. Now, first of all, a few hundred years mean
something in history, and Luther is a little bit older than the
Nazis! But this is not the decisive point. The decisive point is that
the doctrine of the state was a positivistic doctrine; providence
was positivistically understood. Positivism means that things are
taken as they are. The positive law is decisive, and this is connected by Luther with the doctrine of providence. Providence
brings this and that power into existence, and therefore it is
impossible to revolt against these powers. You have no rational
criterion by which to judge the princes. Of course, you have
the right to judge them from the point of view whether they
are good Christians or not. But whether they are or not, they
are God-given, and so you have to be obedient to them. Historical destiny has brought the tyrants, the Neros and Hitlers.

Since this is historical destiny, we have to subject ourselves to it.

This means that the Stoic doctrine of natural law, which can be used as a criticism of the positive law, has disappeared. There remains only the positive law. The natural law does not really exist for Luther. The Stoic doctrine of the equality and the freedom of the citizen in the state is not used by Luther at all. So he is non-revolutionary, theoretically as well as practically. Practically, he says, every Christian must put up with bad government because it comes from God providentially. The state for Luther is not a reality in itself. It is always misleading to speak of the Reformers' theory of state. The word "state" is not older than the seventeenth or eighteenth century. Instead of that they had the concept of *Obrigkeit*, of authority, superiors. The government is the authority, not the structure called the "state". This means there is no democratic implication in Luther's doctrine of the state. The situation is such that the state must be accepted as it is.

How could Luther maintain this? How could he accept the despotic power of the states of his time inasmuch as he, more than anyone else, emphasized love as the ultimate principle of morality? He had an answer to this, and this answer is very much full of spirit. He says that God does two kinds of work. The one is his own proper work; this is the work of love and mercy, the giving of grace. The other is his strange work; it is also the work of love, but a strange one. It works through punishment, threat, the compulsory power of the state, through all kinds of harshness, as the law demands. People who say this is against love ask the question: How can compulsory power and love be united with each other? And they derive from this a kind of anarchism which we so often find in the ideas of Christian pacifists and others. The situation formulated by Luther seems to me the true one. I believe he saw more profoundly than anybody I know, the possibility of uniting the elements of power and love in terms of this doctrine of God's "strange" and "proper" works. The power of the state, which makes it possible for us even to be here or for works of charity to be done at all, is a work of God's love. The state has to suppress the aggression of the evil man, of those who are against love; the strange work of love is to destroy what is against love. It is correct to call this a strange work, but it is nevertheless a work of love. Love would cease to be a power on earth altogether without destroying that which is against love. This is the deepest insight into the relationship between power and love that I know. The whole positivistic doctrine of the state makes it impossible for Lutheranism, from a theological point of view, to accept revolution. Revolution results in chaos; even if it tries to produce order, it first produces chaos and disorder increases. Thus, Luther was unambiguously against revolution. He accepted the positively given gift of destiny.

Nazism was possible in Germany because of this positivistic authoritarianism, because of Luther's affirmation that the given prince cannot be removed. This provided a great inhibition against any German revolution. But I do not believe that this would have been possible anyway in the modern totalitarian systems. But the negation of any revolution did serve as an additional spiritual cause. When we say that Luther is responsible for the Nazis, we are uttering a lot of nonsense. The ideology of the Nazis is almost the opposite of Luther's. Luther had no nationalistic ideology, no tribal or racial ideology. He praised the Turks for their good government. From this point of view there is no Nazism in Luther. There is a connection only from the point of view of the conservatism of Luther's political thinking. But this is nothing else than a consequence of his basic presupposition. The only truth in the theory which connects Luther with Nazism is that Luther broke the back of the revolutionary will in the Germans. There is no such thing as a revolutionary will in the German people; that is all we can say and nothing more.

It is equally nonsensical for people to say that it was first Luther and then Hegel who produced Nazism. It is nonsense, because even if Hegel said that the state is God on earth, he did not mean the power state. He meant the cultural unity of religion and social life organized in a state. In this sense Hegel could say there is a unity of church and state. But for him "state" is not the party movement of the Nazis, or a relapse to a tribal system. State for him is organized society, repressing sin.

B. HULDREICH ZWINGLI

Zwingli was not as original a theologian as Luther was. He was partly dependent and partly independent of Luther. It is not easy to describe the character of Zwinglian Christianity. Zwingli was very much influenced by the humanists. He remained his whole life a friend of Erasmus. Neither he nor Melanchthon separated themselves from Erasmus as Luther did. They were humanists as well as being Christians. They were Christian humanists. This is especially clear in a man like Zwingli. The authority of the Scriptures in Zwingli is based on the call of the Renaissance: Back to the sources! The Bible is the revelation of God. "God himself wants to be the schoolmaster." Luther could never have said such a thing. For Luther God is much more powerful than a schoolmaster. The decisive difference is that Zwingli had a fully developed doctrine of the Spirit, which was lacking in Luther and the other Reformers. "God can give truth, through the Spirit, in non-Christians also." The truth is given to every individual always through the Holy Spirit, and this Spirit is present even if the word of the Bible is not present. This was in some sense a liberation from the biblical burden which Luther placed upon the people.

Luther had a dynamic form of Christian life. Zwingli, and Calvin too, had a static one; faith is psychological health. If you are psychologically healthy, then you can have faith, and vice versa. Actually, these two things are identical. Faith for Luther is a dynamic thing, reaching heights and depths. For Zwingli it is much more humanistically balanced. It is similar to the bourgeois ideal of health. "Christian faith is a thing which is felt in the soul of the faithful like health in the body." In Luther there is a continual dying and rising of the community with the personal God of wrath and love. In Zwingli the union with God is not dynamic in this way. Zwingli is progressive; Luther is paradoxical. It is difficult to speak of the paradox on Zwinglian soil. Either the paradox is dissolved or it has to be accepted as such. The basic difference, then, between Zwingli and Luther is this: The paradox of the Christian life against the rational progressivism of the Christian life.

The Swiss Reformation is a synthesis of Reformation and humanism. Calvin, whom we shall deal with later, was dependent on both Zwingli and Luther, but in spite of the fact that he turned from Zwingli back to Luther, to a certain extent, he was also humanistically educated and his writings show the classical erudition in style and content. However, whenever liberal theology arose from the seventeenth through the nineteenth centuries, it developed more in line with Zwingli than with Calvin. I have already stated that Zwingli believed that the Spirit is working directly in the human soul, that his ordinary way of working is through the Word of the Bible, but that God can also work in an extraordinary way in people who have never had any contact with the Christian message, with people in other religions and in humanists. Zwingli's examples are taken mostly from the Greek philosophers, such as Socrates, etc.

Yesterday I read a hymn to be sung by a congregation of Southern Negroes or Midwestern peasants which included Socrates in it, besides Christ and Luther. I do not think it wise to bring theology into a hymn in this way. If people like Zwingli and Calvin speak of revelation and salvation in men like Socrates and Seneca, they are making a mistake. The mistake is that they choose only certain representatives of pagan piety. However, pagan piety is exactly the same as Christian piety in this respect that it is just as intensive in the common people who are really pious in their knowledge of God, and people in this class should have been mentioned just as much. But since they were good humanists, they mentioned only their own sociological class, people who were not only great men but who also belonged to the intelligentsia. If you are ministers, it is better to decide not to incorporate such things into a hymn. Although I have given you as much Socrates and Plato as I can, nevertheless, I do not sing to them.

Zwingli defines God as the universal dynamic power of being in everything that is. In this sense you can recognize some of my own theological thinking in Zwingli and Calvin, but also in Luther. However, in the humanistic form in which Zwingli conceived of God, it has a much more rational deterministic character. God works through the natural law. Thus, Zwingli's doctrine of predestination is colored by a rational determinism. The same thing is true of Calvin's doctrine, whereas in Luther there is more of Ockhamism and Scotism, and therefore a sense of the irrational acting of God in every moment, which cannot be subjected to any law.

The law plays a different role in the Lutheran and Zwinglian Reformation. In Zwingli it is not the law which makes us sinful, but the law shows that we are sinful, whereas Luther had the profound insight that we have rediscovered in modern psychology that the law produces resistance, and thus, as Paul said, it makes sin more sinful. This was lacking in both Zwinglian and Calvinistic thinking. The concept of law in them has a very positive connotation. This refers generally to natural law. And natural law means in ancient literature primarily the law of reason, the logical, ethical, and juristic law. Secondly, it is also the physical law. We should not think of physics when we read about natural law in books of antiquity. Usually it means the ethical law within us, which belongs to our being and is restated by the Decalogue and the Sermon on the Mount. It exists by nature, by created nature, and is that which we are essentially. This kind of law is much more in the minds of Zwingli and Calvin than in Luther's. Luther detested the idea that God has established a law between himself and his world, between himself and the finite actions and things and decisions. He wanted everything as nonrational, nonlegal, as possible, not only in the process of salvation but also in the interpretation of history and nature. Zwingli and Calvin accepted nature in terms of law. Thus, when Immanuel Kant defined nature as a realm in which physical law is valid, this was much more Calvinistic and Zwinglian; in any case, it was not Lutheran. For Luther nature is the mask of God through which he acts with mankind in an irrational way—very similarly to the Book of Job. The attitude towards nature in Zwinglianism and Calvinism is much more in accordance with the demands of bourgeois industrialized society to analyze and transform nature for human purposes, while Luther's relationship to nature has much more the sense of the presence of the divine, irrationally, mystically, in everything that is. If I had not known this before, I would have learned it when I came to America.

For Zwingli the law of the gospel is law. It is not only this, of course, since he does accept Luther's doctrine of the forgiveness of sins, as did all the Reformers. At the same time he spoke, however, of a new evangelical law, as the nominalists and humanists did. This law should be the basis of the law of the state. Wyclif and Ockham had the same idea; this shows that at this point there is a Catholic element in Reformed thought, namely, the idea that the gospel can be interpreted as the new law. The term, "the new law", is a very old one, appearing very early in church history. For Luther this would have been an abominable term. The gospel for Luther is grace, and nothing more than grace; it can never be the new law. But for Zwingli this new law is valid not only for the moral situation but also for the state, the political sphere. Politically the law of the gospel determines the laws of the city. If cities do not subject themselves to this law, they may be attacked by other cities which do. This law, Zwingli thought, is against Catholicism, so he started the war against the cantons in Switzerland and died in one of the battles. But the principle remained that the law of the gospel should be the basis of the law of the state. This had a tremendous influence in world history and saved Protestantism from being overwhelmed politically by the Roman Church of the Counter-Reformation.

A deeper element of difference between Luther and Zwingli has to do with the doctrine of the sacraments. The fight between Luther and Zwingli in Marburg in 1529 contrasted two types of religious experience, the one a mystical interpretation of the sacrament, the other an intellectual interpretation. Zwingli said that the sacrament is a "sure sign or seal" which like a symbol serves as a reminder; by partaking of it we express our will to belong to the church. The divine Spirit acts beside the sacraments, not through them. Baptism is a kind of obliging sign, like a badge. It is a commanded symbol, but it has nothing to do with subjective faith and salvation, which are dependent on predestination.

In the controversy on the doctrine of the eucharist, the point at issue was on the surface a matter of translation, but in reality it was a question of a different spirit. The discussion centered on the meaning of the word "is" in the statement: "This is my body." The humanists usually interpret "is" to mean "signifies" or "means". Luther stressed that it must be taken literally; the body of Christ is literally present. For Zwingli it is present for the contemplation of faith, but not *per essentiam et realiter* (by essence and in reality). "The body of Christ is eaten when we believe that he is killed for us." Everything is centered on the subjective side. It is the representation of a past event, not in itself a present event. The present event is merely in the subject, in the mind of the believer. He is certainly with his Spirit present in the mind, but he is not present in nature. Mind can be fed only by mind, or spirit by spirit, and not by nature.

Zwingli maintained against Luther that the body of Christ is in heaven *circumscripte* (by circumscription), that is, in a definite place. Hence, the body of Christ is a particular individual thing; it does not participate in the divine infinity. Just like a man with a body, Christ is finite, and the two natures are sharply separated. The Lord's Supper is a memory and a confession, but not a personal communion with someone who is really present. Luther's emphasis is on the reality of the presence, and to underscore this he invented the doctrines of the omnipresence of the body of the elevated Christ. The presence of Christ is repeated in every act of the sacrament of the Lord's Supper. Historical person and sacramental person are identical. To explain this Luther said: "Where you put God, there you must put humanity; they cannot be severed or separated; it has become one person." To say that the divine character of the bodily Christ is only said in symbolic or metaphoric terms is of the devil. Luther completely rejected the idea that the divinity of Christ is separated from his humanity in heaven. Even in heaven the divinity and the humanity of Christ belong together. He expressed this in the profound and fantastic doctrine of the ubiquity of the body of Christ, the omnipresence of the body of the ascended Christ. Christ is present in everything, in stone and fire and tree, but for us he is present only when he speaks to us. But he can speak to us through everything. This is the idea that God drives toward embodiment or corporeity, and that the omnipresence of Christ's body in the world is the form in which God's eternal power is present in the world. If this is carried through in scholastic terms, and taken literally or superstitiously, it is an absurd doctrine, because it belongs to a body to be circumscribed. But if it is taken symbolically, it becomes a profound doctrine, because it says that God is present in anything on earth. He is always also present with his concrete historical manifestation in Christ. Luther meant this quite primitively, but his meaning is that in every natural object you can have the presence of Christ. In a Lutheran service during the Sundays in spring, you always find a tremendous amount of flowers and things of nature brought into the church, because of this symbol of the participation of the body of Christ in the world.

When the discussion on the Lord's Supper came to an end, the Reformers had reached agreement on many points. They denied the doctrine of transubstantiation; but they could not agree on the ubiquity of Christ's presence. Luther stated that there was a fundamental difference between Zwingli and himself when he said: "They have not the same spirit with us." What does this mean? First of all, it involves the matter of the relationship between the spiritual and the bodily existence. In Zwingli you have a humanistic intellectualism which separates the spirit from the body, a tendency which is ultimately rooted in Neo-Platonism. Hence, in Calvinism there is a lack of interest in the problem of expression. For Luther, on the other hand, spirit is present only in its expressions. The interest is incorporation. Oetinger, the mystic, said: "Corporeality is the end of the ways of God." Hence, there followed a great interest in the bodily reality of Christ, in history and in sacrament. The second spiritual difference has to do with the religious meaning of nature. In Zwinglian thought nature is controlled and calculable in terms of regular natural laws. By contrast Luther's dynamic naturalism often goes into the demonic depths of nature, and is not interested in any laws of nature.

Two Latin phrases were used to express the difference. The Lutheran formula is *finitum capax infiniti*—the finite is capable of the infinite. For Zwingli this is impossible. The Reformed formula is *finitum non capax infiniti*—the finite is not able to have the infinite within itself. This is a fundamental difference which shows up first in christology, then is extended to the whole sacramental life and the relationship to nature.

It is perhaps well to say that in the Swiss Reformation the sociological background was codeterminative of the particular form in which these discussions took place. In Germany we have the form of surviving aristocracy. In Switzerland we have the large towns like Zürich and Geneva which were centers of trade and industry. Sociologically the Swiss Reformation drives in the direction of industrial society. In the Lutheran Reformation, especially in northern Germany, the pre-bourgeois situation is retained as much as possible. When you read Luther's *Small Catechism*, you will see evidences of a paternalistic culture of small farmers and some craftsmen in villages and small towns. If, in contrast to this, you read some of the writings of Zwingli and Calvin, you are with men who have a world-wide horizon, due to the trading that went on in the centers in which they lived.

C. John Calvin

1. *The Majesty of God*

Calvin's doctrine of God and man is the turning point of all his other doctrines. Some have said that the doctrine of predestination is the main point. This, however, is easily refuted by the fact that in the first edition of his *Institutes*, the doctrine of predestination was not even developed. Only in the later editions did it acquire a prominent place. It can also be refuted from more important angles.

The doctrine of God is always the most decisive thing in every theology. For Calvin the central doctrine of Christianity is the doctrine of the majesty of God. Calvin states more clearly than any of the other Reformers that God is known in an existential attitude. For him human misery and divine majesty are correlated. Only out of human misery can we understand the divine majesty, and only in the light of the divine majesty can we understand human misery. Calvin applied to God a word which Rudolf Otto rediscovered—*numen*, numinous. God is a *numen* for him; he is unapproachable, horrifying, and at the same time fascinating. He speaks of God in terms of "this sacred numinous nature". He is distinguished from all idols and from the gods of polytheism. God cannot be spoken of directly because of his radical transcendence. Calvin had a very interesting theory of Christian symbolism. The symbols are significations of God's incomprehensible essence. He said that the symbols have to be momentary, disappearing, and self-negating. They are not the matter itself. I think this self-negating is the decisive characteristic of every symbol with respect to God; if they are taken literally, they produce idols. It is Calvin who said this, and not the mystical theology of a Pseudo-Dionysius. Thus, when we speak of symbolism when referring to God, we can refer to one who is certainly beyond suspicion of being less than orthodox.

The truth of a symbol drives beyond itself. "The best contemplation of the divine being is when the mind is transported beyond itself with admiration." The doctrine of God can never be a matter of theoretical contemplation; it must always be a matter of existential participation. The famous statement of Karl Barth, derived from a biblical text (Ecclesiastes 5:2), that "God is in heaven, and you are on earth", is one that Calvin often made and explained. The heavenly "above" is not a place to which God is bound, but an expression of his religious transcendence. This leads to the central attitude in Calvinism of fear of idolatry. Calvin fought against idols wherever he believed he saw them. For this reason he had no interest in the history of religion, which is practically condemned as a whole as being idolatrous. Religion cannot avoid having an element of idolatry in it. Religion is a factory of idols all the time. Therefore, the Christian and the theologian must be on their guard and prevent idolatrous trends from overwhelming their relationship to God.

Calvin fought against having pictures in the churches, and all kinds of things which can divert the mind from the wholly transcendent God. This is the reason for the sacred emptiness of the Calvinist church buildings. There is always a fear of idolatry in the depths of men who have overcome idolatry. So it was with the prophets, so it was with the Muslims, and so it was now with the Reformers. Calvinism is an iconoclastic movement, crushing idols, pictures of all kinds, because they deviate from God himself. This idea that the human mind is a "perpetual manufacturer of idols" is one of the most profound things which can be said about our thinking of God. Even orthodox theology is often nothing more than idolatry.

On the other side, the human situation is described in much more negative terms by Calvin than by Luther. "From our natural proneness to hypocrisy, any vain appearance of righteousness abundantly contents us instead of the reality", which is our sin. Man cannot stand his reality; he is unrealistic about himself. As we say in modern times, man is ideological about himself; he produces unreal imaginings about his being. This is a radical attack on the human situation, but it corresponds to God as the God of glory. When Calvin speaks of the God of love, it is usually in the context of the elect. Among them he reveals his love. Those who are not the elect are from the very beginning excluded from love. If this is true, then is it not also true that for Calvin God is the Creator of evil? This question has to be answered in connection with the doctrines of providence and predestination.

2. Providence and Predestination

Calvin was well aware that his way of thinking could easily lead to a half-deistic concept which places God alongside the world. Several hundred years before the deistic movement arose in England, Calvin warned against the deistic idea of God beside the world. Instead of this he conceived of a general operation of God in preserving and governing the world, so that all movement

depends on him. Deism is a carnal sense which wants to keep God
at a distance from us. If God is sitting on his throne without caring
about what is going on in the world, that leaves the world to us.
This is exactly what the Enlightenment and industrial society
needed. They could not tolerate a God who is continually involved
with the world. They had to have a God who gives the world its
initial movement, then sits beside it without disturbing the businessman in his affairs and the creators of industry. Against this
Calvin says: "Faith ought to penetrate further." God is the
world's perpetual preserver, "not by a certain universal action
actuating the whole machine of the world and all its respective
parts, but by a particular providence sustaining, nourishing, and
providing for everything which he has made." All this implies a
dynamic process of God within the laws he has given. He knew
that the doctrine of natural law could easily make God into something beside reality. Therefore, according to Calvin all things have
instrumental character; they are instruments through which God
works in every moment. If you want to call this pantheism, you
do not know what the word means. If you call it panentheism, that
could be all right, because this means that everything is in God.
Things are used as instruments of God's acting, according to his
pleasure. This is very close to Luther's idea. Calvin also has a
concept of omnipotence which is against the absurdity of imagin-
ing a highest God sitting somewhere and deliberating with himself what he should do, knowing that he could do many other
things or anything he wanted. This would be exactly like a woman
in the household who decides to do this or that. This is an unworthy view of God, and the Reformers knew it. "Not ... vain,
idle or almost asleep, but vigilant, efficacious, operative, and
engaged in continual action; not a mere general principle of confused motion, as if he should command a river to flow through
the channels once made for it, but a power constantly exerted on
every distant and particular movement. For he is accounted
omnipotent, not because he is able to act but does not act, and
sits down in idleness." Omnipotence is omniactivity. Providence
consists in continuous divine action.

This raised the problem with which Calvin was still wrestling on
his deathbed: If this is so, is God not the cause of evil? Calvin was
not afraid to say that natural evil is a natural consequence of the
distortion of nature. Secondly, he said it is a way to bring the elect

to God. But then he made a third assertion: It is a way to show the holiness of God, in the punishment of those whom he has selected for damnation and in the salvation of those who are elected. This says that God has produced evil men in order to punish them and in order to save others who are evil from their evil nature. This exclusively theocentric view which centers everything around the glory of God has understandably been attacked, and Calvin was very sensitive to the charge that he made God the cause of evil.

The suffering of the world is not a real problem for Calvin. Since his first principle is the honor of God, he can show that human suffering is (1) a natural consequence of the distorted, sinful world; (2) a way of bringing the elect to God; (3) a way for God to show his holiness in the punishment of a distorted world. Physical evil here is taken partly as a natural consequence, partly as an educational means, and partly as punishment for sin. But this does not solve the problem of moral evil. Calvin tries to show that the evil acts of Satan and of wicked men are determined by God's counsel. Even Pilate and Nebuchadnezzar were servants of God. God blinds the minds and hardens the hearts of men; he puts an evil spirit in their hearts. Calvin quoted Augustine: "For God, as Augustine says, fulfills his righteous will by the wicked wills of wicked men." "He (Augustine) declares that he (God) creates light and darkness, that he forms good and evil, and that no evil occurs which he has not performed." Such statements which seem to make God the cause of evil are understandable only in the light of Calvin's idea that the world is "the theater of the divine glory". God shows his glory in the scene we call the world. In order to do this, he causes evil, even moral evil. Calvin said that to think that God permits evil because of freedom is frivolous, because God acts in everything that goes on; the evil man follows the will of God although he does not follow his command. By following his will, evil men defy God's command, and that makes them guilty.

This means that Calvin's idea of providence is strictly God-caused; I do not say "determined", but "God-caused". And if—as Calvin realized—some people feel that we cannot say this about God, that this kind of providence is a horrible thing, he answered: "Ignorance of providence is the greatest of miseries; the knowledge of it is attended with the highest felicity." Belief in providence liberates us from anxiety, dread, and care. This period, around the end of the Middle Ages, was one of catastrophes and external changes, and of profound anxiety internally. Calvin's doctrine of providence is not an abstract one; it is supposed to heal anxiety, to give moral courage, and for this reason he praises the divine providence.

Involved with his doctrine of providence is his famous doctrine of predestination. Predestination is providence with respect to the ultimate aim of man. It is providence which leads man through his life to his final aim. So predestination is nothing else than the logical implication and the final fulfillment of providence. What does this doctrine of predestination mean? How does this problem arise? Why is it that most of the great names in religion, from Isaiah, Jesus, Paul, Augustine, to Luther, are adherents of predestination, whereas those who do not adhere to it are nearer to a moralistic interpretation of Christianity than to a strictly religious one? If we deny predestination, we are denying the high line of religious personalities and their theology.

The question behind this doctrine is: Why does not everybody receive the same possibility to accept or reject the truth of the gospel? Not everyone has the same possibility historically, for some have never known Jesus. Not all have the same possibility psychologically; their condition is such that they cannot even understand the meaning of what is said to them. The answer to this question is divine providence, but, as we have said, providence with respect to our eternal destiny is predestination. The moment that Christianity emphasizes the uniqueness of Christ, it must ask why most people have never heard of him, while others who have heard of him are so preconditioned that their hearing has no meaning to them. In other words, all of these who teach predestination have observed something empirically, namely, that there is a selective and not an equalitarian principle effective in life. Life cannot be understood in terms of an equalitarian principle, but only in terms of a selective principle.

Everybody asks questions such as these. Calvin said that we should not suppress such questions out of false modesty; we must ask them. "We shall never be clearly convinced ... that our salvation flows from the fountain of God's free mercy till we are acquainted with his eternal election, which illustrates the grace of God by this comparison, that he adopts not all promiscuously to the hope of salvation but gives to some what he refuses to others." There is another side to this too. Those who ask this question are given a certainty of salvation because predestination makes salvation completely independent of the oscillations of our human being. The desire for the certainty of salvation is the second reason for the doctrine of predestination in Paul, Augustine, Luther, and Calvin. They could not find a certainty by looking at themselves, because their faith was always weak and changing. They could find it only by looking beyond themselves to the action of God.

The concrete character of divine grace is visible in an election which includes me specifically and at the same time excludes others. This leads to the concept of double predestination. "We call predestination the eternal decree of God by which he has determined in himself what he would have every individual of mankind to become, for they are not all created with a similar destiny; but eternal life is foreordained for some and eternal damnation for others. Every man, therefore, being created for one or the other of these ends, we say is predestined either to life or to death." That is Calvin's definition. What is the cause of this election? Only God's will and nothing else. "If, therefore, we can assign no reason why he grants mercy to his people but because such is his pleasure, neither shall we find any other cause but his will for the reprobation of others." The irrational will of God is the cause of predestination. This introduces us to an absolute mystery. We cannot call God to any account. We must accept it purely and simply and drop our own criteria of the good and the true. If someone says this is unjust, Calvin would say that we cannot go beyond the divine will to a nature which determines God, because God's will cannot be dependent on anything else, not even in him. Here we see the full weight of the Ockhamistic-Scotistic idea that the will of God is the only cause of what God does, and nothing else.

Calvin himself felt the horrible aspect of this doctrine. "I inquire again how it came to pass that the fall of Adam, independent of any remedy, should involve so many nations with their infant children in eternal death, but because such was the will of God ... it is an awful decree, I confess!" Nevertheless, when Calvin was attacked, especially in his last years—in face of his death—he answered in a slightly different way: "Their perdition depends on the divine predestination, in such a manner that the cause and matter of it are found in themselves." Hence, the immediate cause is man's free will. Like Luther, Calvin is thinking on two levels. The divine cause is not really a cause but a decree, something which is a mystery and for which the category of causality is only symbolically and not properly applicable. Besides this Calvin knew, as did the other Reformers and every predestinarian, that it is a man's finite freedom through which God acts when he makes his decree of predestination.

If we should criticize this, we should not say that it is a simple contradiction between God's causality and human freedom. This is too easy, because the levels are different, and there is no possible contradiction on different levels. A contradiction must occur on the same level. There is the level of divine action, which is a mystery because it does not fit our categories, and there is the level of human action, which is a mixture of freedom and destiny. Do not think of the Reformers, or any of the great theologians, in terms of a single level of thought. Otherwise you are faced with all sorts of impossible statements which not only contradict each other, but also result in the destruction of your minds, if by a heroic attempt you try to accept a contradiction. Instead, you can think in terms of two levels. For example, you can say: "I cannot escape the category of causality when I speak of God's action, and when I do so, I derive everything from God, including my eternal destiny." This sounds like a mechanical determinism. But this is not what predestination means. On the divine level causality is used symbolically to express that everything which brings us to God is derived from God.

The question this raises for the individual Calvinist is whether he is elected. What gives him the assurance of election? Thus the search for the criteria, the marks of election, begins. Calvin recognized some of them. The first and most decisive one is the inner relationship to God in the act of faith. Then there is the blessing of God and the high moral standing of a person. These are all symptoms. Psychologically this brought about a situation in which the individual could gain certainty only by producing the marks of election in terms of a moral life and an economic blessing. This means that he tried to become a good bourgeois industrial citizen. He believed that if he were this, he had the marks of predestination. Of course, theologically it was known that predestination could never be caused by such actions. But if they are there, the individual can have certainty. Here lurked the danger in this theology which dealt with the marks of election.

It is remarkable how little Calvin had to say about the love of God. The divine glory replaces the divine love. When he speaks of the divine love, it is love toward those who are elected. The universality of the divine love is denied, and the demonic negation, the split of the world, acquires a kind of eternity in Calvin through his doctrine of double predestination. Therefore, this is a doctrine which contradicts the divine love as that which sustains everything that is, a doctrine which Dante expressed when in his *Divine Comedy* he wrote at the entrance of hell: "I also have been created by divine love." However, if something is created by divine love, it cannot be eternally condemned.

3. *The Christian Life*

I want to make only a few statements about Calvin's doctrine of the Christian life. He said: "When they explain vivification of that joy which the mind experiences after its perturbations and fears are allayed, I cannot coincide with them (i.e., with Luther), since it should rather signify an ardent desire and endeavor to live a holy and pious life, as though it were said that a man dies to himself that he may begin to live to God." For Luther the new life is a joyful reunion with God; for Calvin it is the attempt to fulfill the law of God in the life of the Christian. The summary of the Christian life is self-denial and not love. It is departing from ourselves. "Oh, how great a proficiency has that man made who, having been taught that he is not his own, has taken the sovereignty and government of himself from his own reason, to surrender it to God." What describes the Christian life for Calvin is not Luther's view of the ups and downs, the ecstasy and despair, in the Christian. For Calvin the Christian life is a line going upward, exercised in methodical stages.

There are two other elements in Calvin's view of the Christian life. The world is a place of exile. The body is a valueless prison of the soul. These words are more those of Plato than of the Old or New Testament. Yet, Calvin denied any hatred of life. His asceticism was not of the Roman type which tended to deny life itself or to deny the body by ascetic exercises. It was what Max

Weber and Ernst Troeltsch called an inner-worldly asceticism. It has two characteristics: cleanliness, and profit through work. Cleanliness is understood in terms of sobriety, chastity, and temperance. This has had tremendous consequences in the lives of people in Calvinist countries. It has been expressed in an extreme external cleanliness and an identification of the erotic element with the unclean. This latter is against the principles of the Reformation, but it was the consequence of the Calvinist ethics. The second characteristic of this inner-worldly asceticism is activity in the world to produce tools and, by means of them, profit. This has been called the "spirit of capitalism" by Max Weber (*The Protestant Ethic and the Spirit of Capitalism*). This has been so misunderstood that I would like to make a few comments on it. There are some people who think that great scholars like Max Weber and Ernst Troeltsch have stated that Calvinism produced capitalism. Then these clever people answer Weber— probably the greatest scholar in the nineteenth century in the fields of sociology and the humanities—by pointing out that capitalism existed before Calvin was born, especially in the Lombardian plain in northern Italy, in the cities of northern and southern Germany, in London, etc. What Weber said is that there is something in the spirit of Calvinist ethics and some related sectarian ethics which serves the purposes of investment, an important element in the capitalist economy. In pre-capitalist economy the rich man showed his riches in glorious living, in building castles or mansions or patrician houses. But Calvinism tried to show people how to use their wealth differently. It should be used partly for endowments and partly for new investments. One of the best ways of supporting the capitalist form of economy is to make the profits into investments, that is, into means for more production, instead of wasting the profits in glorious living.

That is what Max Weber wanted to say. If you do not believe he was right, I can tell you that in eastern Germany, before the catastrophes of the twentieth century happened, the cities in which the Protestants lived were the wealthy ones, and the ones in which the Catholics lived were the poor ones. Perhaps the poor were happier than the rich, but the towns and cities influenced by Calvinism produced capitalism in Germany, and not the Catholics, or the Lutherans in the East.

4. *Church and State*

Calvin's doctrine of the church is like Luther's; the church is the place where preaching is carried on and the sacraments are correctly administered. However, Calvin makes a much more radical distinction between the empirical church and the invisible church. While for Luther the invisible church is only the spiritual quality of the visible church, for Calvin the invisible church is the body of those who are predestined, in all periods of history, and not always dependent on the preaching of the Word. This is connected with the doctrine of the Holy Spirit in Zwingli and Calvin; the Spirit works also apart from the Christian message, and is therefore universally active.

From this point of view the visible church is an emergency situation, an adaptation of God to human weakness. Thus, it is not a matter of believing in the church, but believing that there is a church. The main function of the church is educational. The church always has to bring people into the invisible church, the body of the predestined, by means of preaching and the sacraments. On the other hand, the emphasis on the educational work of the church is much stronger than in Lutheranism. Although the church is ultimately an emergency creation of God, it is actually the only way for most people to come to God at all. The difference between Calvin's and Luther's doctrine of the church is that instead of having two marks of the church—doctrine and sacraments—as Luther had, Calvin has three marks: doctrine, sacraments, and discipline. The element of discipline is decisive. "As some have such a hatred of discipline as to abhor the very name, they should attend to the following consideration. . . . As the saving doctrine of Christ is the soul of the church, so discipline forms the ligaments which connect the members together and keep each in its proper place." The discipline starts with private admonition; it goes through public challenge (this was ruinous socially) and finally to excommunication. But even excommunication is not able to remove one from the saving power of God. Whereas someone who has been excommunicated cannot be saved while in this state, according to the Roman Church, in Protestantism a person will be saved in spite of excommunication if he is among the predestined.

Besides these three marks of the church, there are other things by divine law. There are four offices: pastors or ministers, doctors or teachers, presbyters, and deacons. The pastors and presbyters are the most important of these four offices. All four are by divine order; they must always be there; they are derived from the Bible.

In its mixed status the church has within itself a community of active sanctification. This community is created by the church and becomes manifest in the Lord's Supper. Thus, discipline precedes the reception of the Lord's Supper. Now, I do not want to go into Calvin's doctrine of the sacraments. The main thing is that he tried to mediate between Luther and Zwingli. Against Zwingli, he did not want the Lord's Supper to be only a commemorative meal; he wanted the presence of God, but not a presence which is superstitious and magical, as he saw in Luther's doctrine, where even unbelievers eat the body of Christ. This is magic, and I think rightly rejected by Calvin. Instead, he spoke of the spiritual presence of Christ, and this is also the presupposition for an effective reading of the Bible.

Calvin was a humanist and, therefore, gave to the state many more functions than Luther. Luther gave it practically only one function: to suppress evil and to preserve society from chaos. Calvin used the humanistic ideas of good government, of helping the people, etc. But Calvin never went so far as to say, with the sectarian movements, that the state can be the kingdom of God itself. He called this a Jewish folly. What he said—with Zwingli —is that a theocracy has to be established, the rule of God through the application of evangelical laws in the political situation. Calvin worked hard for this. He demanded that the magistrates of Geneva care not only for legal problems, the problems of order in the general sense, but also for the most important content of daily life, namely, for the church. Not that they shall teach in the church or render decisions as to what shall be taught, but they shall supervise the church and punish those who are blasphemers and heretics. So Calvin with the help of the magistrates of Geneva created the kind of community in which the law of God would govern the entire life. Priests and ministers are not necessarily involved in it. Theocratic rulers are usually not priests, otherwise theocracy becomes hierocracy; rather, they are usually laymen. Calvin says that the state must punish the impious. They are criminals because they are against the law of the state which is based on God's law.

Calvinism saved Protestantism from being overwhelmed by the Counter-Reformation. Calvinism became a tremendous international power through the alliances of Protestants on a worldwide scale. Another element in Calvinism is the possibility of revolution. Certainly Calvin said that all revolution is against the law of God, as Luther did. But then he made an exception which has become decisive for Western European history. He said that although no individual citizen should be allowed to start a revolution, the lower magistrates should be willing to do so if the natural law, to which every ruler is subject, is being contradicted. This is a possibility in a democracy such as ours in which all of us are lower magistrates; we establish the government by our voting. Under these circumstances revolution is universally permissible. The situation in Western Europe was that the kings and queens were mostly on the side of Catholicism, and Protestantism could be saved only by people who believed they could fight against the rulers in the name of God, rulers who suppress the true gospel, the purified gospel of the Reformation.

5. *The Authority of Scripture*

The doctrine of the authority of Scripture in Calvin is important because on its basis biblicism developed in all groups of Protestant faith. The Bible for Calvin is the law of truth. "At length, that the truth might remain in the world in a continual course of instruction to all ages, he determined that the same oracles which he had deposited with the patriarchs should be committed to public records. With this design the law was promulgated, to which the prophets were afterwards annexed as its first interpreters." The Bible must, therefore, be obeyed above all. It contains a "heavenly doctrine". Although an adaptation, this was necessary because of the mutability of the human mind. This was the necessary way to preserve the doctrines of Christianity. By writing them down, God's instructions become effectual. Calvin also spoke of the Bible as the "peculiar school of the children of God".

All of this can be harmless—or quite the opposite. Much discussion is taking place as to how to interpret Calvin's doctrine of

Scripture. In any case, the answer is that this authority is absolute, but only for those to whom the divine Spirit gives the testimony that the Bible contains the absolute truth. If this happens, we can witness to the whole Bible as an authoritative book. The form of the Bible's authority is derived from the fact that the Bible was composed under the dictation of the Holy Spirit. This term, dictation of the Holy Spirit, led to the doctrine of verbal inspiration which surpassed anything which can be found in Calvin himself, and which contradicts the Protestant principle as such. The disciples were "pens" of Christ. Everything which came from them as human beings was superseded by the Holy Spirit who testifies that the oracles of God are contained in this book. "Between the apostles and their successors, however, there is . . . this difference—that the apostles were the certain and authentic amanuenses of the Holy Spirit, and therefore their writings are to be received as the oracles of God." "Out of the mouth of God" the Bible is written—the whole Bible. Any distinction between the Old and New Testaments, largely disappears. You can find this still today in every Calvinist country.

CHAPTER VI

The Development of Protestant Theology

WE shall now give a survey of the rhythm in the development of Protestant theology in the last centuries. This development is important not only from the historical point of view, but also because elements created during this period are profoundly embedded in our minds and souls and bodies. Although we cannot present a history of Protestant theology, we can show the various tides in its development.

A. THE PERIOD OF ORTHODOXY

The immediate wave which followed the Reformation is the period of Orthodoxy. Orthodoxy is greater and more serious than what is called fundamentalism in America. Fundamentalism is the product of a reaction in the nineteenth century, and is a primitivized form of classical Orthodoxy. Classical Orthodoxy had a great theology. We could also call it Protestant scholasticism, with all the refinements and methods which the word "scholastic" includes. Thus, when I speak of Orthodoxy, I refer to the way in which the Reformation established itself as an ecclesiastical form of life and thought after the dynamic movement of the Reformation came to an end. It is the systematization and consolidation of the ideas of the Reformation, and developed in contrast to the Counter-Reformation.

Orthodox theology was and still is the solid basis of all later developments, whether these developments—as was usually the case—were directed against Orthodoxy, or were attempts at restoration of it. Liberal theology to the present time has been dependent on the Orthodoxy against which it has fought. Pietism was dependent on the Orthodoxy which it wanted to transform into subjectivism. Past and present restoration movements try to recapture what was once alive in the period of Orthodoxy. Hence, we should deal with this period in a much more serious way than is usually done in America. In Germany, and generally in European theological faculties—France, Switzerland, Sweden, etc.—every student of theology was supposed to learn by heart the doctrines of at least one classical theologian of the post-Reformation period of Orthodoxy, be it Lutheran or Calvinist, and in Latin at that. Even if we should forget about the Latin today, we should know these doctrines, because they form the classical system of Protestant thought. It is an unheard-of state of things when Protestant churches of today do not even know the classical expression of their own foundations in the dogmatics of Orthodoxy. This means that you cannot even understand people like Schleiermacher or Ritschl, American liberalism or the Social Gospel theology, because you do not know that against which they were directed or on what they were dependent. All theology of today is dependent in some way on the classical systems of Orthodoxy.

Orthodox theology also had a political significance, because of the need to define the status of religion in the political atmosphere of the post-Reformation period. It was a period which prepared the Thirty Years' War. Under the German emperor every territory had to define exactly where it stood, and this was the basis of its legal acknowledgment within the unity of the Holy Roman Empire. The theology, furthermore, was a theology of the territorial princes. They wanted to know from their theological faculties exactly what a minister was supposed to teach. They had to know it because they were the official lords of the church, the highest bishops, *summi episcopi*. All of the theological problems at this time involved a legal problem. When in regard to the Augsburg Confession you read about the *Variata* or *Invariata*, you might think, "What nonsense!" Not only the unity of Protestantism was threatened, but also people were killed when the *Variata* (the Altered Augsburg Confession) was introduced in place of the *Invariata* (the Unaltered Augsburg Confession) without the permission of the princes. It was more than just nonsense. It was the difference between Gnesio-Lutheranism and Philippism. Gnesio-Lutheranism means genuine or original Lutheranism, and was represented by Flacius, who was also the greatest church historian of Protestantism. Flacius had a point of view similar to the Barthian school today, stressing the total depravity of man. In scholastic terminology Flacius said that the substance of human nature is original sin. This idea, however, was not accepted by Orthodoxy.

Philippism, on the other side, represented the tendency of Philip Melanchthon. It was very similar to Reformed ideas, so that it is even difficult today to find out how much in Philippism is Reformed and how much is Melanchthonian. This group was nearer to what today we would call a moderate liberal theology, against the Gnesio-Lutherans. The result of these struggles at the end of the sixteenth century was the *Formula of Concord* (1580). Many of the territorial churches believed that it contained the pure interpretation of the Augsburg Confession in its unaltered form. The implication of all this is that the doctrinal element becomes much more important in Orthodoxy than in the Reformation, where the spiritual element was more decisive than the fixed doctrines. Luther did not fix doctrines, although he himself could be very tenacious.

1. *Reason and Revelation*

We must deal now with the principles of orthodox thought. One of the first was the relationship to philosophy, a very old issue in Protestantism. Luther, it seems, was disinclined to accept anything from reason, but in reality this is not true. It is true that he made many angry statements against the philosophers, by whom he usually had in mind the scholastics and their teacher, Aristotle. But in his famous words at the Diet of Worms Luther himself said that unless he were refuted either by Holy Scripture or by reason, he would not recant. Luther was not an irrationalist. What he fought against was that the categories of reason should transform the substance of faith. Reason is not able to save but must be saved itself.

It became immediately clear that theology cannot be taught without philosophy, that philosophical categories must be used, consciously or unconsciously, in teaching anything whatsoever. For this reason Luther did not prevent Melanchthon from introducing Aristotle again, and with Aristotle many humanistic elements. However, there were always some who attacked philosophy, humanism, and Aristotle. There was a man, Daniel Hoffmann, who said: "The philosophers are the patriarchs of heresy." This is what some theologians say even today. But when they develop their own theologies, you can easily show from which "patriarchs of heresy", that is, from which philosophers, they have taken their categories. They have said: What is philosophically true is theologically wrong; the philosophers are unregenerated insofar as they are philosophers. This is a very interesting statement because it means that there is a realm of life which in itself cannot be regenerated. This contradicts, however, the emphasis on secularism in Protestantism. "Philosophers", said Hoffmann, "try to be like God because they develop a philosophy which is not theologically given." Hoffmann was not able to carry through this idea, but he produced a continual suspicion against the philosophers in the churches and in theology, a much greater suspicion against philosophy than exists in the Roman Church. And this suspicion is very much alive again in the present-day theological situation.

The final victory of philosophy within theology was the presupposition of all the theological systems in Orthodoxy. Johann Gerhard was the one who developed the classical system in Lutheran theology. He was a great philosopher and theologian, in some ways comparable to Thomas Aquinas for Roman Catholics. He represents the latest flowering of Protestant scholasticism. He distinguished articles which are pure from those which are mixed. Those which are solely revealed are pure; those which are rationally possible as well as revealed are mixed. He believed, with Thomas Aquinas, that the existence of God can be proved rationally. But he was also aware that this rational proof does not give us certainty. "Although the proof is correct, we believe it because of revelation." In this way we have two structures: the substructure of reason, and the superstructure of revelation. The biblical doctrines form the superstructure. What actually happened later—and this is a preview of the centuries which followed—was that the mixed articles became unmixed rationally, and that the substructure of rational theology dispossessed the superstructure of revelation, drawing it into itself and taking away its meaning. When this happens, we are in the realm of rationalism or Enlightenment.

2. The Formal and Material Principles

Protestantism in Orthodoxy developed two principles of theology, a formal and a material principle. So far as I know, however, these are nineteenth-century terms. The formal principle is the Bible; the material principle is the doctrine of justification. They are interdependent, according to Luther. What presents the message of justification in the Bible is that which deals with Christ, and this is what is authentic. On the other hand, this doctrine is taken from the Bible and is, therefore, dependent on it. This interdependence of Bible and justification was maintained in Luther's thought in a free, creative, and living way. The attitude of Orthodoxy became different. The two principles were placed beside each other. The result was that the Bible became the real principle in the realm of authority.

What was the doctrine of the Bible in Orthodoxy? The Bible is attested in a threefold way: (1) by external criteria, such as age, miracles, prophecy, martyrs, etc.; (2) by internal criteria, such as style, sublime ideas, moral sanctity; (3) by the testimony of the Holy Spirit. This testimony, however, gets another meaning. No longer does it have the Pauline meaning that we are the children of God ("The Spirit himself beareth witness with our spirit that we are children of God." Romans 8:16). Instead, it became the testimony that the doctrines of the Holy Scriptures are true and inspired by the Spirit. In place of the immediacy of the Spirit in the relationship of God and man, the Spirit witnesses to the authenticity of the Bible insofar as it is a document of the divine Spirit. The difference is that if the Spirit tells you that you are children of God, this is an immediate experience, and there is no law involved in it at all. But if the Spirit testifies that the Bible contains true doctrines, the whole thing is brought out of the person-to-person relationship into an objective legal relationship. This is exactly what Orthodoxy did.

A very interesting discussion about the *theologia irregenitorum* followed from this, the theology of those who are not converted, the unregenerated. If the Bible is the law of Protestantism, it should be possible for all who can read the Bible and interpret it objectively to write a systematic theology, even though they do not participate in the Christian faith. All they have to do is to

The Development of Protestant Theology   281

understand the meaning of the words and sentences of the Bible. This was absolutely denied by the pietists, who said that there can be only a *theologia regenitorum*, a theology of those who are regenerated. If we look at this discussion in modern terms, we can say that Orthodoxy believed in the possibility of a systematic theology which is not existential, while the pietists believed that it is necessary for theology to be existential.

There is something difficult in both positions. The unregenerated man is able to know that what the Church or the Bible says is essential for salvation, but he is unable to apply this to the present situation. The function of the orthodox theologian is independent of his religious quality. He may be completely outside. On the other hand, the pietist theologian can say of himself, and others can say of him, that he is converted, regenerated, and a real Christian. But he has to state this with certainty. Is there anyone who can do this, who can say: "I am a real Christian"? The moment he does it, he ceases to be a real Christian, since he is looking to himself for certainty in his relation to God. This is most certainly impossible. This problem still exists today in all Protestant churches. In my *Systematic Theology* I have solved the problem in the following way. Only he who experiences the Christian message as his ultimate concern is able to be a theologian, but nothing more than this can be demanded. It may be that one who is in doubt about every particular doctrine is a better theologian than many others, as long as this doubt about doctrine involves his ultimate concern. So one does not need to be "converted" to be a theologian—whatever that term may mean. You are not asked to test whether or not you are a good Christian, so that you can say: "Now since I am a good Christian, I can be a theologian." The pietist would tell you: "You must first be converted before you can really be a theologian." Then you should answer him: "The only thing which is 'first' is that the ultimate concern coming from God has grasped me, so that I am concerned about him and his message, but I cannot say more than this. And sometimes I am not even able to express it in these terms, because even the term 'God' disappears sometimes. In any case, I cannot use it as the basis for believing that I am a good Christian and thus possibly a theologian."

The orthodox doctrine of inspiration took some of Calvin's ideas and made them more radical and primitive. The authors of Scrip-

ture were the hands of Christ, the notaries of the Holy Spirit, the
"pens" by which the Spirit wrote the Bible. The words, and even
the pointings in the Hebrew text, are inspired. Hence, an orthodox theologian, Buxtehof, contested the fact that the consonants
of the Hebrew text received their vowel pointings in the seventh
to ninth centuries A.D.; instead, they must have originated with the
Old Testament itself. The prophets must have invented the system of pointing, which was actually invented fifteen hundred
years later. This is the consequence of a consistent doctrine of
inspiration; otherwise, what would the divine Spirit do with the
Hebrew text, for without the vowels, the Hebrew words are
ambiguous in many places. Then there is the problem with
Luther's and the King James' translations, and with other new
translations. One is driven to actual absurdities with this doctrine
of inspiration. To maintain it one has to make artificial harmoniza-
tions, for there are innumerable contradictions in the Bible on
historical as well as on other matters. Such contradictions are
made out to be only apparent, and one is forced to be ingenious
in inventing ways to harmonize them.

Another deeper principle was the *analogia scripturae sanctae*,
the analogy of sacred Scripture, which means that one part must
be interpreted in terms of another. By this means creeds could be
established on the basis of Holy Scripture. These were the formulae which everybody was supposed to find in the Bible. This
was another inescapable consequence of the doctrine of inspiration.

There was another help for people who had to swallow the doctrine of verbal inspiration. The question was: What about the
many doctrines we find in the Bible? Are they all necessary for
salvation? The Catholic Church had a very good answer. You do
not need to know any of them; you have only to believe what
the church believes. Only the ministers and educated people
need to know the special doctrines. The Catholic layman believes
what the church believes, without knowing what that is in many
respects. Protestantism could not do this. Since personal faith
means everything in Protestantism, the distinction between *fides
implicita* and *explicita* (implicit and explicit faith) is impossible
for it. But then an impossible task arose: How can every ordinary
farmer, shoemaker, and proletarian in the city and the country
understand all these many doctrines found in the Bible, which are

too numerous even for an educated man to know in his theological examinations? The answer was given by distinguishing between fundamental and non-fundamental articles. Such a distinction is popular even today. In principle this distinction should not be made, because if the divine Spirit reveals something, to what extent can we say it is non-fundamental? In any case, non-fundamentals proved later on to be very fundamental, when certain consequences were drawn from non-fundamental deviations.

Although this was a dangerous thing, it had to be done for educational reasons. Most people are just not able to understand all the implications of the doctrines of the church. Two interests were in conflict with each other. On the one hand, the interest of the systematic theologian is to increase the fundamentals as much as possible; everything is important, not only because he is writing about it, but because it is in the Bible. On the other hand, the interest of the educator contradicts this interest of the systematic theologian. The educator wants to maintain as little as possible, so that what he teaches becomes understandable. He would like to leave out all doctrines of secondary importance. In the end the educator prevails. What we find in the rationalism of the Enlightenment is largely a reduction of the fundamentals to the level of popular reasonableness. Education was partly responsible for the coming of the Enlightenment; it was a central concern of all the great philosophers of that period. Even today the departments of education are usually more inclined toward a theology based on the Enlightenment than the other departments of theology are. The reason for this is that the educational needs bring about a limitation of content, whereas the theological needs call for an enlargement of content.

B. PIETISM

Orthodoxy had one doctrine which was a transition to the next great movement—Pietism. In its doctrine of the *ordo salutis*, the order of salvation, the last step was the *unio mystica*, the mystical union with God. For Luther this is the beginning of the faith in justification. The moment that Orthodoxy accepted from the ecclesiastical tradition the *unio mystica* as a definite state which must be reached, the concept of faith became intellectualized. In Luther both are kept together; in Orthodoxy they fall asunder.

Faith becomes the intellectual acceptance of true doctrine, and communion with God becomes a matter of mystical experience. This splits Luther's thought—especially of the younger Luther— into two pieces; the mystical and the intellectual aspects are placed beside each other.

What is Pietism? The term is much less respectable in America than in Europe. There the words "pious" and "pietist" can be used of people, but hardly in America, because here they carry the connotations of hypocrisy and moralism. Pietism does not necessarily have these connotations. It is the reaction of the subjective side of religion against the objective side. Of course, the subjective side in the order of salvation was dealt with in Orthodoxy, but it did not mean very much. Actually Orthodoxy lived in the objectivity of theological and ecclesiastical organization. Yet, this should not be overemphasized. As the hymns of Paul Gerhardt show—he lived during the highest development of this period— there was always a personal religious relationship to God. But for the masses of people it was the license to become licentious; the state of morality was miserably low, especially in the Lutheran countries, where the doctrinal element was decisive and discipline did not exist.

The pietists, and especially the greatest of them, Philip Jacob Spener, wrote in continual reference to Luther. He showed that all the elements of Pietism were present in the early Luther, and that Orthodoxy had removed them in favor of the objective contents of doctrine. Spener tried to show that Orthodoxy had grasped only one side of Luther. Pietism was justified in this respect. Pietism also had a great influence on culture as a whole. It was the first to act in terms of social ethics. The pietists in Halle founded the first orphanage and started the first missionary enterprises. Orthodoxy held that the non-Christian nations are lost, because they had already received the apostolic preaching immediately after the founding of the church, and rejected it. St. Thomas, for instance, had gone to Asia. So it is not necessary to renew the missionary enterprise. The pietists felt altogether differently about it. Human souls, wherever they may be, can be saved through conversion. So they began their missions to foreign lands, and this gave them world-historical perspectives. A man like Zinzendorf, together with Wesley, looked to America, while Orthodoxy restricted itself to its own territorial churches.

The liturgical realm was also changed a great deal. One of the most important changes was the reintroduction of confirmation as a confirming of the sacrament of baptism.

Pietism is important for theology in three respects. It tried to reform theology, the church, and morals. According to Pietism, theology is a practical discipline. In order to know, one must first believe—an old demand of Christian theology. This demand entails, at the same time, the central importance of exegesis. Old and New Testament theology become decisive, not systematic theology. Wherever biblical theology prevails over systematic theology, that is almost always due to the influence of Pietism. Before the theologian is able to edify others, he must first be educated himself.

The church is not only a body of people which exists to listen to the Word. Not only ministers but also laymen are the bearers of the church. Laymen are to have an active part in the priestly function in different places—sometimes in the church, but mostly in their homes, and in special conventicles of piety, *collegia pietatis*, where they came together to cultivate piety. They spent hours in the interpretation of the Bible, and they emphasized the need for conversion. They emphasized the idea of an *ecclesiola in ecclesia*, a small church within the large church.

Pietism also influenced the morals in the Protestant world. At the end of the seventeenth century the moral situation was disastrous in Europe. The Thirty Years' War brought about dissolution and chaos. The form of life became extremely brutal, unrefined, and uneducated. The orthodox theologians did not do much about it. The pietists, however, tried to gather individual Christians who would accept the burden and the liberation of the Christian life. Its main idea was sanctification, a common emphasis in Christian sectarian movements. Individual sanctification includes, first of all, a negation of the love of the world. The question of the ethical *adiaphora* became important in the discussion with orthodox theology. (*Adiaphoron* means that which makes no difference, having no ethical relevance.) The question was whether there are some human actions of no ethical relevance, which can be done or left undone with equal right. Orthodoxy said there is a whole realm of such *adiaphora*; Pietism denied it, calling it love of the world. As it often happens with such things, Spener was mild in his condemnation, then Francke

and the Halle pietists became very radical. They fought against
dancing, the theater, games, beautiful dresses, banquets, shallow
talk in daily life, and in general resembled the Puritan attitude.
In this connection, however, I would like to say that it was not so
much the Puritans who produced this system of vital repression
so common in America; it was more the pietistic evangelical movements of the mid-nineteenth century which were responsible for
this condemnation of smoking, drinking, movies, etc.

The orthodox theologians strongly reacted against the attack
of the pietists. One of them wrote a book with the title *Malum
Pietisticum*, "The Pietistic Evil". They fought against each other
on many points, but in the end the pietistic movement was
superior because it was allied with the trends of the time, away
from the strict objectivism and authoritarianism of the sixteenth
and seventeenth centuries to the principles of autonomy which
appeared in the eighteenth and nineteenth centuries.

It is entirely wrong to place the rationalism of the Enlightenment
in contradiction to pietistic mysticism. It is popular nonsense
that reason and mysticism are the two great opposites. Historically, Pietism and the Enlightenment both fought against
Orthodoxy. The subjectivity of Pietism, or the doctrine of the
"inner light" in Quakerism and other ecstatic movements, has
the character of immediacy or autonomy against the authority of
the church. To put it more sharply, modern rational autonomy is
a child of the mystical autonomy of the doctrine of the inner light.
The doctrine of the inner light is very old; we have it in the
Franciscan theology of the Middle Ages, in some of the radical
sects (especially the later Franciscans), in many sects of the Reformation period, in the transition from spiritualism to rationalism,
from the belief in the Spirit as the autonomous guide of every
individual to the rational guidance which everybody has by his
autonomous reason. From another historical perspective, the third
stage of Joachim of Floris, the stage of the Holy Spirit, is behind
the idea among the bourgeoisie of the Enlightenment that they
have reached the third stage, the age of reason, in which every
individual is taught directly. They go back to the prophecy of
Joel, in which every maid or servant is taught directly by the
Holy Spirit, and no one is dependent on anybody else for the
Spirit.

Thus we can say that rationalism is not opposed to mysticism, if by mysticism we mean the presence of the Spirit in the depths of the human soul. Rationalism is the child of mysticism, and both of them are opposed to authoritarian Orthodoxy.

C. THE ENLIGHTENMENT

Socinianism is one of the sources of the Enlightenment. It was a movement started by Faustus Socinus, who fled from Italy to Poland where he found a haven of security against the Counter-Reformation and the persecutions of some of the Reformation churches. He and his followers wrote the book called *Racovian* *Catechism*, which presents a predominantly rationalistic Protestant theology. Harnack says in his *History of Dogma* that Socinianism was the end of the history of Christian dogma. Protestantism had preserved some dogmas, at least the early dogmas of the church. Socinianism dissolved all the Christian dogmas with the help of the rationalism and humanism of the Renaissance. This movement is more important than either the repetition of it in English deism, where it was radicalized, or in modern liberal theology, including Harnack himself, where it was carried through.

(1) The Socinians accepted the authority of the Bible, but declared that in non-essential things it may be in error. Furthermore, historical criticism is necessary. Its criterion is that nothing can be a revelation of God in the Bible that is against reason and common sense. And nothing that is morally useless can be the revelation of God in the Bible. Socinus spoke of *religio rationalis*, rational religion, which is given in the Bible and is the criterion for the authority of the Bible.

(2) In the doctrine of God Socinus criticized mainly the dogma of the trinity. The Socinians are the predecessors of the later Unitarian movements. He said—and in this he is historically right —that the arguments for the trinitarian dogma do not exist in the Bible as they were later presented in Orthodoxy. The Bible does not contain the dogma of the trinity, although there are some trinitarian formulations. The Greek concepts, he said, anticipating the Ritschlian criticism of the dogma on which we are all dependent today, are inadequate for understanding the meaning of the gospel and are, moreover, contradictory in themselves.

(3) God created the world out of the given chaos (*tohu wabohu*

in the creation story in Genesis) which the pagan religions and also Greek philosophy presuppose. Man is the image of God because of his reason, which makes him superior to the animals. Adam was not a perfect man, but was primitive and by nature mortal. He had neither original immortality nor original perfection. I believe this is closer to the biblical text in both respects than the later glorification of Adam which makes his fall absolutely impossible to understand. The Socinians derive the fall of Adam from the strength of his sensual impressions and on the basis of his freedom. This freedom is still in man.

(4) Hence, the idea of original or hereditary sin is a contradictory concept. Socinus says that there is no sin without guilt. If we are guilty by birth, then we must have sinned before we were born, or at least at the very beginning of our life, which is a meaningless statement. What is really the truth is that we are historically depraved and that our freedom is weakened. This makes it necessary for God to give us a new revelation beyond natural revelation. Christ has a true human nature, but not a divine nature. On the other hand, he is not just an ordinary man. He is a higher type of man, a "superman", so to speak, in the Nietzschean, not the comic-book, sense. For this reason he can be an object of adoration.

(5) The priestly office of Christ is denied. He is prophet and king. The ideas about a substitutionary sacrifice or punishment or satisfaction for sin are meaningless and self-contradictory, because guilt is always a personal thing and must be attributed to individuals. On the other hand, Christ is king and sits at the right hand of God and is really ruling and judging.

(6) Justification is dissolved into a moralistic terminology. In order to be justified, we must keep the commandments. With respect to the state, he favored passive resistance against the power forms of the state.

(7) Eschatology is dissolved; it is a fantastic myth. What remains and is most important is immortality. This must be preserved by all means.

Many of these ideas anticipate the theology of the Enlightenment and modern liberalism. What really survives from Socinianism are the three theological ideas of the Enlightenment: God, freedom, and immortality. I like to quote from Immanuel Kant's *What is Enlightenment?*: "Enlightenment is man's release from his self-incurred tutelage. Tutelage is man's inability to make use of his understanding without direction from another. Self-incurred is this tutelage when its cause lies not in lack of reason but in lack of resolution and courage to use it without direction from another. *Sapere aude!* 'Have courage to use your own reason!'—that is the motto of enlightenment." Kant goes on to show how much more comfortable it is to have guardians and authorities but he says this comfort has to be given up. Man must stand upon himself; it is his nature to be autonomous.

Rationalism and Enlightenment emphasize human autonomy. "Autonomy" is not used in the sense of arbitrariness, of man making himself or deciding about himself in terms of his individual desires and arbitrary willfulness. Autonomy is derived from *autos* and *nomos* (self-law) in Greek. It does not say that "I am a law unto myself", but that the universal law of reason, which is the structure of reality, is within me. This concept of autonomy is often falsified by theologians who say this is the misery of man, that he wants to be autonomous rather than dependent on God. This is poor theology and poor philosophy. Autonomy is the natural law given by God, present in the human mind and in the structure of the world. Natural law usually means in classical philosophy and theology the law of reason, and this is the divine law. Autonomy is following this law as we find it in ourselves. It is always connected with a strong obedience to the law of reason, stronger than any religious idea that seems to be arbitrary. The adherents of autonomy in the Enlightenment were opposed to anything so arbitrary as divine grace. They wanted to emphasize man's obedience to the law of his own nature and the nature of the world.

The opposite of autonomy is the concept of heteronomy. Heteronomy is precisely arbitrariness. Arbitrariness shows up as soon as fear or desire determine our actions, whether this fear be produced by God or society or our own weakness. For Kant the authoritarian attitude of the churches, or even of God if he is seen in a heteronomous light, is arbitrariness. Arbitrariness is subjection to authority, if this authority is not confirmed by reason itself, for otherwise one is subjecting oneself on the basis of fear, anxiety, or desire. The Enlightenment is the attempt to build a world on this autonomous reason.

Just as autonomy is not willfulness, reason is not calculation.

Reason is the awareness of the principles of truth and justice. In the name of this reason, the Enlightenment fought against the demonic authorities of the *ancien régime* in eighteenth-century France and in Europe generally. This reason is the awareness of the principles of truth and goodness, not the calculating and controlling reason of business. The eighteenth century had some heroic elements in it; reason is always seen fighting against the distortions of humanity under the regime of the French kings and the Roman popes and all who cooperated with them for the suppression of humanity. We should not have contempt for the rationalism of the eighteenth century, if we know what it did for us. It is due to the Enlightenment that we have no more witch trials. It was Cartesian philosophy applied to concrete problems which made such a superstition impossible. The general education we all enjoy in the West is a creation of the eighteenth century. And our democratic ideology had its origin in the same century.

Harmony is a third principle of the Enlightenment, following from the principles of autonomy and reason. If we find the principles of truth and justice in the depths of our being, and if each individual has different interests, how are a common knowledge and common symbols of democracy and economy possible? If autonomous reason in each individual is the ultimate arbiter, is not that the end of a coherent society? The principle of harmony is the answer to this question. This principle does not mean that there is nice harmony between everyone. The eighteenth century knew how terrible life really was. Rather, harmony means that if everyone follows his rational, or even irrational tendencies, there is nevertheless a law behind the backs of everyone which has the effect of making everything come out most adequately. This is the meaning of the Manchester school of economics, the meaning of the pursuit of happiness in the American Constitution and of belief in democracy. In spite of the fact that each one decides for himself about the government, a common will, a *volonté générale*, will somehow result from all of this. This is the belief in ethics and education, that a community spirit will be the result of everyone's becoming educated as a personality. This is the principle of Protestantism, that if every individual in his own way encounters the biblical message, a conformism of Protestant character will be the outcome.

The miracle is that this happened, that actually the prophecy under the principle of harmony was really verified in all these realms. The greatest development in economy happened. A Protestant conformism arose, in spite of the numerous denominations. And democracy has worked and is still working, in spite of the disruptive tendencies that are visible today in America. The modern belief in progress is rooted in this principle of harmony, in spite of any lack of authority.

Tolerance is another concept we must keep in mind when dealing with the Enlightenment. One of the main historical reasons for tolerance is that if intolerance had continued, all Europe would have been destroyed by the religious wars. It could be saved only by a tolerant state which is indifferent toward the various confessional groups fighting against each other. However, when John Locke wrote his letters on tolerance, he was well aware that tolerance can never be an absolute principle. So he limited it in an interesting way. Although a leader of the development toward the Enlightenment, he nevertheless said that there are two groups which cannot be tolerated. They are the Catholics and the atheists. Catholics cannot be tolerated because they are by definition intolerant; they aim to subjugate every nation they can by force to the authority of the Roman Church. Atheists are not intolerant, but they threaten the very foundation of Western society, which is based on the idea of God. The greatest witness to John Locke's point is Friedrich Nietzsche, who said that because "God is dead", the transformation of the whole society is at hand. This is what John Locke wanted to preclude in the name of reason.

English Deism is another movement of great importance for modern theology. The deists used philosophy in a practical way to solve theological problems. Deism was a movement of the intelligentsia, and not so much a real philosophy. They wrote attacks against traditional Orthodoxy. They criticized, as the Socinians had done, the problems of biblical religion. All elements of criticism can be found in them which we now associate with liberal theology. The problems of biblical history, the authority of Jesus, the problem of miracles, the question of special revelation, the history of religion, which shows that Christianity is not something so different, the category of myth, which was invented by the deists two hundred and fifty years before Bultmann's essay on demythologization—these are the problems with which Continental theology has had to deal ever since. The great movement of historical criticism began around 1750. Lessing, who was the greatest personality of the Enlightenment, a poet and a philosopher, was the leader in the fight against a stupid Orthodoxy which stuck to the traditional terms. The great critical line of development in theology, running from D. F. Strauss, Schleiermacher, etc. to Johannes Weiss, Albert Schweitzer, and Bultmann, had its origin back there in the middle of the eighteenth century, which itself was carrying through the ideas of the Socinians and others.

It may seem as if there were one all-embracing development in theology, an ocean which flooded over the continents. But this is not true. There were reactions in all these periods. There were high and low tides. There were the reactions of Methodism and Pietism; there was the reaction of Romanticism at the end of the eighteenth century; there were the revivalistic movements in the mid-nineteenth century, and finally there is the reaction of Neo-Orthodoxy at the beginning of the twentieth century. In all of these movements, one question is predominant: What about the compatibility of the modern mind with the Christian message? There was always an oscillation between an attempt at synthesis, in the Hegelian and Platonic sense, which means a creative unity of different elements of reality. In this sense the two men with the greatest theological influence in the nineteenth century were Hegel and Schleiermacher. Together they produced what I call the great synthesis. They took into themselves all the impulses of the modern mind, all the results of the autonomous development. Beyond this they tried to show that the true Christian message can be maintained only on this basis, and not in terms of either Orthodoxy or the Enlightenment. They rejected both and tried to find a way beyond them, Schleiermacher more from the mystical tradition of his pietistic background (he was a Moravian), and Hegel more in philosophical terms out of the Neo-Platonic tradition. By 1840 both of these forms of synthesis were considered to have broken down completely, and an extreme naturalism and materialism developed. At this time, then, another theological school tried to save what it could. This was the Ritschlian school, the leaders of which, beside Ritschl himself, were Wilhelm Herrmann and Adolph von Harnack, who is the teacher of all of us in many respects. This was a new synthesis on a more modest level, on the level of Kant's division of the world of knowledge from the world of values.

The Ritschlian synthesis broke down at the turn of the century, partly under the impact of inner theological developments. Here I can mention Ernst Troeltsch, my great teacher, and Martin Kähler, my other great teacher, who came from the pietistic and revivalistic tradition of Halle. Primarily, however, it broke down from the impact of the events of world history, the World Wars, which spelled the end of centuries of European life. Again the diastasis against the synthesis of Christianity and the modern mind became real under Karl Barth. My own answer is that synthesis can never be avoided, because man is always man, and at the same time under God. He can never be under God in such a way that he ceases to be human. In order to find a new way beyond the former ways of synthesis, I use the method of correlation. I try to show that the Christian message is the answer to all the problems involved in self-criticizing humanism; today we call this existentialism; it is a self-analyzing humanism. This is neither synthesis nor diastasis, neither identification nor separation; it is correlation. And I believe the whole story of Christian thought points in this direction.

Index of Names

Index of Subjects